The Family Matters

The Family Matters

Two centuries of family law and life in Ontario

Sheila Kieran

KEY PORTER BOOKS

Canadian Cataloguing in Publication Data

Kieran, Sheila.
The family matters : two centuries of family law in Ontario

Includes index.
Bibliography: p.
ISBN 0-919493-76-9

1. Domestic relations – Ontario – History.
I. Title.

KEO213.K54 1986 346.71301'5'09034 C86-093972-3

Key Porter Books Limited
70 The Esplanade
Toronto, Ontario
M5E 1R2

Photo Research: Nicholas Stahl, John Wellwood
Text Research: Jill Funimoto, Kathy McDonald, Kathleen Vaughn
Design: Leslie Smart and Associates
Printed and bound in Canada

86 87 88 6 5 4 3 2 1

Contents

Foreword

No area of the law touches our daily lives so intimately or directly as the laws respecting our family relationships. These laws determine how and whom we may wed, the manner in which we are obliged to support our dependents, the rights and responsibilities of partners within marriage, and the obligations to spouses and children if the marriage ends. Our society is organized on the basis of family, and the laws that touch upon it are fundamental to us all.

Consequently it is vitally important that our family law always be in close step with our changing society. As values and relationships change, so must laws change. To be out of step, to fall behind, is to invite distrust and disrespect for our law and its institutions and to impose unnecessary hardship on dependents and children, those least able to protect themselves and exercise their rights.

This book is about the evolution of family life and law in Ontario over the past two centuries. It shows how the law has been out of step with practices in society at various times in our past, how it caught up, and how it began to slip behind again. The Family Law Reform Act of 1978 and its related statutes represented more than a century of catching up. But society and its values continued to change at a fast pace. By the early 1980s further reform was necessary. Ontario has taken a long step forward with the passage of the Family Law Act in January, 1986.

Among other things the Act provides for an equal distribution of property between spouses on marriage breakdown or death, with certain exceptions, strengthens mutual support obligations, and generally recognizes marriage as an equal partnership. It further recognizes the obligations of parents to support their children even beyond the age of majority, where they can, to enable them to obtain a higher education, and the obligation of grown children to support their aged parents.

The pace of change has quickened. The first major step took over a century. The second took less than a decade. Society is evolving more rapidly, and Government must respond to, encourage, and sometimes lead the process of change.

Sheila Kieran's book traces the course of the historic evolution of the family in terms of both social attitudes and laws which touched upon it. The research was commenced under my predecessor, the Honourable R. Roy McMurtry. It has been my pleasure to continue and complete the work that he started.

This book shows us the family is the most vital and central institution in our society. Its social evolution and the state's responses to it through legal development must be studied and analysed. History's lessons can guide us in the future. This book is an excellent beginning to that process.

Ian G. Scott
Attorney General for Ontario
April, 1986

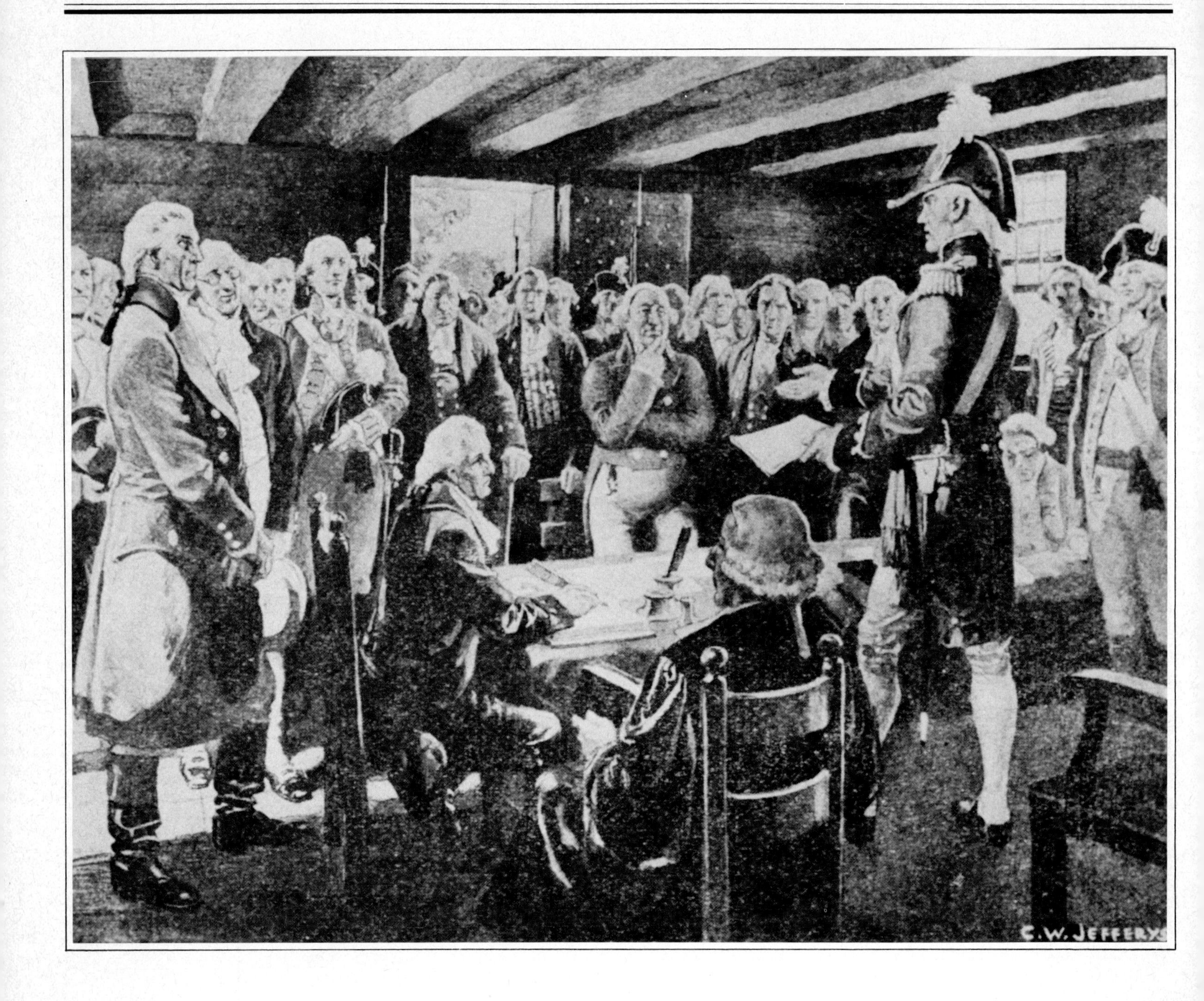

John Graves Simcoe opens the first Legislature of Upper Canada at Newark, September 17, 1792.

Preface

I am very pleased to have been invited to contribute this preface to Sheila Kieran's important history of Family Law Reform in Ontario.

During the almost ten years that I was privileged to serve as the province's Attorney General, the reform of clearly out-of-date Family Law became a priority of the government.

When I was sworn into the Ontario Cabinet in 1975, a great deal of important research had already taken place, including a major report by the *Ontario Law Reform Commission*.

As well, my seventeen years' experience as a trial lawyer had convinced me of the fundamental inequality existing in relation to marital litigation, particularly in respect to support obligations and property sharing.

Notwithstanding the obvious need for reform, there still existed at that time a certain lack of political will to tackle reforms which would alter traditional concepts of property ownership and principles of fault finding as a necessary ingredient of domestic litigation.

The process of reform, therefore, involved lengthy debates fueled by both legal and sociological arguments. The search for some reasonable degree of social and political *consensus* was inevitably protracted. In the circumstances the Family Law Reform Act of 1978 was landmark legislation.

However, it was intended not to be the final word but a very important beginning. Experience would dictate future reform. Indeed, my proposals to extend the presumption of equal sharing of family assets to include business assets on marriage breakdown became a contentious issue during my leadership campaign of 1984-85.

I am delighted that Ms. Kieran has recorded this important history of Family Law in Ontario and that the present Attorney General, the Honourable Ian Scott, is carrying forward vital new reforms.

Roy McMurtry
Former Attorney General for Ontario
April, 1986

Introduction

The modern history of this province begins in another country where 80,000 men and women who thought of themselves as loyal and worthy subjects woke in the aftermath of a revolution to find they were despised, legally disenfranchised, discriminated against, and, in some cases, beaten and tortured.

Some went to the West Indies, to Florida, or to England; most fled to what is now Nova Scotia. Six thousand left the nation they had helped to create and moved through a physical and social wilderness to carve out a new province in what was then the western portion of Quebec. There, by their beliefs, their behaviour, and their laws, they moulded what became Ontario. This is the story of how they interpreted one aspect of the law – that concerning the family – to shape their society and how both society and family law changed from their day to ours.

When Ontario's Family Law Reform Act was passed in 1978, it represented the most complete overhaul of legislation in more than eight centuries; less than eight years later, it showed signs of wear and was changed once again.

The process of change is continuous and, like everything else, has speeded up; this book offers as complete a record as possible of the recent major reforms to family law and examines how and why change took place. Although some things remain to be done – some things *always* remain to be done – Ontario's present-day law is among the world's best.

Why focus on family rather than on other kinds of law? Because it is (aside from our occasional forays into traffic court) the most frequent reason, and almost always the most important one, that brings any of us in contact with the law. Few of us (our Walter Mittyish dreams to the contrary) will ever play a role in a criminal court; more and more of us, however, live in relationships that were not envisioned when either the older etiquette books or law books were written; we separate and/or divorce at an increasingly hectic rate; we give kids up for adoption, adopt them, help them seek their natural parents or object to their attempts to do so. We conceive, carry, and bear children according to the ancient laws of nature, but we will need society's laws to guide us through the maze created by reproductive technology. All of those are issues in family law.

But the study of family law has another important function: it tells us more about contemporary social and political reality than we generally acknowledge. In the Middle Ages people believed that the importance of life was found in one's relationship with God – and, as a reflection of that belief, family law was the purview of the church. In the eighteenth century people sought meaning through reason – and family law moved from the church to Parliament. In the nineteenth century people believed that redemption lay in a social Gospel, and systems of social support grew around the family. Today people believe that the greatest chance for fulfillment lies in development of the self, and family law stresses the autonomy of individuals.

Or, to use another example and another perspective, Victorian society was paternalistic, based on the assumption that those of higher rank knew best – an exact replica, written large, of how the law believed families should be organized and how it encouraged them to organize themselves. It was not until the reform movement began, even before Victoria ascended the throne of Britain, that society started to reshape itself. And it is no coincidence that one constant focus of that change was family law.

Despite its importance to us, as much as to English Victorians, there has never been an account of our history viewed through the prism of family law. Most legal histories of Ontario begin somewhere near the middle of the nineteenth century and, even then, some contain errors of fact. But family law in this province goes back, literally, to the first days of Upper Canada. It was understood as essential by that original influx of immigrants and it remains a useful tool for understanding how we became what we are.

Seventeen eighty-four is taken as a starting point for this history because there is evidence that the original settlers and their immediate descendants used it to date the existence of this province: in 1884, for example, a "Circular to Editors, Country and Township Municipal Officers, and Others" asked for their cooperation "in promoting the Centennial Celebration of the First Settlement of Upper Canada" in "the month of June next." It was signed by prominent citizens promoting the United Empire Loyalist Centennial, a group whose names dot the province to this day, among them: Dr. Henry Scadding, John Playter, Lieutenant-Governor John Robinson, the Methodist Church's General Superintendent Albert Carman, Egerton Ryerson, S.J. VanKoughnet, and both the Reverend Mr. William H. Withrow and his cousin, Alderman John J. Withrow.

Although examining the context of the past involves writing about men and women well known to most of us, it also reveals others elbowed aside by time, their contributions unknown or unmarked. Between those two extremes, there are people and events that have been carelessly pigeonholed so that, for example, John Graves Simcoe comes down to us as a whey-faced British prig; how then to explain the more complex human being who, with all his airs and failings, walked into a small colonial outpost and, against the wishes of supposedly more liberal folk, managed to make this province one of the first jurisdictions in the world to legislate against slavery?

I am neither a historian nor a lawyer and would not presume to don the mantle of either; like writers, lawyers and historians examine and attempt to impose some shape on human experience and behaviour. Human experience and behaviour, in all their variety and subtlety, are the focus of this book.

A work that carries only the author's name is incomplete without the names of the dozens of people who helped transform it from idea to reality. I am deeply indebted to the ineffable Joan Taylor, who found Peter Teeple and the story of Caroline Norton; to Kathleen Corlett, who was a patient tutor in the law of the first half of the twentieth century; to Kathy McDonald and Jill Funimoto, who dropped everything to bring order out of a tonne of later legal material. Kathleen Vaughn, for whom interesting facts apparently leap nimbly off library shelves, found several hundred crucial books, articles, papers, and clippings and then subdued them into coherent chronologies.

David Hall-Humpherson kindly shared letters, pictures, and recollections of his mother, the late and much-missed Nell. Information, books, documents, or assistance were generously supplied by: H.T.G. Andrews, Chief Judge, the Provincial Court (Family Division); Moira Armour; Judi Beaman; Wendy Bryans; Professor J.M.S. Careless; Ian Carman; the Honourable Sean Conway, MPP; Henry Cartwright; Judge Ian Cartwright; Linda Silver Dranoff; Doralen Erb; Stephen Grant; June Gibson; Frances Gregory; John C. Hodgson, Chief Librarian of New York's *Daily News;* Stephen Ireland; Kenneth Jarvis, Secretary of the Law Society of Upper Canada; Dr. Mark Kieran; David Kilgour; Brian Land and Natalie Litwin of the Legislative Library; Juliet Mannock, Barry Morgan, and Eva Varengu, who provided some of the research for chapters one and two;

Elizabeth Marsh of the Metropolitan Toronto Children's Aid Society; Ross McLean; Olive Navis; the Honourable Robert Nixon, MPP; Gerald Owen; Ivon Owen; Elliott Pepper, Q.C.; Professor George Rawlyk of Queen's University; Dr. Charles Roland of McMaster University; Helen Riley; Ruth Seeley; Cathy Shepard of the Ontario Archives; Maxine Sidran; the family of Louis and Mary Trudeau of Wikwemikong, Manitoulin Island; Barbara Wilson of the Public Archives of Canada; Judge Norris Weisman of the Provincial Court (Family Division); William Withrow; Scott Young; the staffs of the Art Gallery of Ontario, the Metro Toronto Reference Library, the Baldwin Room, the Rare Books Room, and, especially, of the Ontario Archives, who were helpful in providing material. Frances Kieran successfully searched for several key articles and facts, and assisted in organizing the bibliography. In the very early days of the project, Judge Rosalie Abella gave it crucial support; as always, Barbara Moon was a patient listener and made useful suggestions for tackling difficult writing problems.

Harold Rosenberg and members of the University of Toronto staff helped trace Irving Reider's scholastic career; Ben Rosenberg and Albert Gallander spoke candidly and at length about their old friend. Without bitterness or sentimentality, Dr. Maurice Adelman recalled university life in the '30s; my sister, Myra Kates, supplemented my memories with her own recollections and she helped to bring out of the shadows of forty years the young man who had been our Uncle Irv.

Pressed by her own deadline, Michele Landsberg was unfailingly supportive in the way that only another writer who is "with book" can be. Betty Jane Corson is a diplomatic editor (as well as a true connoisseur of the subjunctive). Andrew Kieran took time from his hectic professional schedule to give urgently needed technical assistance; on the truly terrifying occasion when an error threatened three months' work, he was kind enough both to solve the problem and to resist commenting on its origins.

Professor Gerald Craig of the University of Toronto set aside his own project and spent hours correcting some howlers in the early chapters, as if there were nothing he enjoyed more than poring over the work of an eager neophyte.

Within the Ministry of the Attorney General, assistance was provided by: David Allen; Val Clare; Annie Coté-Kennedy; Allan Dickie; Craig Perkins; Allan Shipley; Deborah Wilkins. Peter Lukasiewicz, knee deep in a new career as executive assistant to a new minister in a new government, nonetheless took time to listen – and to help.

According to *The Oxford Companion to Law*, the concept of "the reasonable man" (sometimes known as "the man in the street" or "the man on the Clapham omnibus") has existed since 1837; he (the *Companion* notes the absence of a "reasonable woman" in the common law) is that mythical being whose foresight, care, and caution are a standard against which the behaviour of others may be judged. For example, a reasonable man, whether a family court judge or the newly appointed director of continuing education in his profession, would ration the time he took from his professional and private life and would probably not answer an endless stream of naive, repetitive, and confused questions, would not point out structural holes in writing, help an author find a legal researcher or restrain her from over-researching, or spend hours arguing points of law as with a colleague – tactfully and with precision. It was my great good fortune that George Thomson has never been on a Clapham omnibus.

Professor H.R.S. Ryan, Professor Emeritus of the Faculty of Law, Queen's University, is a legal scholar, philosopher, and historian, a gifted teacher and a stickler for accuracy, a man less cowed by change than all of the world's self-appointed "futurists" taken together. He, too, was wonderfully imprudent in spending time, hours and hours of it, correcting this work and patiently explaining both the broad sweep of history and its essential details. Generosity on that scale is rare and it is treasured.

All of the material regarding current law was checked by senior staff members of the Ministry of the Attorney General and reflects their knowledge of it; flaws in a large mass of historical and social material, despite the generous assistance of the many people involved, are probably inevitable. I, of course, take full responsibility for those.

This book would not have been possible, quite literally, without the support of the man who was Attorney General of Ontario while it was being written: the Honourable (now His Excellency) Roy McMurtry. From the first, he readily agreed to sponsor its writing and commercial publication and he asked only that it be an accurate and readable account of a major element in Ontario life. When Ian Scott was appointed Attorney General, the first with the power to succeed McMurtry in other than title, even I wondered, briefly, what he would do about both a law and a book that were identified with his predecessor. He turned out to be generously enthusiastic about this history and took time from a staggering work schedule to discuss family law issues with me.

Of greater importance, he briskly set about, even before the pictures were hung in his office, to bring in the reforms McMurtry had been forced to abandon, first in 1978 and then in 1985. This would have been a slender volume, indeed, without the ten years in which Roy McMurtry unswervingly supported family law reform and the determination with which Ian Scott took up the challenge.

Like Caroline Sheridan Norton, I "learned the . . . law, piecemeal, by suffering under it." People still suffer, although perhaps less obviously than in the past. But let the record show that the law today is at least an attempt to bring fairness, compassion, and reason into an area totally lacking in those qualities for nearly a thousand years and that reform in Ontario owes a great deal to the work of two decent men.

Sheila Kieran
Toronto
June, 1986

English Law: "The Rule of Decision in All Matters"

Today it is antique chic, self-consciously dainty, in the way of towns that live by the tourist trade. In 1792 it was a "poor wretched straggling village" able to accommodate the Governor and his lady in only a tent, since the Naval Hall, its grandest building, was being renovated. Its modern name is Niagara-on-the-Lake; in those days, it was called Newark.

There, on September 17, 1792, the new Legislature met for the first time in Newark and passed its first statute, to establish the English civil law in Upper Canada. Like all choices people make in governing themselves, this one signified more than what lay on the surface of its dusty legal circumlocutions. Because, the bill said, the province had "become inhabited principally by British subjects, born and educated in countries where the English laws are established," English law would be "the rule of decision in all matters of controversy, relative to property and civil rights."

Not long after, an anonymous English traveller, thought to be of "some standing and learning, especially in the law," wrote to a friend that

> . . . [not] all the laws of England are introduced into this province, but such as are suited to its circumstances. Many of our laws would be to them totally useless and inapplicable, and the source of much confusion. To have proffered them such a gift, would have been like placing the armour of a giant in the custody of a dwarf.

Nonetheless, at the same session the representatives of "the dwarf" passed a second statute, decreeing that all facts at issue before the courts should be "determined by the unanimous verdict of twelve jurors, which jurors shall be summoned and taken conformably to the law and custom of England."

" . . . summoned and taken conformably to the law and custom of England." That, of course, was the point. It was, after all, the right to live under English law that had been a major factor in bringing these particular people to this place of endless forests and hills, to the narrow belt between water and brooding rock where they would shape their communities. They had lived in the colonies of a King who signified five and a half centuries of protection under the law. Mad he might be, but he represented order, civilization, and certainty in a world that seemed to them to be turning itself inside out and, given

Court portrait of George III.

the choice, they had sacrificed much in order to continue living under the symbol of the Crown.

In making that decision, they were committing themselves to a complex of laws rooted, in part, in twelfth-century England and, in part, in religious laws – themselves founded on the Old Testament and on Roman law. Inevitably, all would have to be reshaped to the needs of a new society in a new country – a process that would begin almost immediately and would focus on the law of marriage.

Few of those who lived in Upper Canada and were subject to the new laws were themselves British. For more than a hundred centuries the area that comprised the new province had been inhabited by Indians; they had seen their first Europeans only in 1640, when the Jesuits came to evangelize them. By the 1760s there were, in addition, French farmers on either side of the Detroit River (site of the first permanent non-native settlement) merchants, soldiers, and the fur traders who sent pelts by boat down the St. Lawrence to the bustling port at Montreal.

A handful of those settlers had arrived more than a decade before the Loyalists, when the land was still a part of "Quebec," those 3,000,000 square kilometres of casual sprawl across the upper half of the continent. Its eastern boundary was Labrador, then moved southwest to the juncture of the Mississippi and Ohio rivers, dipping in an uneven line into what are now New York, Pennsylvania, and Ohio and north to Detroit. Only the bleak lands farther north, given the Hudson's Bay Company in 1670, kept Quebec from reaching the bay itself.

Originally "New France" but commonly called "Canada," Quebec had been an English possession since the French defeat at Quebec in 1759; it then took its new name and administration from the Quebec Act of 1774. Sensitive to the French majority amongst the white settlers of the time, the Act decreed that, although English criminal law would be the rule, civil law was that of the Canada that had been French.

But, in the colonies to the south, events that would alter that situation were moving toward their inevitable end – and thus to a new beginning.

The rising tide of the American Revolution had probably been inevitable since 1764, when colonists became embittered by various measures of the British Parliament and, in the words of future U.S. President John Adams, "the child of independence was born." By 1765 dissatisfaction had changed to violence: on August 26 of that year a mob burned the home of the Lieutenant-Governor of Massachusetts and, along with it, his magnificent library. Later, when import duties were placed on lead, glass, paint, and tea, the colonists boycotted those goods – a further irritation between them and the authorities.

In the spring of 1770 a mob harassed a sentinel in the town and, in the resulting mêlée, troops firing in his support killed five men, further inflaming tensions between those who supported British rule and those opposed to it.

The deterioration continued until, in the winter of 1773, matters came to a head with the so-called "Boston Tea Party": three ships carrying tea sailed into Boston harbour where a group disguised as Indians boarded the vessels and dumped the tea chests into the water; the manoeuvre was so elegantly carried out that its careful planning was unmistakable.

The rebels set up Committees of Public Safety (within a few years, the name would turn up, in an even more blood-chilling context, as the French Revolution turned to the Reign of Terror). With the arrogance traditional to such groups, they took upon themselves the right to decide whose beliefs were of a satisfactorily revolutionary hue: in most of the American colonies each person, according to a Test Act, was required to carry with him a certificate stating that he was free of suspicion of loyalty to King George III. In other words, like all revolutions, this one, when it came, would be essentially a civil war, fought between former friends and neighbours and within families.

Amongst the more than 2,000,000 Americans of the day, perhaps a third had Loyalist sympathies. Long before the opening shot of the Revolutionary War, it was apparent to 80,000 of them that they could not stay in an America that, as much as it was going to fight against an external power, was going to war within itself; it was equally apparent that these people would not be *able* to stay in the country born of such a war.

Some were eager to move north; others, although they were Loyalist sympathizers, wanted to remain; harassed because of their views, they reluctantly emigrated. (Many in this

Sir Frederick Haldimand.

latter group returned to the United States as soon as hostilities died down.) Others just wanted to be left alone to get on with lives that were filled enough with uncertainty and hardship. Having spent long years building their homes, tilling their farms, educating their offspring, they had no taste for either war or relocation. Staying put and keeping quiet was a small enough added price for hanging on to what had already taken the major part of several lifetimes to acquire.

The rebels, however, did not permit neutrality or pacifism: those who refused to embrace The Cause were considered as traitorous as those who opposed it. This placed an intolerable burden on, amongst others, the Quakers whose pacifist beliefs do not countenance war, whatever its reasons or outcome. Threatened by the rebels, many responded quickly to promises by the British authorities to respect their religion if they settled in the northern colony.

Then there were the Palatines (sometimes, with the Quakers, referred to as the "Plain Folk"), also pacifist by religious conviction, and one of the few groups in the American states who revered the English King, George III. He was of German extraction, and it was he whom they trusted – even if that faith required yet another in a series of moves that their families had begun nearly a hundred years before.

The history of the Palatines, in fact, is testimony to the awful durability of the human behaviour that makes refugees of the innocent: they were originally French Huguenots, German and Scandinavian Protestants who had settled in the area of Germany then known as the Lower Palatinate, on both sides of the lush Rhine Valley. By the beginning of the eighteenth century, they had fled in large numbers to England and Ireland as a result of religious persecution and endless wars (some Irish Dulmages and Sparlings were originally German Dolmetsches and Von Sperlings).

Many acted on the King's promise of religious freedom in his American colonies and moved eagerly across the ocean, hoping at last to find peace. Then, when they seemed permanently settled, mostly in Connecticut and Pennsylvania, the prospect of another war and the rebel refusal to respect their pacifism forced many to begin searching for yet another refuge where their customs and beliefs would be accepted.

One hallmark of their culture was the inimitable cuisine that uses black walnuts in soups and pickles; their route – quickly dubbed "The Trail of the Black Walnut" because so many of those trees grew in its hospitable limestone soil – led them to settle across the southern rim of what is now Ontario, where their culture is still maintained in communities stretching from Belleville to Kitchener. The "late Loyalists" from among these groups (some did not start the northward trek until about 1794) included descendants of the Dutch founders of New York City as well as of Pennsylvania German – "Deutsch" – whose customs and food still make them famous. By the time they reached permanent homes at last, some families had been on the move for more than seventy years and had come across the world in an age when even the most intrepid seldom moved a hundred kilometres from the places of their birth.

Migration into the part of the province of Quebec that would become Ontario had started even before the formal declaration of hostilities; some came via Sorel, a few by way of the Detroit River, most by land, crossing by boat at the Niagara River from Fort Niagara. On March 17, 1776, with the revolution now begun in earnest, General William Howe evacuated Loyalist sympathizers from Boston along with his troops, and the search for refuge became more urgent. Of those who eventually left the United States as Loyalists, approximately a third went to what are now New Brunswick and Nova Scotia; others headed for Florida (then Spanish territory) or the Caribbean or sought to retrace roots back to England.

But 6,000 came to what is now Ontario – some drawn by promises of land or of compensation for farms and properties lost in the American colonies. The land aside, they were drawn by their unshaken belief in the advantages of life under a politically powerful Britain, with its secure social and legal traditions.

Two hundred years later, it may seem tactless or mean-spirited to detail the savagery of the American rebels that inspired the Loyalist migration, but a proper understanding of the circumstances of the Loyalists – and a desire to give them their due – requires it. Experience had shown what they could expect in the breakaway colonies: there were laws that forbade them to keep arms, that required them to produce certificates of character before they were permitted to take lodgings in an inn, and that imposed special taxes on them. A Loyalist could not practise medicine or the law, could not teach, be a member of a jury, act as guardian or executor of an estate, buy or sell land, sue a debtor, or seek legal redress for wrongs committed against him. This effectively denied a day in court to people whose lives and belongings were frequently endangered. Loyalists were beaten, their homes burned; some were tortured – tarring and feathering was a favourite mode – and some were murdered. According to one historical account:

> . . . it seemed appropriate to revolutionary justice to carry through jeering crowds a loyalist gagged and bound, astride a rail with sharp angles, or (on) an unsaddled horse, with his face to the tail and coat turned inside out [a "turncoat"]; to cause a hot Tory [the designation

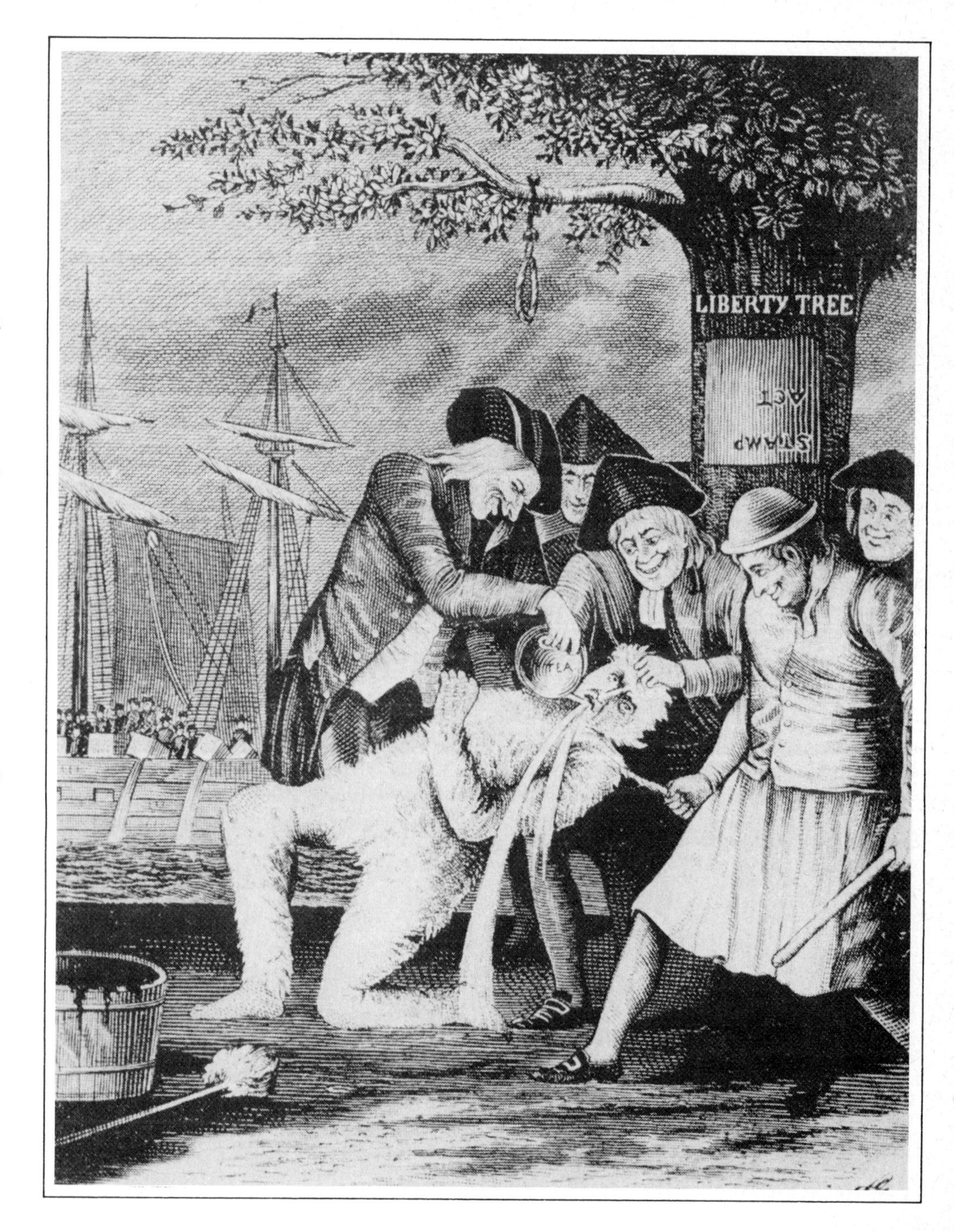

A 1774 Boston cartoon suggests how revolutionaries think Loyalists should be treated.

Loyalists on the trail to Upper Canada, a sketch by C.W. Jefferys.

> was used to identify Loyalists, irrespective of their actual political leanings] to sit long on a lump of ice and so be cooled; or to hoist these enemies of liberty upon a liberty pole and for a time keep them there with perhaps a dead animal hanging beside them . . . It was a grim pleasantry to brand High Church Tories with the cross. Sometimes there was added whipping, a cropping of ears, and exposure in the pillory. Savage mobs expelled aged people from their houses, which might then be burned; sometimes they destroyed the mills of loyalists and maimed their cattle . . . To hang a loyalist in effigy before his own door, or to fire at his lighted windows was an evidence of patriotism.

By comparison, perhaps even the hardships of seeking refuge paled: many families slogged long distances through swamp and forest to reach their new homes. According to one John MacLennan, a woman

> . . . carried two young children on her back. In the weary journey through the woods she thought her burden had become lighter and discovered that she had dropped one. On retracing her steps for some distance, she found the youngster sleeping quietly beside a decayed log . . . his hands begrimed with earth . . .

Thomas Gummersall Anderson, whose Loyalist father settled in Cornwall, points out briskly that "the Loyalists, having sacrificed their property to their politics, were, generally speaking, poor"; he goes on to describe "sup-on," the family's "morning and evening repast," which, he said, was made "of Indian corn, ground, and boiled for several hours, then eaten with milk, butter, sugar, etc., to suit the taste." Some would have considered sup-on an extraordinary treat: John MacLennan says that one traveller, "coming all the way from Georgia, told the story of the company feasting on a dog, to avoid starvation – his meagre share being a paw."

The bitterness of their memories stayed with some Loyalists as long as they lived and was given fresh life within a generation, when, in 1812, Canada and the United States were once more at war. William Canniff, writing in the mid-nineteenth century, claimed that "no history can parallel the deeds of atrocity enacted by the villainous "Liberty men" and went on to tell of

> . . . an old lady, on the verge of the grave, and with voice tremulous in remembrance of fiendish acts she had witnessed [who said that] the rebels, on one occasion entered a house and stripped it of everything, even the bed on which lay a woman on the point of confinement . . . upon a winters night . . . who, before morning, became a mother.

A more poignant note is struck in a letter that Sir John Johnson, member of a large and enormously influential family, a stepson of Molly Brant (of whom more later) wrote to his brother-in-law Robert Watts, who lived in New York:

> Neither time, distance nor the unhappy Revolution that have taken place can make me forget My friends or lessen in the least the sincere regard I had for you and your good Lady. Few Men, if any, have greater reason to regret

A stained-glass window in Grace United Church, Napanee, incorporates a Loyalist motto.

> their Separation from friends than myself, particularly as my fate puts an end to the prospect of our ever meeting in the same happy situation we once experienced.

But it is not the saddened participants who write history; that task usually falls to the victors and explains the tradition by which Loyalists are pictured as a small band of British elitists fleeing dynamic change in order to preserve a rotting colonialism on the shores of the St. Lawrence. According to a relatively recent *Encyclopaedia Britannica*, for example:

> In general, loyalism was strongest among officeholders and others who served the crown or proprietors; Anglican clergymen and their parishioners in the north; Quakers and other conscientious pacifists, such as members of German religious sects; large landholders, particularly in the north; and wealthy merchant groups in New York, Philadelphia, Baltimore, Charleston and elsewhere whose businesses and properties were affected by the war.

The implications of that characterization, at least as applied to those in Upper Canada, are simply not true. All Loyalists were American: in order to be designated "Loyalist," the refugee had to have been *born* in the United States. A large proportion of those who made land-grant applications as Upper Canada Loyalists were illiterate and used a "mark" as a signature; records show that most were farmers from the lower social and economic strata of Pennsylvania and Upper New York State.

General Frederick Haldimand, that decent man and competent administrator who was responsible for immigrants of the period, reported to London in 1784 that 6,152 refugees had arrived. Some had been soldiers and in 1785 Sir John Johnson described those who had settled in eight townships: 1,568 men; 626 women, 1,492 children, and ninety servants. In a day when servants were paid little or nothing, ninety amongst more than 1,500 families indicated a group with modest means indeed.

Some Loyalists were people of extraordinary spirit and determination – for example, Adam Young (the first generation of his family to anglicize the German surname Jung), who by 1775 had spent more than thirty years clearing and working his hundred-acre farm in New York State. Young had been harassed by rebel neighbours and was imprisoned for eleven months when he refused to take an oath of allegiance to the new regime; his home was burnt, his fields laid to ruin, and his stock stolen from him. When war came, Young served the Loyalist forces as a guerrilla fighter.

As a result, his lands were later confiscated and he started again the daunting work of pushing back the frontier and making a home and a livelihood for himself and his family. Adam Young was then sixty-six years of age – in an era when the death certificate of a fifty-one-year-old man gave the cause as "old age."

An affecting portrait of another Loyalist family was provided, with haphazard punctuation and spelling, by an elderly woman, Catharine White, writing in 1812 in support of her request for a U.E.L. land grant:

Loyalist Charles Inglis, consecrated by the Church of England in 1787, was the first bishop appointed overseas. His diocese covered British North America (including the West Indies).

> My father and Mother came from England, settled in the United States, in St. Lawrence upon a farm which they purchased there, planted some trees and were beginning to prosper when the revolutionary War broke out . . . Hearing that sugar was made from Trees in Canada, and being thorough Loyalists, and not wishing to be mixed up with the Contest about to be carried on, we packed up our effects and came over to Canada . . . Mother used to chop down Trees, attended the house hold duties and as the children grew up, they were trained to Industrious habits, we were very useful to her, attended the cattle, churned the butter, making cheese, dressing the flax, spinning, in those days the spinning Wheel looked cheerful, made our own cloth, and stockings . . . The Bay of Quinte was covered with Ducks of which we could

obtain any quantity from the Indians. As to fish they could be had by fishing with a scoup I have often speared large Salmon with a pitchfork . . . A tree fell one day and hurt Mother's back very much, we sent for the old woman (the Chief physician of the surrounding County as it gradually settled) who came steeped some wheat made lye, applied it very hot in a flannel, in a very short time, she was well as ever.

Another woman – hardly a colonial eager to re-create a British court on the shores of the Great Lakes – was a Loyalist from a very different background. Energetic, outspoken, and strongly influential, Molly Brant has stood too long in the shadow of her brother Joseph. An instinctive leader from the matriarchal Mohawk society, she lived for twenty-two years as the consort of a white man, one of the most respected ever to come into contact with the Indian people.

There are few solid facts about the early years of Kōnwatsi'tsiaiéñni or Gonwatsijayenni ("Someone Lends Her a Flower"), English name, Mary, known most of her life as Molly. She was born about 1736 and was always close to Joseph, six years her junior. Descended from a chief of the Mohawk Nation and thus royalty in their own culture, they were, according to neighbours, "a Family of Distinction." Their lineage gave them considerable influence within the Six Nations which they used repeatedly when war came. The Six Nations' tradition of loyalty to the British – a commitment that played a decisive part in Canada's early history – was one of the major influences on Molly Brant's adult life.

Another was the remarkable Irish-born Superintendent of Indian Affairs for the province of New York, Sir William Johnson. The widowed father of a half-dozen children, he lived with Molly Brant from 1759 until his death on the eve of the Revolutionary War; she bore him at least eight children and, on his death, made her own contribution to the war and her own proud path through two disparate societies.

She was particularly suited to be his partner and to wield influence on events after his death. Molly Brant had been brought up in a society unafraid of its powerful females (the respected women of the tribe, the Matrons, chose the chief). Moreover, as the member of a great family, she had been treated with exquisite courtesy and affection by an intelligent man who was himself a long-time friend and ally, and idolized by her people.

Sadly, there is not a single drawing, sketch, or contemporary description of Molly Brant, although there are many portraits of her brother, including two famous full-length paintings (one by the great English portraitist, George Romney). A man who met her in the winter of 1754-55 later said only that an English captain "fell in Love wth. Ms. Mary Brant who was then pretty likely not havg. had the small pox" – and that is the sum of what we know of her person.

Of her character, happily, there is much more evidence: the commander of a Six Nations settlement at Carleton Island, where she urged her people to remain loyal to the British cause, said their "uncommon good behaviour is in a great Measure to be ascribed to Miss Molly Brants Influence over them, which is far superior to that of all their Chiefs put together." Brant worked hard, first feeding those who sought refuge in the Mohawk Valley, then sending ammunition to supporters of the Loyalist cause. In August of 1777 she sent Indian runners to warn a British force at Fort Stanwix (now Rome, New York) of the approach of a large rebel contingent, which, as a result, was ambushed by Indians and Loyalists at the battle of nearby Oriskany.

In retribution a force of Oneida Indians, who were rebel supporters, harassed the Mohawks, Brant especially, and made it necessary for her to seek refuge with a cousin who was the chief in a Cayuga village. At the urgent request of the British authorities, she moved herself and her family to Fort Niagara and, later, to Cataraqui (now Kingston).

The British treatment of Brant, whom they respected – and needed – might best be described as "give her anything she wants," whether it was help in settling family members in Montreal, financing the education of her children, or awarding her a considerable pension of £100 a year. In 1784 the British built homes at Cataraqui, one for Joseph and one for Molly.

The Americans, who wanted her to persuade the tribes of the Ohio Valley to accept their government policy of westward expansion, were equally eager suitors for her support. After the fighting ended, they promised her "if she and Her Family would return to that Country . . . a sum of Money equal to the sum their lands were sold for by the Commission of Confiscation" – an offer she rejected "with the utmost contempt." Clearly, they never understood the depth of Brant's bitterness at the Oneida attack or her fierce devotion to Loyalism.

At the end of the trail, a home carved from the new province's dense bush.

The last account of Molly Brant was written during the 1790s by an anonymous traveller who said he saw

> . . . in the church in Kingston . . . an old Indian woman, who sat in an honourable place among the English. She appeared very devout during the Divine Service and very attentive to the Sermon . . . When Indian embassies arrived, she was sent for, dined at Governor Simcoe's and was treated with respect by himself and his lady.

Molly Brant was in her sixty-first year when she died at the home of her daughter Magdalene, in Cataraqui on April 16, 1796. She was buried in St. George's (now St. Paul's) churchyard. Other than the minister's notation of Brant's name and the date in the parish records, there is no description of her funeral. According to a history of the church, published in 1937, no grave or stone marking Molly Brant's resting place has ever been found.

In later years historians with a sense of propriety appropriate to their times and temperament – but perhaps not to Brant's and Johnson's – declared that the two had married in the rites of the Anglican Church, possibly in a deathbed service performed for the sake of their children. There is no evidence to substantiate this claim, and considerable reason to doubt it. Johnson, after all, would have known that the children, born in the Mohawk Valley, were subject to the common law of England and, according to that law, they could not be legitimated retroactively.

Certainly, Brant was Johnson's wife according to Mohawk custom, but there is nothing to indicate that they had ever married in the Mohawk ritual. Clearly, the relationship as it existed suited them both: in his will Johnson refers without embarrassment to "my present housekeeper, Mary Brant" and to his "natural children," and Brant always distinguished between her surname and theirs. Perhaps she wished to protect her status as a Matron in the Mohawk society while ensuring that her children, carrying their father's notable name, would be welcome in his culture – bastards or not. If that is the case, her hopes for them appear to have been fulfilled: according to a contemporary letter "(the children) are, I believe, with the exception of one son, all daughters. Sir William bequeathed handsome fortunes to the whole family. The Misses Johnson are married respectably in the country."

The land of Molly Brant's birth had been Indian and Dutch; by the time of her death, across a new border, it was unmistakably different – not British, to be sure, and certainly not American – but headed in a direction uniquely its own. She had been a force in its foundation.

The more precise shape of the new community would remain blurred until another battle was fought – not in a field or on the sea, but in the Legislature – attacks mounted, positions defended, skirmishes won, losses counted – in the cause of a law. On the evidence of Brant's life, it was a law she would not have considered of much importance. But it mattered greatly to the type of society that was beginning to take form at the time of her death and it would be debated for more than half a century. Specifically, it was a law that defined under whose auspices valid marriages would be performed in Upper Canada.

Today's couple, standing in the presence of a clergyman, two witnesses, and their chosen guests, inherit more than seven centuries of tradition. Some choose a service filled with the stained-glass solemnity of the old vows: "with my body I thee worship"; "I take thee to be my wedded husband . . . to love, honour and obey"; "forsaking all others, cleave you only to her." Others are inspired to write their own "may-your-love-be-a-shining-big-bird-of-happiness" prose or to compose a solemn declaration of their most optimistic hopes for the future.

But the choices were not always so broad. In the beginning, the law of marriage and unmarriage was the law of England – and in *its* beginning, the marriage law of England was the law of the Western Catholic Church. As celebrated by the church, "sacramental marriage" – a sacrament conferred, one on the other, by two baptized persons and completed only by physical consummation – is indissoluble except by the death of one of the parties. Before it existed in the religious form, couples simply exchanged vows with each other, or sometimes in front of the community.

In the Britain of the Middle Ages, the Ecclesiastical Courts had total jurisdiction in matters affecting marriage: whether a couple had been wed validly, whether the behaviour of husband or wife was cause to allow them to live apart and, in that event, what arrangements would be made for the maintenance of the wife and children.

The early church had complex rules that prohibited marriage between people who were related by blood (extending even to sixth cousins), by status (widowed spouses could not marry in-laws, for example), or by sacramental relationship (a baptized person could not marry his or her sponsor).

The validity of marriage was commonly challenged, sometimes after both its principals were dead, thus casting doubt on the legitimacy of children. Even a couple who had later validated their marriage could not confer retroactive legitimacy on offspring: according to a famous dictum of English civil law (in force until 1926) "once a bastard, always a bastard."

The word "bastard" comes from a phrase in Old French, *fils de bast* – the son born in a barn, idiomatically the "acknowledged son of a nobleman, born out of wedlock"; it, in turn, came from a word that referred to concubinage and was derived from *bansti*, "barn" in Teuton. The etymology is instructive because it reflects social attitudes toward illegitimate birth throughout several centuries of law. In medieval England, a bastard had no rights and no responsibilities for either of his parents. He could not look to them for support in their lifetimes or for bequests afterward. They had no right to his custody or guardianship; the law's Latinate description of him as *filius nullius* – nobody's child – was depressingly accurate.

The consequences could be devastating in a society in which the main source of wealth was the inheritance of land – and in which, according to the law, bastards could not inherit.

What we call divorce was unknown, although there were two kinds of separation (*dīvortium* in Latin): divorce from bed and board (separation) and divorce from the bond of matrimony (annulment).

With the Reformation, which had its beginnings in the marital problems of Henry VIII, the Ecclesiastical Courts became those of the Church of England and gradually lost exclusive jurisdiction over marriage. In the time of the first Elizabeth, the British Parliament established Parliamentary divorce, its first involvement in what had been exclusively a church matter (although, by the end of the 1600s, just one or two divorce bills had been passed). Church courts still concerned themselves with certain tangled questions of validity, but the number of prohibited degrees of blood or status relationship had been reduced; the civil courts dealt only with those marital matters which affected rights of property and inheritance. In the sixteenth and seventeenth centuries there was continuous church debate on whether divorce from bed and board dissolved the marriage or was separation only. By the end of the 1600s the accepted position was that the divorce was just a separation, not a dissolution of the marriage.

The procedure for obtaining a Parliamentary divorce was difficult and expensive, available only to the wealthy and favoured and only on grounds of rape, adultery, sodomy, or bestiality.

Over the years Parliament developed a divorce procedure in cases of adultery, but it was very different for men than for women. A husband first sued his wife's lover on grounds of "criminal conversation" (in the words of one Canadian legal historian, "for an act that was neither genuinely criminal nor conversational"); he then sued in the Ecclesiastical Court for separation from bed and board, and in Parliament for divorce. If the adultery was that of the husband, however, the wife could sue only in the Ecclesiastical Court for separation and in Parliament for divorce – she was not entitled to support or any damages. The Parliamentary bills, introduced separately in each case, allowed the plaintiff but not the respondent, who was regarded as the "guilty party," to remarry.

By the middle of the eighteenth century, Parliament was becoming further involved in the process of legislating matrimony: in 1753 it passed an Act dealing with the solemnization of marriage. According to the Act, a wedding, to be valid, had to take place in a parish church, cathedral, or chapel in the presence of a minister of the Church of England and two other witnesses; the couple's intentions to marry had to have been announced ("the banns published") on three successive Sundays before the wedding or, if that was not possible, after a special license had been obtained. The Act affected England only and did not apply to Quakers and Jews, who were "authorized to solemnize marriage according to their own rites."

By 1792 the civil courts were declaring marriages null and void from the beginning when it could be shown that they were bigamous or the result of coercion. They were also nullifying marriages in which parents had not given permission to children who were under age or lacked the intellectual capacity to give consent. Both Ecclesiastical and civil courts were ruling on issues of validity or in cases in which the marriage had not been solemnized according to the 1753 Marriage Act. Now, only matters of impotence or a challenge on grounds of prohibited degrees of relationship were being heard exclusively in the Ecclesiastical Courts.

And it was at that moment, with jurisdiction over marriage and divorce split between church and state – but, increasingly, held by the state – that Upper Canada adopted the English law for its own.

The Merchant and the Member from St. Mawe's

Two persistent religious and political battles, begun in the late eighteenth century, would prove crucial in defining the province that was to come. Only one, the fight over lands set aside for the church ("the Clergy Reserves") is remembered: even today's schoolchildren learn about the one-seventh of surveyed lots set aside in 1791 under that title. But it was the other – a marriage law controversy that dragged on long after its original combatants were in their graves – that began first. Unknown today, even to many lawyers, the issue was so crucial in its time that it was the subject of debate in every one of the first eleven Parliaments of Upper Canada.

It was fuelled, as such fights usually are, by the fiercely held ideals of two powerful, vastly different men. One was the Honourable Richard Cartwright, a successful merchant and Kingston's leading citizen; the other was John Graves Simcoe, chosen in England in 1791 to become the province's first Lieutenant-Governor. It was an inevitable fight, given Simcoe's character and that of the people he had been sent to govern. The Simcoe remembered today, when he is remembered at all, is a stiff ultra-Tory, the veritable caricature of a haughty soldier who came here as a stranger when the old province of Quebec was carved into Upper and Lower Canada.

Simcoe saw in the western of the two provinces a "Canada" that, in reality, would be nothing less, or more, than an England writ small; it would be ruled from the top, its aristocracy founded easily on the upper-class shoulders of the half-pay officers who had fought in the Revolution. Simcoe was genuinely dismayed that voters in the province chose for their Legislature men "of a Lower Order, who kept but one Table, that is who dined in Common with their Servants." On the evidence of such words, history's Simcoe is an imperious patrician, blind to both the singularity and the challenge of the new province entrusted to him.

All of which he was. But he was more: a complex, unfulfilled man, physically brave but in uncertain health, who cared to the roots of his soul for his King and his God and, aside from those, probably only for his children and the quite remarkable wife who bore them. Ambitious, his plans and ideas humming with intelligence and energy, the real Simcoe was not a man who had just been dropped into the laps of those he governed: he had earned the right to his ideas of the new country, however wide of the mark they were.

The son of a naval officer who had died while on his way to fight with Wolfe at Quebec (his future wife's father had actually served in the Battle

A flattering portrait of John Graves Simcoe.

of the Plains of Abraham), Simcoe had come to America to fight in the early days of the Revolution; he was commended for his active part in operations on Long Island and in New Jersey, evacuated from Boston with Howe, wounded badly at the Battle of Brandywine, and, after narrowly escaping with his life, taken prisoner of war by rebels in Pennsylvania.

His unyielding patriotism and devotion to duty cloaked a man who, at least on occasion, was a romantic. In 1782, the year after he returned to England from war service, Simcoe met Miss Gwillim; she was sixteen and an orphan, her widowed mother having died in childbirth. The heiress to Colonel Gwillim's not inconsiderable estate, sombrely christened Elizabeth Posthuma, was pretty and an accomplished linguist with a boundless curiosity about the world around her. The future Mrs. Simcoe was of Welsh descent, a spirited youngster who must have been a wondrous contrast to the solemn young officer fourteen years her senior. Although her guardian was unhappy about the hasty courtship, the two were quickly engaged and married within months of meeting.

The marriage was a happy one for the Simcoes and a piece of great fortune for posterity: Mrs. Simcoe was a sharp observer with a fine eye for detail; she had ready access to people at all levels of her society, especially to those powerful citizens whose decisions were influencing the direction of the new province. Moreover, she was skilled enough to write an incomparable day-to-day record (with her own sketches) of our earliest history. There were, of course, limitations on both Simcoes: they were, like us all, creatures of their time. In order to understand the first Lieutenant-Governor's attitudes, it is

A decidedly unflattering portrait of Elizabeth Posthuma Gwillim Simcoe, when she was in her twenties.

necessary to take a closer look at that time.

In 1791 a group of enraged peasants at Varennes caught Louis XVI, Marie Antoinette, and members of the royal family frantically fleeing toward the Austrian border, and returned them to Paris. Three and a half weeks later hundreds of people, lining up in the centre of Paris to sign a petition, became embroiled in a fight, and troops, trying to quell the ensuing disorder, fired into the crowd; fifty people were killed in what became known as the Massacre of the Champs de Mars. In the name of democracy, the French, no longer a people, were dissolving into a mob.

Though manageable by contrast, England had problems of its own: several dissenting denominations had split from the Established Church, the largest group being the 60,000 English Methodists whose ties to Anglicanism were steadily eroding. Englishmen like Simcoe, for whom the Church was the rock of existence, believed, as readily and unquestioningly as they breathed, that any move that strengthened Methodism was intolerable.

And there was more than religion at stake: an assault on the Church was an assault on its head, the English sovereign, and, by extension, on English institutions. To a man of Simcoe's station and class, this had to be fought at all costs; English life, after all, was the apotheosis of civilized society: power was held by those whose breeding, education, and wealth had fitted them for it. Of course, the privilege of aristocracy carried responsibility (*noblesse oblige*) and Simcoe had been the Member of Parliament for St. Mawe's, Cornwall, since 1790.

To such a man nothing but anarchy could come from giving responsibility to the poor, the illiterate, the mob. One had only to look across the Channel or across the ocean to understand what confirmation Simcoe saw for this view of the world: in France, regicide would be committed and, as for America – well, there Simcoe had already suffered greatly. And, packing this mental baggage, along with two of their six children, the Simcoes headed for Upper Canada.

Although they were wined and dined when they arrived in the town of Quebec after a forty-six-day trip across the Atlantic, Simcoe must have chafed before he reached his final destination. There was no quorum of councillors in Upper Canada and therefore no one to administer his oath of office, so he cooled his heels in the eastern province for another seven months. Finally, on July 1, 1792, the Simcoes arrived at Kingston where, one week later at St. George's Church, "attended . . . by the Magistrates, and principal inhabitants," Simcoe took his oath as Lieutenant-Governor.

One of those "principal inhabitants" was almost certainly Richard Cartwright, a founder of the church in which the ceremonies of office took place. He, too, judged the world on the basis of his perceptions of it. But he had experienced that world differently and therefore held basic beliefs that were the opposite of Simcoe's. Still, Simcoe quickly nominated him to sit in the provincial Legislature, which then, and for the first half-century of Upper Canada's existence, was a bicameral body with an elected Legislative Assembly and an appointed Legislative Council. The appointment was a decision that Simcoe would quickly and needlessly regret: in misunderstanding Cartwright, he would misunderstand the people he had come to govern and, despite his formidable energy and essential decency, he would be of lesser importance to them than, clearly, he wanted to be.

And, although Richard Cartwright is almost unknown today (a grandson, Sir Richard Cartwright, who was first a minister in the Laurier government and then Senate leader, cuts a wider swath in the history books), it was his sensibility that, in the long term, proved more accurate than Simcoe's. He was, in fact, the quintessential Loyalist: born in Albany in 1759 of an English father and Dutch mother, he was no democrat but a pragmatist with firm allegiance to the English Crown who had come to the northern colony because of his political sympathies.

Cartwright was now a prosperous businessman, well liked and influential. The only existing portrait of him is contained in a friend's description of him: ". . . a boy in playing, struck him with a stone in his left eye, which deprived him almost entirely of its use, and turned the ball outwards, by which his countenance, otherwise remarkably fine, was somewhat deformed." Although not a lawyer, he was an unpaid judge of one of the courts of Common Pleas, courts – one in each district of the province – that handled small personal disputes not involving the Crown.

Cartwright, a deeply religious man, had been forced by the war to abandon plans to enter the Anglican ministry. Nonetheless, he indirectly influenced the religious life of the province for nearly three-quarters of a century by

Banns of Marriage ~~between Robert &~~

Numb. 60 Lieutenant Colonel John Graves Simcoe of this Pariſh

and Miſs Elizabeth Posthuma Gwillim of this Pariſh were

Married in this Church by Licence

this 30th Day of December in the Year One Thouſand Seven Hundred and eighty two by me Thos. Roskilly, Curate

This Marriage was ſolemnized between Us { John Graves Simcoe / Elizabeth Posthuma Gwillim

In the Preſence of Saml. Graves. Margaret Graves

The Simcoes' marriage certificate.

influencing the young Scots Presbyterian immigrant who lived with the Cartwright family and tutored the children. In 1803, when the young man, John Strachan, presented himself for ordination in the Church of England, he carried a letter of reference from Richard Cartwright. He later became the province's first Anglican bishop and mentor to the second generation of its power elite.

For some time, there had been a matter that deeply troubled Richard Cartwright. In 1784 he had married Magdalen Secord (whose sister-in-law would later walk a cow into history) at the British military post at Niagara; the marriage had not been solemnized in the presence of a minister of the Established Church. However, according to what was now the prevailing law of Upper Canada, that was the only way couples were considered to be legally married and their children legitimate.

That law, which came from England, had been designed for the majority in *that* country, living in its small area, compelled, for certain purposes, to conform to the rites of a single church. In the sparsely settled colonies, however, where there were few ministers, vast distances, and poor roads, many couples were married by magistrates, commanding officers of military posts, regimental surgeons acting as chaplains, or by other public officials who simply read the service from *The Book of Common Prayer*. As matters stood, these couples were living in sin, their children irrevocably marked as bastards, ineligible to inherit.

Richard Cartwright had two sons and a daughter and he was now anxious to regularize his marriage and legitimize his three heirs. (Sadly, they would not live to benefit from his substantial estate. Those three and another of the five children subsequently born to the Cartwrights would grow to adulthood, then die in the three years prior to Cartwright's own death.) In the first session of the First Parliament he introduced as the first bill one that would validate irregularly contracted Anglican marriages and, contrary to long centuries of English tradition, retroactively confer legitimacy on the children of such unions.

But Simcoe thought the bill "hasty and ill drawn" and it was withdrawn on Simcoe's explicit promise that the plight of Anglicans who had not been married by their clergy would be taken up with the authorities in the British Home Office, the ministry responsible for the colonies.

In the Legislature's second session, even before word arrived from London, Cartwright reintroduced his bill in the Upper House and there it passed rapidly. When it was sent to the House of Assembly, however, the Lower House amended it to allow ministers of other denominations to validly solemnize marriages of *their* members. It seemed that men who ate at the same table as their servants could not see why one religion should be preferred within the law over others.

The amended Act passed the Assembly but was unacceptable to the Legislative Council and was defeated; it was then withdrawn, again with positive assurances to the Lower House that representations would be made to the Home Office on the issue of allowing non-Anglican clergy to perform valid marriages.

Simcoe, not to put too fine a point on it, was stalling with no real intention of getting such an agreement. Writing to one of the King's Principal Secretaries, Henry Dundas, he said:

> The general cry of Persons of all

> conditions for the passing the Marriage Bill was such, that I could no longer withhold under the pretence of consulting any opinions at home, having already availed myself of that excuse for delay; There are very few Members of the Church of England in either house and the disposition of the house of Assembly is to make Matrimony a much less solemn or guarded contract than good Policy will Justify. They returned the Bill with a rider giving power to Ministers of every sect and denomination, (of which in this Country there are not a few), to solemnize Matrimony. And it was only on a compromise that they were prevailed upon to withdraw it . . .

Moreover, Simcoe was not above a small piece of sophistry, blandly assuring the Home authorities that any move to extend the rights of marrying to other denominations would cause unrest.

> . . . on the first day of the meeting of the House [he reported to Henry Dundas] petitions from Menonists, Tunkers [a Baptist sect], and others were brought forward praying that their ministers might be authorized to solemnize marriage with validity. The petition was disregarded, but it was found that had the question been stirred in any respect whatever the various pretensions and prejudices of the different sectaries would have produced great animosity and confusion; it was, therefore, thought that it was most advisable to suspend all proceedings on the subject . . .

A seemingly deft ploy: since there were a variety of denominations wishing to be treated equally with the Church of England, the entire question should be shelved.

But ideas have their own momentum and, once it had become an issue, the recognition of the rights of various religious denominations simply would not disappear. First, there was the numerical reality that Anglicans were a minority in Upper Canada. But there was an even more decisive factor – one that was as alien to Simcoe as the idea of pluralism: in fleeing the rebels of the American Revolution, the Loyalists had declared their adherence to the Crown but not to the totality of English custom and practice. They had been born and had lived in a society of many faiths and opinions and had no intention of building one in which they were going to be denied previously held rights.

In hindsight, it is easy to oversimplify the entire rights issue and to assign heroes and villains. Sides changed, for example, when it came to the matter of slavery. In 1772 the English jurist Lord Mansfield, ruling in the case of a slave named Somerset, decreed that a person living in England was, by virtue of that fact alone, free; as a result, it was illegal to bring slaves into England. Influenced by that decision, which did not have force in the colonies, Simcoe pushed for abolition shortly after he arrived in Upper Canada.

But he faced stiff opposition: writing again to Dundas to describe events in the Assembly, Simcoe said:

The Reverend John Strachan, 1827.

> The greatest resistance was to the Slave Bill, many plausible Arguments of the dearness of Labour and the difficulty of obtaining Servants to cultivate Lands were brought forward. Some possessed of Negroes knowing that it was very questionable whether any subsisting Law did Authorize Slavery, and having purchased several taken in War by the Indians at small prices wished to reject the Bill entirely, others were desirous to supply themselves by allowing the importation for two years. The matter was finally settled by undertaking to secure the property already obtained upon condition that an immediate stop should be put to the importation and that slavery should be gradually abolished.

Cartwright, on the other hand, owned slaves and saw nothing wrong with the practice. The law that resulted from Simcoe's efforts was, as he knew, far from perfect: it forbade the slave trade but it freed only those slaves born after 1793 and, even then, only when they reached the age of twenty-five. Virtually ignored today, it was liberal legislation in an era when the idea of people owning people was still acceptable in much of the "civilized" world: such renowned "democrats" as George Washington and Thomas Jefferson owned slaves and Benjamin Franklin owned *and* dealt in them.

The fight over rights that centred on marriage was, in fact, about much more than who could perform the happy duties; it became an emotional shorthand for attitudes toward people as diverse as the British sovereign and the rebels of the United States. Within its vocabulary, men were defining the society they wanted for themselves and the one they bequeathed to us.

The importance they attached to the issue made them fierce in their judgements of each other: just a year after his appointment of Cartwright to the Legislative Council, Simcoe dipped pen in venom to write Dundas again, describing Cartwright and his partner, Robert Hamilton:

> Mr. Hamilton is an avowed Republican in his sentiments and altho' the merchants are justly obnoxious to the settlers of this Province, and He is particularly so, yet the ascendancy He and his friend, Mr. Cartwright *must acquire*, by being Agents for the Contract which supplies the King's Troops with provisions, is of that nature, that there is nothing to prevent them from exercising it to the detriment of Government, if they have any particular Object to promote, that may gratify their avarice, ambition or Vanity.

Elsewhere, he further vilified Cartwright as "a republican" (a considerable insult in post-Revolutionary Canada) and "disloyal."

Cartwright was more thoughtful – and accurate – in his judgements of Simcoe, but no more generous; after the end of each session of Parliament, he created an imperishable record of the time by setting down a detailed account of events in letters to his friend, the Montreal merchant Isaac Todd. One such report, written on the first of October, 1794, offers particularly sharp pictures of Simcoe, of the issues underlying the ongoing disputes, of feelings in the province at the time, and, ultimately, of Richard Cartwright himself.

> It seems . . . that every man who will not be a mere tool, and pay implicit respect to the caprice and extravagance of a Colonial Governor, must be an object of jealousy and malevolence, not only here but at home. Yet ask these gentlemen for what purpose they gave me a seat in the Legislative Council? I presume they will tell you it was from a desire to avail themselves of my knowledge of the country and acquaintance with the inhabitants, derived from long residence and familiar intercourse with them, to assist in framing such laws as might be most applicable to the situation of the colony; not merely to show my complaisance to the person at the head of the Government. Such, at all events, is the duty which I conceive that my appointment imposes on me; and do they expect that I should either approve of or be silent upon measures that are totally inapplicable to the state of society in this country, that are inconsistent with its geographical situation, and must shock the habits and prejudices of the majority of its inhabitants?
>
> I do not doubt the disposition of the Governor to consult the welfare of the Province, yet this disposition sometimes puts on an odd appearance. He is a man of warm and sanguine temper, that will not let him see any obstacles to his views; he thinks every existing regulation in England would be proper here . . . he seems bent on copying all the subordinate establishments without considering the great disparity of the two countries in every respect. And it really would not surprise me to see attempts made to establish among us Ecclesiastical Courts, tithes and religious tests, though nine-tenths at least of our people are of persuasions different from the Church of England, though the whole have been bred in a country where there was the most perfect freedom in religious matters, and though this would certainly occasion almost a general emigration . . .

Cartwright went on to quote part of an address he had made not long before to a grand jury:

> "We are happily exempt from those political dissensions that are now covering Europe with crimes and blood. . . reposing under the protection of a Government from whose bounty we possess a soil that furnishes to the industrious every necessary of life – a Government that hath liberally assisted us in converting our forests into comfortable habitations and fruitful fields -- we seem little disposed to forget,

> and base would we be if we could forget, the ties of gratitude as well as duty by which our allegiance is secured . . ."

Then, returning to the matters at hand, he told Todd that

> . . . though I do not think it necessary to bow with reverence to the wayward fancies of every sub-delegate of the Executive Government, I will not hesitate to assert that His Majesty has not two more loyal subjects, and in this Province certainly none more useful, than Mr. Hamilton and myself, nor shall even the little pitiful jealousy that exists with respect to us make us otherwise . . . I am ashamed to have said so much on this subject, but I cannot help being provoked by such unhandsome conduct . . .

Clearly, Simcoe and Cartwright represented two very different ideas of the new province. Would it be governed by a constitution that was, in Simcoe's glowing phrase, "the very image and transcript of that of Great Britain"? Or would it take its shape from the ideas of Cartwright and men like him? He thought it "as impolitic as it is unjust" to form "a new government, as in the present case, among a people composed of every religious denomination . . . to attempt to give to that Church the same exclusive political advantages that it possesses in Great Britain, and which are even there the cause of so much clamour . . ."

Neither man would live to know the outcome – in that maddening, mysteriously workable way that Canadians think of as theirs, the answer would take time – sixty-seven years! – and compromise.

The passage of the first Marriage Act in 1793, in fact, settled very little: aside from regularizing already existing unions, it provided only that a magistrate in any district of Upper Canada – there were four – might validly marry couples until there should be at least five "parsons or ministers of the Church of England" in the district; first, however, the magistrate must have put up a notice in the most public place in the township or parish and then have waited for three Sundays to elapse.

Having urged the Home Office in 1794 to do nothing more about the marriage question, Simcoe did likewise in 1795 when Presbyterians presented a petition urging that their ministers be given the right to perform valid marriages. In 1796 it was the turn of the Baptists of Bastard Township (which took its name from an old Devonshire family and not from the unhappy situation of many of its younger residents). The Presbyterians of Grenville County tried again, pointing out to Simcoe that, in Scotland, their church enjoyed the right to celebrate marriages, a right they should therefore have in Upper Canada. Far from convincing Simcoe, this moved him to describe the petition as "a product of a wicked head and most disloyal heart."

Of course, Simcoe alone could not have imposed his ideas of church-sanctioned marriage and, in fact, he was being encouraged by Henry Dundas's letters. Moreover, he had worries other than the vexing marriage question. In 1789 the province had suffered "The Hungry Year," a devastating drought, and recovery was slow; nonetheless, there was now a plentiful supply of grain – more even than could be sent over the scant road system and exported. Farmers were distilling the excess and it was natural that, in a new country with its harsh winters and isolation, much of the product of their stills got no farther than the nearest kitchen table.

Then there was the matter of the provincial capital: the Lieutenant-Governor had pushed hard for a site on the River La Tranche – he renamed it the Thames River – at what is now London. But geography and settlement patterns made the idea so unrealistic that, on October 21, 1792, Cartwright was able to place pen in hand – and tongue in cheek – to report to Isaac Todd:

> The River Tranche is still talked of as the seat of government, but I hope this plan will not be persisted in, for it appears to me as complete a piece of political Quixotism as I recollect to have met with . . . it is a scheme perfectly utopian, to which nature has opposed invincible obstacles; unless Mongolfier's ingenious invention could be adapted to practical purposes, and air balloons be converted into vehicles of commerce.

Simcoe's immediate superior, Guy Carleton, Lord Dorchester – a man he often ignored or fought with – obviously agreed, and the seat of government moved from Newark to York on Toronto Bay.

Visitors often noted the number and sophistication of the entertainments offered at the new capital, but the province was inevitably isolated by the gulf between events in Europe and receipt of the news in Upper Canada. On March 1, 1794, for example, Mrs. Simcoe wrote, "The news received of the death of the Queen of France. Orders given out for mourning, in which everybody appeared this evening, and the dance postponed." By that date the hapless Marie Antoinette had been dead four and a half months.

Newspapers were a vital source of information and there was one at Newark by the spring of 1793; others were published in Kingston and, before long, at York, occasionally providing pungent footnotes to any account of family life of the time: Abraham Matice, who signed with "X, his mark," announced that

> Whereas my wife Sarah refuses to go live with me on my farm on Yonge Street, where I have for her a comfortable house, and as I am not able to support her in town, from the high price of provisions and the heavy expense of house rent, I therefore caution the Public not to harbour or credit her on my account, as I will pay no debt of her contracting from this date.

An unidentified man stated that "my wife Nancy refuses living with me without any manner of cause, she being influenced by her vile parents." At Niagara, when a husband issued a public notice refusing responsibility for his wife's debts, she, in turn, announced that his announcement was a joke since everyone knew her husband was worthless and that, in fact, she frequently paid *his* bills; she therefore warned merchants she would not be responsible for them any longer. One Hebsebah Burton was moved to write the editor of the Niagara *Herald* that "husbands advertising wives and wives advertising husbands has become no small part of your business."

But discord was not the only family problem: in the province's early days even routine illnesses threatened the lives of adults and their children. In February, 1793, Mrs. Simcoe proudly wrote her friend Mrs. Hunt, to "inform you that my little Katherine goes on well, eats, sleeps and grows fat, so I hope she will not feel the want of a wet nurse, which was what I could not procure for her."

Fifteen months later, in a poignant letter to Mrs. Hunt, she wrote:

> It is with pain I take up my pen to inform you of the loss we have sustained & the melancholy event of our losing poor little Katherine, one of the strongest, healthiest children you ever saw . . . She had been feverish two or three days cutting teeth, which not being an unusual case with children I was not much alarmed; on good Friday she was playing in my room, in the afternoon was seized with fits, I sat up the whole night the greatest part of which she continued to have spasms & before seven in the morning she was no more.

Unhappily, the Simcoe family's experience was not rare at a time when fever-reducing drugs were unknown, leaving infants vulnerable to high temperatures and the resulting convulsions.

The most common illness, however, was the one described as "ague and fever," from which Mrs. Simcoe, among others, suffered frequently. Contemporary descriptions of both the malady and its remedy (Jesuit's bark from Peru, which contains chincona and from which quinine is refined) reveal its true, astonishing, identity: malaria. Many of the Loyalist soldiers or those who served later in Upper Canada had been stationed, at some point in their careers, in the Caribbean or Asia and carried malaria in the bloodstream. Once they were bitten by the hardy local mosquitoes that bred in the still waters and hot summers, the disease spread quickly. (In fact, the last major epidemic of malaria in the province occurred in 1895, when the disease swept the Peterborough area.)

It is not clear whether Simcoe ever suffered from malaria, although he was frequently laid up with fevers and coughs. Professional problems did plague him however: he continued at loggerheads with Lord Dorchester who, as Governor-in-Chief, was superior to the Lieutenant-Governors in both provinces. Simcoe ignored that chain of command, writing directly to London rather than reporting through Dorchester. Nonetheless, he had lost his campaign to increase the number of troops available for the province's defense, Dorchester insisting that the main threat from the Americans was through Vermont into Lower Canada.

There was, of course, good news for Simcoe as well: the prosperity of Upper Canada after the end of the drought

Lord Dorchester.

owed much to him. He was determined to build a solid economic foundation in the province as rapidly as possible and to improve commerce and communications by driving roads through the wilderness. By the time he was called back to London after four years in Upper Canada, two vital arteries, Yonge Street running north and south and Dundas Street going west, were under way.

In the hot summer of 1796 John Graves Simcoe left the province, having done at least a creditable job amongst its people. His nemesis Dorchester was about to retire and return to England, while Simcoe's own career was flourishing. He was only forty-four and had every reason to expect that he would be returning to Upper Canada before long. Perhaps his wife was less certain. Her entry for Thursday, June 21, 1796, reads:

Took leave of Mrs. McGill and Miss Crookshank. I was so much out of spirits, I was unable to dine with them. Mrs. McGill sent me some dinner, but I could not eat; cried all day. The Governor dined with Mr. McGill and at three o'clock we went on board the "Onendaga", under a salute from the vessels. Little wind, soon became calm.

Neither of the Simcoes ever saw Canada again.

H.M. Schooner "Onondaga."
(From a Drawing by Mrs. Simcoe.)

Mrs. Simcoe's sketch of the *Onondaga*.

In 1794 the Simcoes built Castle Frank, named for son Francis, as a summer retreat on the banks of the Don River.

The Toronto Fish Market at the foot of Jarvis Street, 1838.

Should Methodists Marry?

With the departure of John Graves Simcoe, political life in the province began to take on a subtly new shape – at least in part because the Lieutenant-Governor had so resolutely stamped his own personality and beliefs on major issues.

But there were other reasons. The geometry of French quarrels with Britain, American quarrels with Britain, and American ambitions in Canada were leading, inevitably, to conflict. When the War of 1812 began, American leaders blithely assumed that the large number of their sympathizers in Canada would make subversion easy: Canada would become what, in their opinion, it should always have been: part of the United States. When the war ended a year and a half later, it was at best a draw for the major combatants. But, for the time being, the result for Canada's future was unambiguous: the two provinces existed and would continue to exist separate from the American republic.

The period leading up to the war was one of population growth for Upper Canada: the population, which numbered 70,000 in 1806, was 95,000 by 1814. But newer immigrants were different from the Loyalists who had preceded them: many were committed to American-style democracy and had come here, not because of any particular political belief, but out of a desire for cheap land. Within twenty years, the relative homogeneity that had existed in 1784 was only a wistful memory.

The results were predictable: as in any society, the existence of a larger population with fewer shared assumptions and goals meant an increase in the number and complexity of problems. Recent settlers were not eligible for the generous assistance – from land grants to livestock – that the Loyalists had received from the British government. The towns were attracting newcomers, many without community roots, who did not want to farm and had no other specific skills. Moreover, although this resulted in a population of poor people, there was no clear-cut way to provide for them.

That first provincial statute, with its "summoned and taken conformably to the laws and custom of England" had an exclusion: according to the final section of Chapter I ". . . be it enacted . . . That nothing in this Act contained, shall vary, or interfere or be construed to vary or interfere with . . . the jurisdiction of the Courts . . . or to introduce any of the Laws of England respecting the maintenance of the poor. . ." Perhaps in the Upper Canada of Simcoe's vivid dreams, poverty would not be permitted to exist. More likely, the reason was practical: in England direct taxes were raised to pay for care of the indigent and direct taxation was anathema to the settlers of Upper Canada.

In order to live in those very early years, the poor depended almost entirely on family and private generosity, although there was occasional public assistance. An early call for government help was contained in a commentary written in 1787 by the magistrates of Kingston: "Humanity will not allow us to omit mentioning the Necessity of appointing Overseers of the poor, or the Making of some Kind of Provision for persons of that Description who from Age or Accident may be rendered helpless." Later, indigents, the "insane," and the homeless were housed in the jails of the four provincial districts – an unhappy solution to social problems that lasted for far too many years.

The concern for helpless children, although Dickensian by today's standards, was enlightened for its time: a statute of 1799 provided that a youngster who had been abandoned by his parents or whose parents were unwilling or unable to provide care might be bound as an apprentice until the age of twenty-one in the case of a male, or eighteen for a female. Those who were more than fourteen years of age had the right to refuse an apprenticeship.

But Alexander Wedge was only a small child, according to the notes taken in his case in the early nineteenth century:

> The Magistrates in General Quarter Sessions, taking into consideration the helpless situation of Alexander Wedge, a boy of about Six Years of age, abandoned by his father and left without an adequate provision by his mother, do order and direct, that the said Alexander Wedge shall be duly indented and apprenticed to James Mitchell Esquire, his heirs and assigns untill he shall have completed His Twenty first Year, He the said James Mitchell and his heirs and assigns furnishing the said Alexander Wedge with sufficient wearing apparel and victuals and teaching him or causing him to be taught, to read and write and at the expiration of his apprenticeship to furnish him with two suits of wearing apparel, a Yoke of Oxen worth Fifty Dollars with a Yoke and chain.

Although generally humane in intent, such a system lent itself readily to abuse and youngsters often ran away; once more, newspapers were crucial in keeping the community informed. A typical ad offered a reward of sixpence for the "apprehension" of an apprentice, followed by the warning: "All persons in this Province are forbid harbouring the above described apprentice, under pain of prosecution." Parents might themselves agree to indenture of their children: a Kingston mother contracted for her son to "perform all such services and business whatsoever" his mistress might order, in return for board, lodging, clothing, and lessons in reading English.

Sometimes indenture had a happy ending, like that described by Loyalist Amelia Harris:

> In the summer of 1800, my mother had a very nice help as a nurse. Jenny Decow had been apprenticed to a relative and at the age of 18 she received her Bed, her Cow and two or three suits of clothing. Those articles it was customary to give to a bound girl and was considered legally of age with the right to earn her own living as best she could. My mother soon discovered that Jenny had a wooer. On Sunday afternoon Daniel McCall made his appearance with that peculiar happy awkward look that young lads have when they are keeping company, as it is called.
>
> At that time when a young man wanted a wife He looked out for some young Girl whom he thought would be a good helpmate and, watching the opportunity, with an awkward Bow and blush, He would ask her to give him her company the ensuing Sunday evening. Her refusal was called "giving the mitten," and great was the laugh against any young man if it was known that He had "got the mitten." All hopes of success in that quarter would be at an end, but young McCall had not "got the mitten," and it was customary on those occasions when the family retired to bed for the young wooer to get up and quietly put out the candles and cover the fire if any, then take a seat by the side of his lady love and talk as other lovers do, I suppose, until 12 or 1 o'clock, when He would either take his leave and a walk of miles to his home that He might be early at work, or lie down with some of the Boys for an hour or two and then be away before daylight.
>
> Those weekly visits would sometimes continue for Months, until all was ready for marriage. . . [One day Daniel McCall told us]

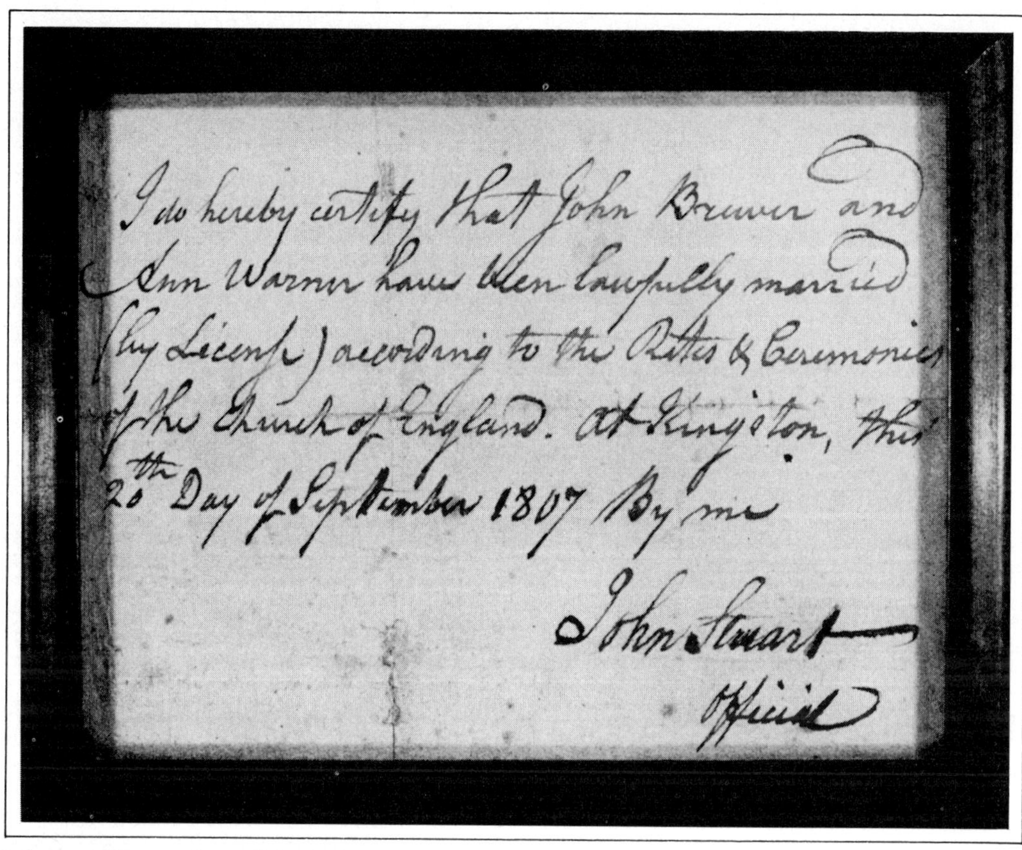

I do hereby certify that John Brewer and Ann Warner have been lawfully married (by License) according to the Rites & Ceremonies of the Church of England. At Kingston, this 20th Day of September 1807 By me

John Stuart
Official

The certificate of a valid marriage.

> they would be married; in an hour afterwards they were man and wife. They were married in their working dresses, he in his buckskin trowsers and she in her homespun. She tied up her bundle of clothes, received her wages, and away they walked to their Log house in the woods. Thirty years after they used to show me some little articles that had been purchased with Jenny's wages and they appeared to look back upon that time with pleasure. They became rich.

The customs and behaviour that underlie such vignettes were the foundations of a society slowly created in the province – a society that had been in the making since the arrival of the Loyalists. The process would remain subtle and complex, but certain of its outlines were becoming steadily more visible in the ongoing battle over the Marriage Law.

In 1797, the year after Simcoe's return to England, a new Marriage Act had been passed by the Parliament of Upper Canada. It gave to

> . . . the minister or clergyman of any congregation or religious community of persons professing to be members of the Church of Scotland or Lutherans or Calvinists . . . (the right) to celebrate the ceremony of matrimony between any two persons one of whom shall have been a member of such congregation or religious community at least six months before the said marriage.

That seemed like a victory, a large step toward recognizing the right of various clergies to perform valid marriages. But, despite apparent liberalization, the Act, which took effect in 1798, actually reaffirmed the old inequality of religion. Under it, an ordained minister wishing the right to perform marriages had to appear before the Quarter Sessions (a court that presided over criminal and civil trials) in the district in which he lived. He was required to bring at least seven "respectable persons" who were members of his congregation and who would declare that he was their minister. He then had to take the oath of allegiance to the King. If the magistrates thought it proper, they could issue a certificate authorizing him to perform marriages, although only in his own district. But none of these requirements applied to the Anglican clergy; their special status was therefore unchanged. Moreover, although the Act applied to Presbyterians and Lutherans as well as to Calvinists, including Baptists and the Dutch Reformed, it still omitted the province's largest single denomination, Methodists. (Nobody questioned the right of Roman Catholic priests to solemnize marriages, since they had done so in the old province, before the creation of Upper Canada, and it was probably assumed that their right in this matter continued.)

The exclusion, of course, was deliberate. While Canadian Methodists were indisputably loyal, that was not always the case with their ministers – all of whom, in the early years, were Americans. Sermons were often filled with exhortations on democracy, separation of church and state, and other subjects that, for Upper Canadians, were inextricably linked with American politics.

Furthermore, the issue was exacerbated by American leaders like Thomas Jefferson and Henry Clay who harrumphed loudly about freeing Canada from colonial rule. Their presumption, politically naive, had the opposite effect to what was intended: rather than waiting eagerly to fall into American arms, Loyalists – and other Canadians – remembered past grievances more vividly and totted up scores they would settle when war finally came. In the meantime such mischief played into the hands of those who favoured discrimination against non-Anglican clergy. They argued that both the oath and the Methodist exclusion were necessary to outwit ministers whose aims were less concerned with the Kingdom of God and more with the subversion of Canada.

So the fight for equal recognition of all religious denominations continued. A petition was read in the House of Assembly on June 29, 1799; it was from Darius Dunham and 119 others who described themselves as "Members of a Methodist Society praying that by a Parliamentary provision the same toleration be extended to them as to other sects in this Province, so as to give validity in law to their marriages." Permission to bring in a bill to this effect was refused.

The Third Parliament of Upper Canada was elected in 1800 and, at its second session, in 1802, three petitions were presented "from the Society of people called Methodists" emphasizing their loyalty to the Crown and asking that "an Act may be passed in our favour giving authority to our Preachers (most of whom are Missionaries from the States) to solemnize the religious rites of marriage as well as confirm all past marriages performed by them." A bill to that effect was passed in the Assembly after some procedural wrangles and was brought to the Legislative Council; it was given first reading there and "ordered to lie upon the table" (tabled) and never heard of again.

If, in those first years of the new century, it was business as usual inside the commodious wood Parliament Buildings that were the focus of the town of York, life outside was changing. That change, from wilderness to community, was so significant that it bears closer examination. If nothing else, it was a clear signal that the provincial law would also have to change in order to reflect an increasingly complex and diverse society.

At the end of the 1700s the capital was a village of twelve city blocks close to the waterfront at what is now Berkeley Street; six blocks lay to the north and six to the south of the present King Street. (Church, to the west, was far from the business district and King and Yonge was not even a crossroads.) Bay Street was said to have been called "Bear Street" – to mark an attack by a bear on horses pasturing nearby. Wolves were also a problem: on November 3, 1800, Joseph Willcocks reported that

> . . . there was a great depredation committed the night before last by a flock of wolves that came into the Town. One man lost 17 sheep; several others lost in proportion . . . two great bears . . . took away two pigs. They carried the pigs in their arms and ran on their hind legs.

By 1803 the capital was a village of 456 people; according to a bylaw, hogs younger than three months could "have liberty to run at large, provided they be yoked or ringed, but if found without a lawful yoke and ring to the nose, shall be subject to impoundage until the owner pays one dollar for each hog." William Cooper ran the Toronto Coffee House (on a site probably quite near the present Parliament Buildings) and promised "genteel board and lodging" with "the best liquors, viands, etc. . . . a large and convenient stable . . . with hay and oats of the very best quality."

There was a distillery on the banks of the distant Don River but none at York, since the gentry preferred imported wines; by 1805 those less fortunate were making do with the beer being produced by Henderson's and Stoyell's, the two new breweries in town. There were several bakers, an auctioneer, a watchmaker, a chandler, a tailor ("Evean Eveans, taylor and habit maker. . . ") and a hairdresser:

> Rock, Hair Dresser from London, begs leave to inform the ladies and gentlemen of York and its vicinity that he will open shop . . . in Mr. Cooper's house, next the Printing office. All orders left for him at said place will be punctually attended to.

There were several ash dealers, including Mr. Allen, Collector of Duties and Inspector of Port and Pearl Ashes and Flour, who offered to buy ashes but warned that "he conceives it his duty to inform those who may have ashes to dispose of, that it will not be in his power to pay cash, but [to offer] merchandise at cash price." There were two general stores and a farmer's market that was held weekly in a five and a half acre square formed by Front, New (now Jarvis), King and Church streets.

Kingston was the grander city and much older, having first been a French fort in 1673 and then surveyed as a town before the arrival of the original Loyalists. By the end of the 1700s, there were 130 houses in Kingston, its church was eight years old and it had had a post office for a decade. The British Post Office, which ran postal service in all of British North America until 1851, did not establish an office in the capital town of York until about 1800.

Farther east, Bytown was a frontier settlement that looked across the Ottawa River to Hull, a bustling town in Lower Canada that had been founded by an American, Philomen Wright. Although Bytown would eventually become Ottawa, in the early nineteenth century it was a backwater. It began to develop only in 1825 when Nicholas Sparks, Wright's employee, paid $240 – his savings of many years – to buy a bush farm near what is now the intersection of Sparks and Bay streets. A man who apparently thought of himself as both Sparks's friend and a poet immortalized him in some of the lumpiest doggerel ever committed to paper – or committed, period:

> 'Tis not my business here to flatter,
> Or with enconiums to bespatter
> The shadows of departed men
> Whom we shall never see again.
> Yet I may say, who knew him well,
> And of him would not falsehood tell,
> That as poor human nature ran,
> He was an honest upright man.

William Jarvis.

Mrs. William Jarvis.

In Cornwall, in the southeast of the province, John Strachan founded a school that, in 1803, offered science, classics, and maths, and in addition, stressed "the ability to observe and make judgments," at a time when teaching by rote was the standard. There were various schools at York; one promised to "instruct 12 boys in Writing, Reading, and Classics and Arithmetic for . . . eight guineas *per annum* . . . and one cord of wood to be supplied by each boy on opening the school." By 1807 the Legislature had passed an Act providing for a grammar school in each of Upper Canada's four districts, the masters to be paid out of public funds.

Although the pull of Montreal's historical and economic importance assured eastward development in Upper Canada, there were communities to the west as well. In 1799 a group of Pennsylvania Dutch families settled between the present villages of Doon and Blair, on the banks of the Grand River – eleven on the west side and one on the east. Brantford was the centre of the Six Nations community while, a hundred kilometres to the southwest, London was a busy mill town. It would suffer greatly during the War of 1812 but, within a few years, rebuild itself with added vigour and become the principal city between York and Sandwich at the American border.

The penalties for crimes in this formative society were severe, in the

European manner: death for forgery or counterfeiting, burning of the hand in one case of theft and seven years' banishment from the province in another, whipping for petty larceny. Flogging was common and pillories were still in vogue: Elizabeth Ellis was sentenced in 1804 to six months' imprisonment for some unstated crime and, in addition, was "to stand in the pillory twice during the said imprisonment, on two different market days, opposite the Market-House in the town of York, for the space of two hours each time"; a man named Campbell received the same sentence for "seditious language."

Duelling, that socially sanctioned ritual of upper-class slaughter, was less severely punished and was therefore used to "settle" increasingly trivial quarrels. The lawyer Edward Weekes was killed when he challenged William Dickson, a colleague and friend, for criticizing his manner in court. In fact, this province lost its first Attorney General, thirty-eight-year-old John White, in a duel. In 1800, White was accused by Major John Small of making "statements derogatory to the character of a lady in the official class" – Mrs. Small. The major, Clerk of the Executive Council, challenged White to a duel that took place on the third day of the new century, in a grove behind the Parliament Buildings. Felled by the pistol shot, White lived for only thirty-six hours and was buried near the present Bloor Street, east of Sherbourne, which was then the site of his back garden. On January 20, 1800, Small was tried for murder before a judge and jury and was acquitted.

William Jarvis, the Provincial Secretary, was the foreman of that jury; seventeen years later, with the grim symmetry believable only in real life, his son, Samuel Peters Jarvis, killed John Ridout in a duel worth noting because it indicated both the stupidity of the custom and the tight-knit society of the time. In 1815, Mrs. Thomas Ridout, member of a leading family of Upper Canada, passed on gossip, based on a misunderstanding, about one of the Jarvises. The Reverend Dr. Strachan was able to avert one duel but, within two years, bitterness between the two families had reached such a point that eighteen-year-old John Ridout, a veteran of the War of 1812 – in no way involved in the original incident – felt he had to challenge young Jarvis to a duel.

James Small (son of the man who had killed White) was Ridout's second; Jarvis was attended by Henry John Boulton (shortly to be instrumental in a happier moment of the province's history). In the early morning light, at Chief Justice Emsley's barn (near what is now the northwest corner of Yonge and College streets) young Ridout nervously fired before the warning count was finished, entitling Jarvis to his shot. Jarvis fired and Ridout fell, dying a short time later.

Jarvis was arrested, charged with murder; Small and Boulton were indicted as accessories. Jarvis was acquitted, Small and Boulton discharged. According to one account:

> The unhappy mother whose unguarded words were the beginning of the troubles between the families . . . never forgave either principal or second for her son's death; for years she used to wait after the morning service at the door of St. James' Cathedral until Boulton came out and would then solemnly curse him for his part in what she called the murder of her son.

The horror of the Ridout-Jarvis affair helped to dampen enthusiasm for the duel as a method of settling differences; there are records of two that took place in the 1830s, but nothing after the very early 1840s.

Even a cursory biography of John White shows what his community lost when he was killed: one of early Upper Canada's two trained and practising lawyers, he had been instrumental in setting up the legal profession in the province. By an Act of 1794 the Lieutenant-Governor had been permitted to grant licenses to no more than sixteen British subjects whom he should "deem from their probity, education, and condition in life, best qualified to act as Advocates and Attornies in the conduct of all legal business in this Province." (Richard Cartwright's sardonic comment: "without any previous study or training, and by the mere magic of the Privy Seal, [they] are at once to start up adepts in the science of the law.")

A Roll was to be kept on which were inscribed those who "shall be holden as duly authorized to receive fees for practicing in any of His Majesty's Courts within the Province." The Roll was made up of sheets of paper on which the names of early generations of lawyers were inscribed – even now, when the method is no longer followed literally, a solicitor who is dismissed from practice, who resigns or dies, is "stricken from the Rolls." (A barrister dismissed from practice is said to have been "disbarred.")

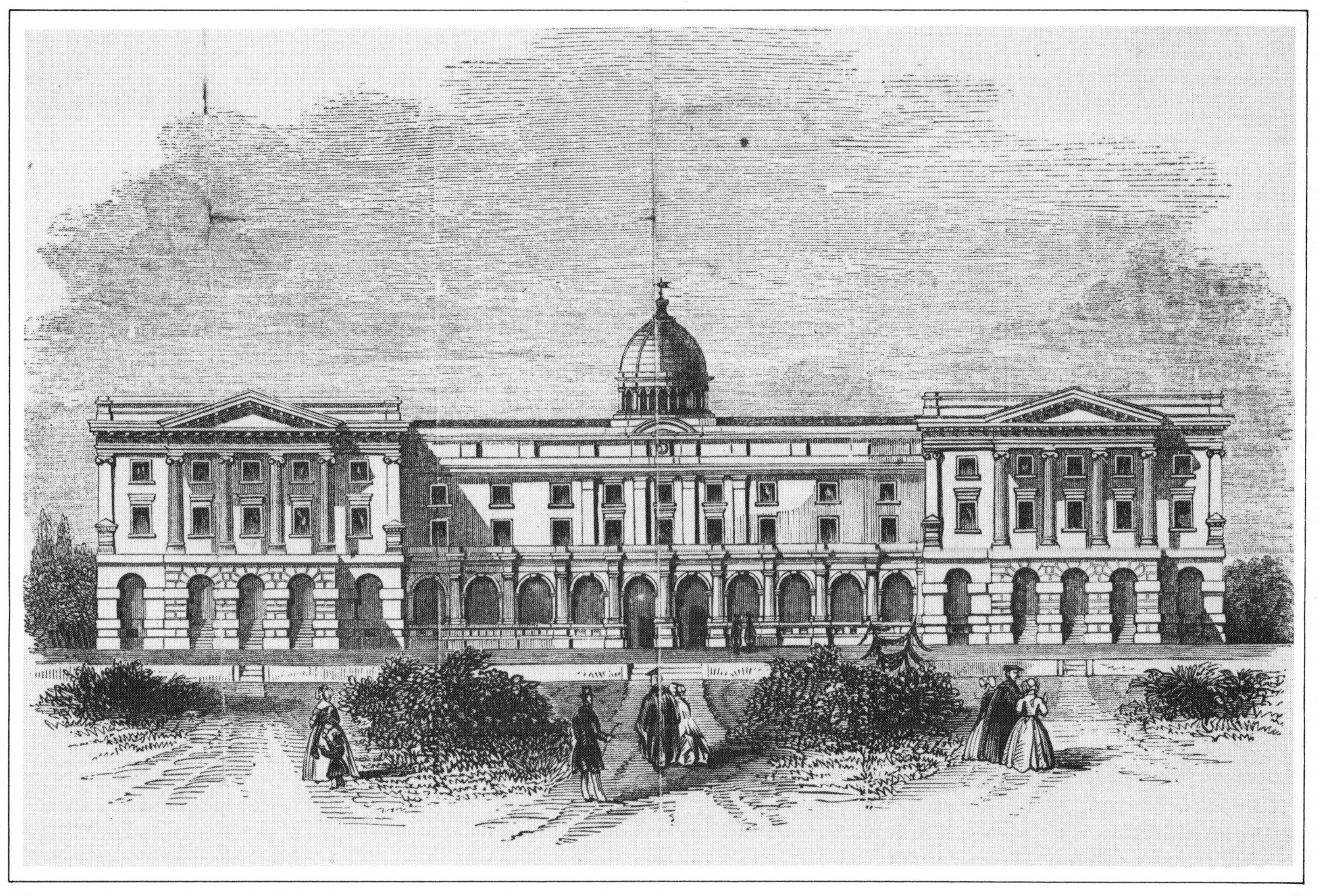

The new Courts of Law, built in 1831, were commonly called Osgoode Hall, but the law school of that name did not begin full-time operation until 1889.

In 1797 an "Act for the better regulating the Practice of Law" was passed by the Legislature; it granted lawyers who were planning to form themselves into a professional group, the Law Society of Upper Canada, the exclusive right to practise law in the province. Two weeks later the Society's first ten members met at Newark, called themselves and five others to the Bar of Upper Canada, and elected John White to be the "Treasurer" (head) of the "Benchers," the name still given members of the Society's governing body. (The first name on the Roll, the first one on the list of Benchers and of treasurers, was that of the doomed John White. The thirteenth Bencher was Edward Weekes; his murderer, William Dickson, was number nineteen.)

Despite the foundation of English law, the English system of separating the practice of solicitor – responsible for property transfers, wills, and other out-of-court transactions – from that of the barrister pleading cases in court, was copied here only briefly. (Until 1857 some lawyers practised as attorneys or solicitors only and a few as barristers only.) Possibly the reason had historical roots: when Upper Canada was still part of the old French province of Quebec, the same person was permitted to practise as an *avocat* (roughly equivalent to the English barrister), *notaire* (a notary with many of the same responsibilities of the solicitor), and even the *arpenteur* (land surveyor). In Upper Canada, land surveying became a distinct profession, but the combined *avocat/notaire* was the pattern for the practice of law in the province.

However, in setting educational standards for lawyers, the English system of articling, by which prospective members of the profession are apprenticed to practising lawyers, was followed – and is a major part of every law student's training today. Although Osgoode Hall was founded in 1831, it did not become a full-time law school until 1889, after several short intervals of operation. At various times the University of Toronto, Victoria and Trinity (when they were independent universities), Queen's, Ottawa, and the University of Western Ontario operated law schools; but these, too, occasionally fell dormant when they failed to attract enough full-time students.

Although the province that John Graves Simcoe had once governed was, by the middle of the century, a vastly different place, some things might have been recognizable to him. There were still the English-style courts, the highways he had initiated, the busy mills he believed would be the province's economic base. The debates in Parliament would also have seemed familiar to the first Lieutenant-Governor since they frequently centred on the Marriage Act. In 1806 (the year of Simcoe's death in England) in the second session of the Fourth Parliament, there was again a petition from Methodists calling for

> . . . an Act . . . giving authority to our preachers most of whom are missionaries from the States and a number more who are resident in this Province regularly ordained to solemnize the religious rites of matrimony as well as to confirm past marriages performed by them.

Such a bill passed the Lower House but was "given the three months' hoist" (a procedural tactic for sidetracking legislation after second reading) and disappeared forever. In 1807 a marriage bill was once again presented, passed by the Lower House, and rejected by the Legislative Council.

This was an especially tense and fractious Legislature: in Europe the English Reform movement, with its talk of democracy and equality, was taking on new respectability and causing a general sense of unease. There was dissent closer to home: Robert Thorpe, an Irish-born judge, had been using his courtroom as a political arena, urging people to tell him their grievances and making political speeches to them. Finally, abandoning all pretense of impartiality, he ran and was elected to the new Legislature. Dismissed by the Lieutenant-Governor, Thorpe returned to England and tried, unsuccessfully, to be reinstated. There were many other vociferous critics but, for the time being at least, the *status* would remain *quo.*

One change, however, did seem possible in the new Parliament's second session, in 1808: the Marriage Act, now being promoted by D'Arcy Boulton, the Solicitor-General, might pass. It did win in the Assembly, but the Legislative Council struck out clauses that would have validated existing Methodist marriages. Their novel reasoning: recognizing irregular Methodist marriages would encourage future irregularities! When the Upper and Lower chambers could not reach a compromise, the bill was lost and was not proposed again in the province's Fifth Parliament.

The next Parliament took office in 1812 and, for the time being, all talk of marriage, democracy, the so-called "common man" and his rights, was set aside. Members of the Legislature were turning their attention to worsening relations between Britain and France and between Britain and her breakaway North American colonies. War was declared on June 19 and within a month American forces had crossed into Upper Canada at Sandwich, across from Detroit. (That winter, provincial leaders organized the Loyal and Patriotic Society to aid the troops and give medals for "instances of courage and fidelity in defence of the Province." The Society's medals were not ready for six years and were never distributed, but its unused funds helped to establish the Toronto General Hospital.)

Seen through a mushroom cloud, nineteenth-century war, with its unsophisticated weapons and stiff formalities, has a kind of naive charm. Notes were passed back and forth between the British general, Sir Isaac Brock, and William Hull, commander of the American forces – Brock demanding surrender, Hull refusing – all in the genteel locutions of the time: "Sir," Brock began, "The forces at my disposal authorize me to require of you the immediate surrender, etc., etc." Hull: "I have no other reply to make, than to inform you that I am prepared to meet any force . . ." The following day Hull surrendered.

Queenston, October 14, 1812, from the letter of an unknown member of the York militia:

> [The Americans] . . . were driven by a furious and avenging enemy, from whom they had little mercy to expect, to the brink of the Mountain which overhangs the

The death of Isaac Brock at the Battle of Queenston Heights.

> river. They fell in numbers – the river presented a shocking spectacle, filled with poor wretches, who plunged into the stream from the impulse of fear, with scarcely the prospect of being saved. Many leaped down the side of the Mountain to avoid the horrors . . . and were dashed to pieces by the fall . . . The invasion of our peaceful shores by its unprincipled neighbours, has terminated in the entire loss of their army . . . the view of dead bodies which strewed the ground, and the mangled carcases of the poor suffering mortals, who filled every room in the village, filled us with compassion.

Amongst the British dead lay Isaac Brock, killed before he could be informed that he had been knighted for the capture of Detroit.

York, April 26, 1813, from the diary of an American Army surgeon:

> . . . nothing but the Groans of the wounded and agonies of the Dying are to be heard. The Surgeons wading in blood, cutting off arms, legs . . . to rescue their fellow creatures from untimely deaths. To hear the poor creatures crying . . . "Oh, my God, my God! . . . Doctor, Doctor! . . . cut off my leg . . . relieve me from misery! I can't live, I can't live!" would have rent the heart of steel, and shocked the insensibility of the most hardened assassin . . . It awoke my liveliest sympathy, and I cut and slashed for 48 hours without food or sleep.

Nostalgia often lies; misery seldom varies.

When the fighting ended, in Christmas week of 1814, the exhausted families of Upper Canada were eager to return to their ordinary lives. According to an English jurist, "The War of 1812 . . . had made for a development on British rather than American lines, and had laid the foundation of a Canadian nationality." Part of that process meant questioning the existence of a Legislature in which one house of unelected members could safely ignore public opinion – as it had done for so long on issues like the Marriage Act. The elected Assembly did not even control all provincial revenues or initiate all spending – making it an Assembly of limited power.

Early in 1815 the peace treaty ending the war was officially ratified; in the summer a veteran of that – and other – wars, died in Montreal: the Honourable Richard Cartwright, of throat cancer, aged 56.

The bill that Cartwright had first introduced continued to be presented, amended, trimmed, passed in one house, defeated in the other: 1816, 1818, 1820, 1821, 1823, 1826, 1827, 1828.

There were other issues that concerned the government: heavy American immigration, which began shortly after the war, levelled off and the colonial administration worried about effects on the provincial economy; by the 1820s, generous government subsidies stimulated emigration from Ireland and Scotland. The first Scots settlers in the Ottawa Valley had come here in 1816 and were followed, four years later, by another 2,000 of their countrymen. In 1825 it was the turn of the wretchedly poor Irish, weary of the economic troubles haunting their homeland. Two thousand used the free passage offered by the British government, their immigration into the Peterborough area undertaken, organized, and supervised by Irish philanthropist Peter Robinson. It was perhaps the most successful settlement of farmers anywhere in the province. All over Upper Canada there were increased demands for schooling, libraries, transportation, roads, land, services to veterans, aid to the destitute – for all the social scaffolding necessary to orderly growth.

In the meantime, of course, people continued to marry, although probably none as colourfully as those who applied to Captain Peter Teeple, a Loyalist and justice of the peace for the District of London. According to a description based on the recollections of Pellum Teeple, youngest of the magistrate's thirteen children:

> The laws or custom of that place required that where no regular license had been procured, the ceremony might be performed at some public cross-roads, at the hour of midnight, the contracting parties appearing in their night-clothes, the justice and one or more others acting as witnesses. In company with his son, Pellum, the Squire repaired to the spot, a lonely cross-road, on a very dark night. Presently two groups approached from opposite directions, one with the bride, the other with the groom. Upon meeting, and the two principals clad in white robes stepping forward at the hour of twelve, they were duly married according to law. Pellum, then a young man of sixteen, said it made a lasting and weird impression on his memory.

The major issue in the election of Upper Canada's Tenth Parliament was the exclusive right of the Church of England to benefit from the Clergy Reserves. When the Legislature assembled in January, 1829, it was dominated by Reformers, most notably William Lyon Mackenzie, he of the ginger hair and matching temper. In the first hour of the Legislative session of 1829 Peter Perry, a Reform member (and founder of the town of Whitby), moved to bring in a marriage bill, which was passed; it was amended insignificantly and reserved "for the signification of His Majesty's pleasure" by the Lieutenant-Governor Sir John Colborne.

Colborne openly detested Methodism and, shades of Simcoe, was writing London charging that its preachers were "undermining the loyalty of the people but their hostility is directed against the established church . . ." Members of the Legislative Council stalled, claiming that the bill was a duplicate of the one already being considered by His Majesty and, members insisted, ought not to be presented "until expiration of the constitutional period within which the Royal pleasure can be signified." There the matter rested.

When the Eleventh Parliament of Upper Canada met in its first session in 1831, much of its membership had changed and there was less rancour than in the previous Legislature. The Marriage Act was now, quite literally, in its second generation: on the first day of the new Parliament the Attorney General, Henry John Boulton, son of the Solicitor-General whose efforts twenty-three years earlier had failed, brought in

Lieutenant-Governor Sir John Colborne.

a bill that would enable ministers of all religions to perform marriages between persons who were members of their respective denominations. It was being given second reading in the Legislative Council on March 2, 1831, when Colborne sent word that the bill of 1829 had been approved by His Majesty and was therefore enacted.

Among the provisions of the 1829 Marriage Act: any marriage previously contracted publicly before any minister, clergyman, or justice of the peace in the province was validated; clergymen of any church or congregation "professing to be members of the Church of Scotland, Lutherans, Presbyterians, Congregationalists, Independents, Methodists, Menonists, Tunkers or Moravians" were authorized to solemnize marriages after obtaining the usual certificate, taking the oath of allegiance, and proving that they were regularly ordained. Only one minor irritant remained: clergymen of the Church of England were not required to obtain the court certificate.

The social change in Upper Canada symbolized by enactment of the bill had its parallels elsewhere: in England and the northern United States the Industrial Revolution had begun, giving the western world a new host of concepts – and realities: burgeoning cities, grimy factories, urban slums, child labour, machine-made goods, the emerging middle class.

There were hospitals in York and Kingston, each receiving government grants and offering free care to the needy. There were unions in Hamilton and in York, where the York Typographical Society was asking for a minimum wage, a ten-hour day, and payment for overtime.

Although the first crude threshing machine, harbinger of the mechanized farm, was in operation in 1832, there

A winter wedding at Niagara, 1843.

was less evidence of an industrial society in Upper Canada. Despite its small cities and tightly knit ruling class, this was a province of farms and villages whose cautious citizens admired things American but revered things British.

In the winter of 1837 both Britain and the United States suffered severe economic setbacks after enjoying periods of rapid business expansion and speculation. British investors began to liquidate their holdings in the United States; at the same time new, tougher American government monetary policies led to the closing of several hundred banks. In Upper Canada the Legislature was carrying a large debt load and could not meet all its commitments; several banks in the province were in financial trouble and faced severe criticism from radical Reformers, including Mackenzie. (A shopkeeper in Sandwich, probably responding to leaner times, announced that his firm, "having determined to close their credit business, respectfully beg leave to inform the public that after the first day of April next, they will only sell for current money, payable on delivery of the goods.") The Lieutenant-Governor's attempted solutions were unpopular, and even the most conservative businessmen in York were beginning to wonder whether the idea of responsible government – a fully elected Legislature in which the majority party initiated money bills and presented them for debate – might not have merit.

One description of politics and society in Upper Canada, written in 1836, gives clues to the cause of increased unrest which, within a year, would lead to the upheaval of rebellions in Upper and Lower Canada:

> We have here a petty colonial oligarchy, a self-constituted aristocracy, based upon nothing real, nor even upon any thing imaginary . . . it is curious enough to see how quickly a new fashion, or a new folly, is imported from the old country, and with what difficulty and delay a new idea finds its way into the heads of the people, or a new book into their hands . . . The very first elements out of which our social system was framed, were repugnance and contempt for the new institutions of the United States . . . the slightest tinge of democratic, or even liberal principles in politics, was for a long time a sufficient impeachment of loyalty, a stain upon the personal character, of those who held them . . . There is among all parties a general tone of complaint and discontent . . . they bitterly denounce the ignorance of the colonial officials at home, with regard to the true interests of the country . . .

The words, which would not have seemed strange coming from the pen of William Lyon Mackenzie himself, were in fact written by the English diarist Anna Jameson, separated wife of the provincial Attorney General of the day.

The uprisings of 1837 were brief, but their effects were not: in the immediate aftermath the province was torn with bitterness, mistrust of reform, and anxiety that the Americans, heartened by the upheaval, might invade again. (There were several such attempts, two across the Detroit and Niagara rivers in June of 1838, by an American group that had fought alongside the rebel forces. On the St. Lawrence, near Prescott, a Polish idealist named Nils

Nils von Schultz, later hanged as a traitor.

Szoltevcky von Schultz led an invasion in what became known as the Battle of the Windmill. Tried by court-martial at Fort Henry, near Kingston, he was found guilty and executed, after an unsuccessful defense by John A. Macdonald.) Even moderate reformers like Peter Perry, author of the successful Marriage Act of 1829, were discouraged by the poisonous anti-reform climate in Upper Canada, and left for the American West.

If 1837 was marked by revolt and suspicion in Upper Canada, it was, at least on the surface, a more auspicious year in "the Mother Country." A girl of eighteen had ascended to the throne of an empire and a coronation and new coinage were being planned under the Prime Minister, Lord Melbourne, to mark the beginning of her reign. Beneath all the excitement, however, this was a period of economic and political problems, both at home and abroad. In 1838, the year of the Queen's coronation, Melbourne sent a colleague, John George Lambton, first Earl of Durham, to report on the political unrest in the North American colonies and to make recommendations about the future of Upper and Lower Canada.

In that same season a young woman, Elizabeth Van Rensselaer Stuart, came to Upper Canada's capital, now officially the City of Toronto, from London, Ontario – and got involved in an affair that, three years later, would mark a new page in the history of family law in the province.

According to An Act for the Relief of John Stuart, presented in the Legislative session of December, 1839, Mrs. Stuart, the mother of three small daughters, was "seduced by one John Grogan, then a Lieutenant in Her Majesty's Thirty-Second Regiment of Foot, and . . . committed adultery with the said John Grogan and eloped from him the said John Stuart, and has continued ever since to live apart from him . . ." Stuart had already sued Grogan civilly and had won judgement for more than £670; Royal Assent to the Act for Relief was given on June 18,

Mackenzie's band of rebels march down Yonge Street, 1837.

SUPPLEMENT
TO THE
COLONIAL ADVOCATE.

Thursday, Sept. 26. 1833.

[From Mackenzie's Sketches of Canada and the United States.]

UPPER CANADA—KING, LORDS, AND COMMONS.

"It may easily be seen to what fate a colonial governor is exposed. He may become the instrument of the ambition or of the interest of those whose advice he is obliged to take. These latter escape as well censure as punishment, whilst he is answerable for errors and injustice which are the means of their acquiring honours and emoluments which should be the recompense of services, the reward of merit."—*Letter—The Hon.* D. *B. Viger to Viscount Goderich in the matter of Attorney-General Stewart.*

☟ ☟ ☟ ☟ ☟ ☟ ☟ ☟ ☟ ☟

A Political Union.

The following curious but accurate statement will convey to the minds of liberal Englishmen a tolerably fair picture of colonial rule. When I left Upper Canada last year, some of the offices, sinecures, and pensions of the government were divided as follows:—

No. 1. *D'Arcy Boulton*, senior, a retired pensioner, £500, sterling.

2. *Henry*, son to No. 1, Attorney-General and Bank Solicitor, £2400.

3. *D'Arcy*, son to No. 1, Auditor-General, Master in Chancery, Police Justice, &c. Income unknown.

4. *William*, son to No. 1, Church Missionary, King's College Professor, &c., £650.

5. *George*, son to No. 1, Registrar of Northumberland, Member of Assembly for Durham, &c. Income unknown.

6. *John Beverly Robinson*, brother-in-law to No. 3, Chief Justice of Upper Canada, Member for life of the Legislative Council, Speaker

a dozen of nobodies and a few placemen, pensioners, and individuals of well-known narrow and bigoted principles; the whole of the revenues of Upper Canada are in reality at their mercy;—they are paymasters, receivers, auditors, King, Lords, and Commons!

Against such a phalanx, it is probable that at present the people, or any representatives they may select, can effect but little, unless supported in right earnest by Mr. Stanley and Mr. Hay. Their truly noble predecessors began to show a disposition to do what it had never entered into the mind of a colonial secretary to do before; namely, to begin to place some real confidence in the honour, generosity, gratitude, and good feelings of the people, the landowners of the colony. Nor have I the least reason to suspect that Mr. Stanley will show that he has left any of his Whig principles at the gate of the Colonial Office, but the contrary. Of Mr. Hay, as I said before, I know nothing; but there cannot be a doubt entertained of his being a very distinguished Whig and thorough Reformer; he would not have received or accepted office else.

The enemies of Canadian freedom say we want to quarrel with England. If that had been true, these pages had never seen the light—if that had been true, nothing would have been more easy for the people than to have effected the change.

Of course the colonial reader must not for a moment mistake the generous Whig-reforming Mr. Hay, of 1833, for an under-secretary, a namesake of his, who held office in the darkest days of Toryism, and was and is, (as I well know and can prove,) as thorough and consistent a Tory (*i. e.*, an enemy to human freedom) as the Duke of Wellington himself. The North American colonists would have had very good cause for doubting the sincerity of any liberal

Prescott may be presumed to have made a convert of Judge *Jonas Jones* whose cruel and unkind acts to this country it has been our unceasing employment to narrate from year to year during the last ten years. Jonas and Hiram are become inseparable companions—they are linked together in every thing. Mr. Norton is now burthened with as many employments, trades and professions, and official and unofficial duties, as must have required a heavy capital, besides good credit with the Chief Justice and Sir John, (for whose public conduct Mr. Norton, by the way professes to entertain a much more profound veneration than he said he felt before he was sent to York as a representative.) It is said that his friend Jonas, will probably accompany him to York next Parliament upon the reform ticket. We always expected that Mr. Norton would perform wonders when sent to legislate, but his conversion of Jonas Jones, if, like his own patriotism, there be any reality in it, is beyond all praise!!! We would not wish in the slightest degree to detract from the merits of Mr. Norton in this achievement, but perhaps Ogle R. Gowan had no small share in the affair.—Ogle fed the Joneses for years on assafœtida till at length they sickened, and Hiram bled them "till they came round again."—*Communicated.*

TASTE!—Is Sir John Colborne veering round towards democracy! If not, how are we to account for his having selected John O'Neil, *tavern keeper* in London, as a commissioner of the Court of Requests? WE have no objections to John O'Neil if "John Colborne" has none. Governer Gilmer is an excellent tavernkeeper, as we formerly stated, and presides in his courts and in his tavern with due decorum. John Colborne may come round yet.

It appears that "the August number of the

William Lyon Mackenzie's special supplement listed names and numbers in his campaign against the "Family Compact."

1841. The Stuarts were now legally free to go their separate ways – the province's first divorcées.

The province itself had undergone change: in February, 1841, in keeping with the recommendations of Lord Durham's report, Upper and Lower Canada were reconstituted as the Province of Canada. Although each retained certain of its own statutes, constitutional and some criminal laws were common to both parts of the union. This province, officially designated Canada West, was still popularly referred to as Upper Canada.

While Durham had been here apparently (but only apparently) solving the colony's political difficulties, London gossip had centred around a court case involving both the English Prime Minister and a woman who eventually left her mark on the law of England – and therefore on the law of Upper Canada.

It took more than twenty years after the upheaval of 1837 for the Legislature of Upper Canada to settle the inequities of the previous rules regarding the solemnization of marriage; in 1859 it passed an Act declaring that:

> . . . the Ministers and Clergymen of every religious denomination in Upper Canada, duly ordained or appointed according to the rites

Lord Melbourne rides with the young Victoria in Sir Francis Case's portrait.

> and ceremonies of the Churches and denominations to which they shall respectively belong, and resident in Upper Canada, shall have the right to solemnize the ceremony of Matrimony, according to the rites, ceremonies and usages of such Churches and Denominations respectively . . .

No distinction was made between the clergy of the Church of England and those of any other denomination. Sixty-seven years had passed since Richard Cartwright's first attempt to change the rules of marriage in Upper Canada.

Today, under the Marriage Act of 1975, only those persons "authorized by or under section 24 or . . . registered under this section as a person authorized to solemnize a marriage" may validly marry couples in Ontario. Registration for this purpose comes under the ministry responsible for all types of business – from movie theatres to mortgage companies: the Ministry of Consumer and Commercial Relations.

Perhaps only the sharp wit and social perceptions of a Jane Austen would do justice to a scene in which Cartwright and Simcoe come back and learn the outcome of their battles.

Caroline Elizabeth Sarah Sheridan Norton.

4 "... My Ox, My Ass, My Any Thing"

"She is my goods, my chattels; she is my house
My household stuff, my field, my barn
My horse, my ox, my ass, my any thing."

The Taming of the Shrew

Those words, used to describe a wife, come from Shakespeare but the sentiments come from several centuries of English law. From the Middle Ages to the late 1800s the language of that law, although more suave in tone, was – if anything – more dismissive. In the view of Sir William Blackstone, famed English legal commentator: "In law husband and wife are one person, and the husband is that person." Of course.

That reality, however, was not acknowledged in ritual or social custom: the bride marching solemnly down the aisle toward her own legal extinction would soon hear her new husband's pledge: "With all my worldly goods I thee endow." It was an empty boast. In fact, by the nineteenth century, the precise opposite was true. The husband was expected to maintain his wife but was not legally *obliged* to give her a farthing – ever. On the other hand, the law *required* her to endow him with everything she had: land, furniture, money, the clothes on her body, the wedding ring he was placing on her finger.

The legal roots of her situation were to be found in the early church's view of sacramental marriage, as succinctly stated in St. Paul's Epistle to the Ephesians 5: 22-25: "Wives, submit yourselves unto your own husbands, as unto the Lord. For the husband is the head of the wife, even as Christ is the head of the church ... Husbands, love your wives, even as Christ also loved the church, and gave himself for it ..."

In keeping with that exhortation, early law had balanced the power of the husband by stressing his obligation to behave wisely and in his wife's best interests. In time, however, that moral imperative faded as the law began to reflect society's emphasis on the wife's subservience and her husband's rights over her. By the nineteenth century the fantasy of the husband and father who protected helpless women and children hid an ugly reality: they were in most danger from him. A married woman's legal position in England – and therefore in Upper Canada – was more invidious than it had been in the Middle Ages, her status that of an infant or institutionalized incompetent.

The history of how that situation changed is a long and complex one, with its roots in the English reform movement and its concern centred on two vital issues: children and possessions. If it sometimes reads like a history of the fight for women's rights, the fact is that the law affecting the woman and her children was most in need of repair. The lot of the middle-class English male and his Canadian counterpart, after all, barely needed improvement.

A home-grown reform movement was a factor in altering the law of Upper Canada as well, although change here had a different speed and rhythm than in England. For example, the first improvement to the legal status of women came in 1839 in England and in 1855 in Upper Canada, when the law acknowledged that mothers, as well as fathers, might be entitled to access or custody of their small children. The fight for the separate property of married women followed a different course: although the issue was hotly debated for several decades in England, the first substantial victory was won in Upper Canada.

The 1830s marked the onset of a fifty-year period when reform ideals engaged the minds and feelings of the English political, social, and artistic elite. The influence and significance of the English reformers are easily misunderstood now because their time is still popularly assumed to have been stodgy, smug, and prim – all that is culturally stereotyped in the term "Victorian." It was anything but, although the era is still confused with the attitudes of the woman for whom it was named. Victoria might be content to play *hausfrau*-Queen to Prince Albert's bedroom-Emperor, but a vastly different world existed outside her palace gates.

There were, to be sure, those of the upper class who assumed, as the Queen did, that they were living in the best of all possible worlds, one in which the future would be much like the past. There was also a new middle class, whose money came from "trade" and whose ancestors from nowhere, but not

Victoria Regina.

all its members were materialistic Forsytes or unrepentant Scrooges. There were the poor, those expendable soldiers in an Industrial Revolution being waged with their underpaid labour, subhuman working conditions, and the virtual enslavement of their children. But not everyone believed that the poor should be content with misery in this world since they had prospects of happiness in the next.

Among those made fortunate either by birth or by brains, there were an extraordinary number of ethically fastidious and intellectually rigorous men and women with roots in the upper classes. While of differing political, social, and religious persuasions, they shared a passionate sense of indignation at the injustices of their society. Reformers, radicals, religious dissenters, feminists, pacifists, suffragists – many of them writers, poets, novelists – they rallied to each other's causes, married into each other's families, published each other's works. Among their number was Caroline Sheridan Norton, a writer named in 1840 by *The Quarterly Review*, an influential journal of the day, as the most talented woman poet in all England. (Elizabeth Barrett Browning was runner-up.)

On the evidence, the *Review*'s editors must have been a quirky lot – nothing in the works of the winner even approaches the imagery and erotic delicacy of Mrs. Browning's sonnets and love poems. But, thanks to her own remarkable qualities of bravery, steadfastness, and energy, Caroline Norton's historical place is secure – if not in slender collections of poetry, then in the bulky volumes of the law.

In London in the spring of 1836 all the talk was of Caroline, separated wife of George Norton, a man for whom the terms "bounder" and "cad" appear to have been coined. His taste for domestic violence had driven her from their home and he had spitefully refused to allow her to see their three young sons. Caroline was twenty-eight, emotional – sometimes to the point of indiscretion – but she was intelligent, well connected, and strong-willed. She and her two sisters were "the three Graces," the trio of beautiful granddaughters of playwright Richard Brinsley Sheridan. ("What a batch of them," the King of France once declared admiringly.)

George Norton, brother of Lord Grantley, was a barrister whose judgeship was directly attributable to Caroline's influence with the Prime Minister, Lord Melbourne. Norton had repaid this kindness by instituting a suit for criminal conversation, naming Melbourne as his wife's lover. But the evidence was so weak – depending almost entirely on the testimony of servants previously dismissed for misconduct – that Melbourne's lawyer saw no point in calling witnesses for the defense. Clearly, the jury agreed: on June 22 it found for Lord Melbourne without even bothering to leave the box.

With the failure of his action, Norton had no grounds for seeking a divorce – but he did have three powerful hostages in his continued battles with Caroline: Fletcher, almost seven; Brinsley, four and a half; and William, not quite three. The children were being cared for by Margaret Vaughan, a relative of Norton with a taste for violence that matched his own.

> The first step she made in their education [Caroline wrote a friend] was to flog [the eldest, then aged six] . . . to impress on his memory that he was not to receive letters from me. Having occasion to correct one still younger, she stripped it naked, tied it to the bedpost, and chastised it with a riding whip.

The law of the day was clear: the boys belonged to Norton. The concept that children were the chattels of their father was so strongly embedded in the law that it extended even beyond the grave: by an act of 1660 only the father had the power to appoint a guardian for his minor children; he might choose their mother for this role – but he might not. The power was solely his.

Like most bullies, George Norton was a weakling whose opinions and intentions wavered according to his mood or the persuasiveness of his family – people who fought amongst themselves and loathed Caroline. Sometimes George relented and promised that she would be allowed access to their children, but this word was written on water. He soon made outrageous proposals for the conditions of such access, leaving Caroline increasingly frantic with uncertainty and the isolation from her sons. Nevertheless, she coldly refused George's offer to barter visits for money.

Although outspoken and at times even daring, Caroline Norton was conventional at heart and certainly did not fancy herself either a pioneer or a feminist:

> I, for one [she declared] (I, with millions more), believe in the natural superiority of man, as I do in the existence of a God. The natural position of woman is inferiority

> to man. Amen! That is a thing of God's appointing, not of man's devising. I believe it sincerely, as a part of my religion. I never pretended to the wild and ridiculous doctrine of equality.

However, the frustration of dealing with the odious George, of his seesawing demands and decrees, finally made it clear to Caroline that she would have to find another solution if she was ever to have access to her children. She decided that, if the law kept her from her sons, then she would just have to get the law changed. In view of the reality of her times, this seemed wilfully blind, even arrogant.

But perhaps not. Her friends included powerful members of the nobility: the Duchess of Sutherland had gone to special pains to signal her support of Caroline to all London society; Georgiana, Caroline's younger sister, was married to the Duke of Somerset's heir. (Her older sister, Helen, was married to Price Blackwood, the Fourth Baron Dufferin; their son Frederick, later Marquis of Dufferin and Ava, served from 1872 to 1878 as the Dominion of Canada's third Governor General.)

Caroline herself was so influential that Mary Wollstonecraft Shelley appealed successfully for her help in securing a pension for the widow of philosopher William Godwin – Mrs. Shelley's father. Caroline's circle of friends also included mathematician Charles Babbage, inventor of the first mechanical computer, as well as many Members of Parliament. There was the Prime Minister, of course, but there were others as well, including Thomas Noon Talfourd, one of the lawyers who had defended Melbourne against George Norton.

Caroline had written a pamphlet, *The Natural Claim of a Mother to the Custody of her Children as affected by the Common Law Right of the Father* but had not found a publisher; in 1837 she decided to have 500 copies "privately" printed. By the beginning of that year, she had convinced Talfourd to introduce the Infants Custody Act into Parliament, in support of which she had written yet another pamphlet. In the spring, however, Talfourd gave notice that he would not press for second reading of the bill – a move widely supposed to have been inspired by a new round of George's promises that Caroline would be allowed to see the children.

In May, George volunteered to have the children brought to London so that they could see their mother, but he again changed his mind. Caroline's response was a written shriek of pain ("You said my children should come! It is most barbarous to deceive me . . . to renew my hope, my anxiety . . . only to destroy me by inches . . .")

Norton invited her to discuss access to the children and once more promised her a visit with them. Two days later he wrote her a lengthy, arch account of how he purchased antiques – a letter so eerily inappropriate that it raises questions about the quality of his sanity. (". . . not that I have bought anything useless, except, perhaps, a mosaic table, which . . . I *believe* is the handsomest in London of its sort, or of any sort. I got it for £26, with an extra rosewood top . . .") Caroline finally saw her sons a few weeks later – the first time in fourteen months. It was probably just as well that, on that exciting day, she did not know that it would be four more years before she saw them again – and that, for most of that time, she would not even know where their father was keeping them.

The Norton battles continued to titillate through the autumn of 1838. In Parliament, Talfourd had introduced the Infants Act again and, although it passed the Commons, it failed in the House of Lords. One reason may have been the appearance of an article in the journal *The British and Foreign Review,* calling Caroline a "she-devil" and hinting at improprieties in her relationship with Thomas Talfourd. (Caroline's status as a married woman ensured that the publication was safe from a libel suit; when a wife had cause to sue, she could do so only together with her husband, even if he was in no other way involved. George, the beneficiary of this deliberate malice, had no reason to take action – and even if he had decided otherwise, and libel had been proved, only he could have collected damages.)

But if 1838 was seasonless gloom, the days of the following summer were a catalogue of triumph: Caroline was presented to the Queen, a royal signal of approval despite her "irregular" – separated – status. In Parliament the Infants Custody Act, presented again by Talfourd, passed both houses. According to its provisions, a mother had a right to seek custody or access if her child was in the custody of the father or a person chosen by the father, or a guardian appointed by the father to act after his death. If the child was younger than seven, the court could now give the mother custody until the child reached that age; if he or she was older, she could ask for regular access. However, if she had been guilty of

Anna Jameson.

adultery (proved either by a sentence of the Ecclesiastical Court or by her husband's success in suing another man for criminal conversation), she had no rights under the legislation.

And, if social approval and Parliamentary vindication were not enough, there was a small but sweet added revenge: Caroline had refused to pay a draper's bill of £146, thus forcing the hapless merchants to sue George, the person legally responsible for his wife's "necessariese" (those items of food, shelter, clothing, and recreation consistent with the family's station and style when its members lived together). She must have found the court's ruling against George little enough; they had been separated for two years and he had everything: her £50 yearly from her father's estate, her jewels, wedding presents, clothing, most of her papers, and, above all, her children.

The pleasure of vindication proved fleeting: the children were in Scotland, beyond the reach of the English courts, and it was 1841 before their father brought them home to go to school. Caroline could finally use the law resulting from her own efforts; George grudgingly gave way and allowed the children to spend a part of that Christmas with their mother.

Her happiness was poignantly brief: nine months later, William, aged eight, died of blood poisoning resulting from neglect of a cut sustained in a fall from a horse. In anguish, Caroline wrote a friend:

> [Son Fletcher's] forethought, tenderness, and precocious good sense will, if God spares him, be the blessing of my life . . . [he] watches me as if I, not he, was the helpless one; and God knows I am helpless! But my child is out of the storm; he is in heaven. Too young to have

offended, he is with those whose "angels do always behold the face of our Father."

In the early summer of 1853, the talk of London was still the Nortons: they were in court battling over unpaid bills and in the letters columns of *The Times* hurling accusations and counter-accusations against each other. George Norton had had the effrontery to rehash the putative affair with Melbourne, offering the story as a matter of fact rather than as a discredited allegation. That injustice brought public support from an unexpected source: John Bayley, a lawyer who had represented George in the criminal conversation trial, wrote the newspaper in defense of Caroline and told how his former client's vindictiveness and Caroline's own genuine concern for her children had changed his views in her favour.

Caroline, who had been working on a novel, put it aside and in 1854 privately published a 144-page pamphlet, *English Laws for Women of the Nineteenth Century.* Her pen dipped in corrosive rage, she recounted the many injustices suffered at Norton's hands; but the tone of the work was so bitterly personal that the context of her argument was easy to ignore. Moreover, her timing was unfortunate: in March, 1854, England and her allies were at war with Russia; attention was focussed on the Crimea.

Caroline Norton was now forty-six years old, still married to the man who inspired only her contempt and with whom she had not lived for eighteen years. She was widely admired for her intelligence and determination, pitied for the relentness sadness of her life. She was, as always, haunted by financial problems, although she was well aware that there were women who were suffering even greater hardships. She had lost none of her determination to change the law, but she was now suspect in the eyes of younger reformers; in their zealous purity, they saw her enthusiasm for their cause as related almost solely to her own problems rather than as a disinterested attempt to improve life for others. In time Caroline's voice would prove to be powerful and influential and, if she could not claim the next victory as hers alone, she certainly played a useful part in bringing it about.

For more than a decade, the reformers had been calling for revision of the laws of divorce and property. Shrewdly, they had done more than simply urge change – they had organized for it, and they had chosen a target that was ripe for overhaul. By the mid-1800s the English legal system, much-vaunted cornerstone of British justice, was a tangle of courts dispensing vastly different rules for the rich and the poor. At the time of the Norman Conquest, when the courts began, they were designed to ensure a fair hearing for nobles and peasants alike; but they no longer reflected the needs of the society they were meant to serve – either in England or its colonies.

This was especially true as it applied to married women: the court structure, in fact, had exacerbated existing injustices, especially in the lives of the less wealthy. There was a dawning recognition of that fact and an emerging social consensus that would bring change – slowly – to the courts and to the law.

Once again, the problem was rooted in the past, when kings at court sat amongst their nobles considering matters of gravest importance to the realm; by the thirteenth century, disputes were settled and wrongdoers punished in one of three courts: Exchequer, where revenue matters were decided; Common Pleas, where civil disputes were settled; and the King's Bench, where, until the fourteenth century, the King himself sat listening to the most important cases – civil, administrative, and sometimes criminal. But, as Parliament became a stronger body, it wanted more forms of the law to come from its deliberations and, in time, a need grew for yet another court that would protect the poor and powerless against the rich and powerful lawmakers. Appeals were heard by an adviser to the King (a chancellor) in the "Courts of Chancery," which, next to the House of Lords, were the highest courts of England.

In them, unlike the others, cases were not decided according to the laws that had evolved from the customs and practices of old (still known as "the common law"). Instead, the chancellor, often a clergyman, made his rulings in "equity and good conscience" and could settle matters in ways not available in the common law. He could, for example, issue orders or injunctions and summon citizens to justify their actions. In time, it was this equity court that protected "lunatics" and children, called trustees and administrators to account for their stewardship of estates, ensured that ordinary citizens were safe from oppression, undue influence, and extortion. Its mandate to protect the weak against the strong extended to wives: in the common law the husband was all-powerful. In the Courts of Chancery, therefore, his wife needed protection against him and the husband was an enemy against whom "unceasing war" was waged.

By the sixteenth century men of wealth (those who had large landholdings) found in the equity courts a way to protect their daughters against fortune-hunting husbands who wanted only to take possession of a wife's inheritance. A rich man conveyed the family's most precious asset, the land, to a friend who would act as trustee and hold it for the use of his widow and daughters, safe from the King's tax collectors and from greedy sons-in-law. Before long, chancellors, who held the designation of "keeper of the King's conscience," took it upon themselves to protect the trusts against trustees – a friend, after all, might turn out to be as greedy as an in-law.

By the seventeenth century the separate property trust (or settlement), protected by the principles of equity, could be composed of jewelry, shares, and furnishings as well as land. But the separation of property, while it kept a husband from flagrantly abusing his wife's wealth, still imposed severe limitations on her use as well. Moreover, since such separate property was held in a trust, it was impractical except for wealthy women who could afford to set aside large assets. In addition, costs in the courts of equity had become prohibitively high (it cost £100, the yearly salary of a prosperous small businessman, to draw up a marriage settlement) and its services were beyond the reach of 90 percent of England's married populace.

Ironically, a court set up to deal in good conscience with the powerless had become a refuge for the wealthy, irrelevant to the needs and concerns of a growing middle class. By the mid-nineteenth century there were, after all, an increasing number of women who were earning income by labouring in other people's homes, businesses, and factories; their pay was subject to the common law that denied them any right to the money they worked hard to earn. This situation, with its protection for the wealthy while the common law left poor married women to fend for themselves, was clearly in need of reform.

Reform, however, depends on more than organization or even on the search for justice that inspires it. Change depends on chance and, in the 1850s, events conspired to make possible certain fundamental shifts in attitudes toward women. First, it was the beginning of a quarter-century of relative prosperity and, at such times, a sense of security makes society more amenable to change. Second, reform often needs a figure around whom people rally and whose life they perceive as symbolic of a cause. Caroline Norton was, in her misery, one such person. Florence Nightingale was, in her passionate concern for the English soldier, another. The Crimean War focussed attention on her – a woman stronger and more dedicated and energetic than England had seen since the first Elizabeth.

She was a thirty-six-year-old nurse who had been sent to the front to supervise the care of 5,000 wounded or dying British soldiers. Nightingale had found appalling conditions: almost nonexistent supplies and dilapidated hospitals that exposed soldiers to as much danger as on the battlefield. Briskly, she set about bringing order from the chaos and, when that task was completed, sailed home. There, she put all her considerable energies into telling Britons that their fathers, brothers, and sons had suffered unspeakable miseries because of official mismanagement and stupidity. As a result, she was arguably the country's second most-loved woman, next to Victoria – arguably only because there were those who held that she was *more* popular than the Young Queen. Nightingale, after all, combined the tender, nurturing qualities that society cherished in women with the strength and forthrightness it assigned to men. In other words, Florence Nightingale might have been designed by fortune to make society feel well disposed toward her sex. Not unaware of her influence, she chose to lend her name to a small committee seeking reform of the laws affecting women.

The group had been organized by Florence Nightingale's cousin, Barbara Leigh Smith, admired in her own right as the author of *A Brief Summary, in Plain Language, of the Most Important Laws Concerning Women, Together with a Few Observations Thereon.* The small book, its manner calm and factual, delivered exactly what its title promised. At a time of renewed interest in the Nortons, the book attracted favourable attention and Leigh Smith decided to capitalize on that fact by forming the committee. Among its members were Lord and Lady Amberley, whose contributions to posterity would include their son, the mathematician and philosopher Bertrand Russell. Mary Wollstonecraft Shelley – daughter of a suffragist, wife of a poet, and, in her invention of Victor Frankenstein and his monster, author of a masterpiece – was a prominent member. Another leading light was Anna Jameson; in Upper Canada she might have been considered little more than the separated wife of the Attorney General, a woman whose *Winter Studies and Summer Rambles in Canada* contained many tart observations about the colony. But in England she was a greatly admired author and feminist; the fact that her husband's will had left her nothing while it conferred his considerable estate on a wealthy Toronto clergyman, George Maynard, had aroused considerable public sympathy for her.

The committee members were far too shrewd to ignore the fact that such a group would accomplish very little without the sympathy and support of men in positions of power. Which describes exactly the Society for Promoting the Amendment of the Law, which had been formed by Henry Lord Brougham, a leading reform politician of the day. Years before, women had helped Brougham in another campaign, the successful drive to abolish slavery, and he was quite ready to help them now. The Law Amendment Committee and its members were involved in the most contentious issues of the day: reform of the courts and reform of divorce law and of the law regarding married women's property. Now it had agreed to work with Leigh Smith's group.

In 1855 her committee began its most effective work: collecting signatures on petitions asking Parliament to reform the laws affecting the property of married women. The campaign was conducted with consummate skill and obtained more than 26,000 signatures within a few months. No detail was overlooked: the most glittering names were collected first – Elizabeth Barrett Browning, Anna Jameson, Elizabeth Gaskell (friend and biographer of Charlotte Brontë), Marianne Evans (better known at a later time as the novelist George Eliot), Jane Carlyle, and, of course, Florence Nightingale. It was "most needful to have an eye to the moral status of the persons supporting this movement," and therefore only happily married or highly esteemed single women were asked to sign the petitions. Caroline Norton, of course, was not included.

But she would still make a considerable contribution, this time in the form of a professionally published and widely distributed pamphlet, *A Letter to the Queen on Lord Cranworth's Marriage and Divorce Bill;* it appeared in 1855, when Cranworth, the Lord Chancellor, had been twice unsuccessful in introducing divorce legislation.

The "letter," which is still credited with having helped stir public sentiment in favour of Cranworth, is a catalogue of despair, a crisply worded description – and indictment – of the treatment of married women in England and therefore in Upper Canada. Quoted at length, it remains the most accurate and compelling picture of the injustices it helped to end in both places:

> A married woman in England has no *legal* existence. Her being is absorbed in that of her husband. Years of separation or desertion cannot alter this position. Unless divorced by special enactment in the House of Lords, the legal fiction holds her to be *one* with [him], even though she may never see or hear of him. She has no possessions, unless by special settlement; her property is *his* property . . . An English wife has no legal right even to her clothes or ornaments; her husband may take them and sell them if he pleases, even though they be the gifts of relatives or friends, or bought before marriage.
>
> An English wife cannot make a will. She may have children . . . whom she may earnestly desire to benefit; – she may be separated from her husband, who may be living with a mistress; no matter: the law gives what she has to him, and no will she could make would be valid. An English wife cannot legally claim her own earnings. Whether wages for manual labour, or payment for intellectual exertion, whether she weed potatoes, or keep a school, her salary is the *husband's;* and he could compel a second payment, and treat the first as void, if paid to the wife without his sanction.
>
> An English wife may not leave her husband's house. Not only can he sue her for "restitution of conjugal rights," but he has a right to enter the house of any friend or relation with whom she may take refuge, and who may "harbour her" . . . and carry her away by force, with or without the aid of the police.

If the wife sue for separation for cruelty, it must be "cruelty that endangers life or limb," and if she has once forgiven, or, in legal phrase, "*condoned*" his offenses, she cannot plead them; although her past forgiveness only proves that she endured as long as endurance was possible.

If her husband take proceedings for a divorce, she is not, in the first instance, allowed to defend herself. She has no means of proving the falsehood of his allegations. She is not represented by attorney, nor permitted to be considered a party to the suit between him and her supposed lover, for "damages" . . .

If an English wife be guilty of infidelity, her husband can divorce *her* so as to marry again; but she cannot divorce him [in the same manner] however profligate he may be . . . The House of Lords grants [a divorce] almost as a matter of course to the husband, but not to the wife. In only four instances [two of which were cases of incest] has the wife obtained a divorce to marry again . . .

She cannot claim support, as a matter of personal right, from her husband. The general belief and nominal rule is, that her husband is "bound to maintain her." That is not the law. He is not bound to *her* . . . If it be proved that means sufficient are at her disposal, from relatives or friends, her husband is quit of his obligation, and need not contribute a farthing: even if he have deserted her; or be in receipt of money which is hers by inheritance . . .

Separation from her husband by consent, or for his ill usage, does not alter their mutual relation. He retains the right to divorce her *after* separation, – as before, – although he himself be unfaithful. Her being, on the other hand, of spotless character, and without reproach, gives her no advantage in law. She may have withdrawn from his roof knowing that he lives with "his faithful housekeeper": having suffered personal violence at his hands; having "condoned" much, and being able to prove it by unimpeachable testimony: or he may have shut the doors of her house against her: all this is quite immaterial; the law takes no cognisance of which is to blame. As *her husband,* he has a right to all that is hers: as *his wife,* she has no right to anything that is his. As her husband, he may divorce her (if truth or swearing false can do it): as his wife, the utmost "divorce" she could obtain, is permission to reside alone, – married to his name. The marriage ceremony is a civil bond for him, – and an indissoluable sacrament for her; and the rights of mutual property which that ceremony is ignorantly supposed to confer, are made absolute for him, and null for her.

Caroline Norton's story was undoubtedly well known in the North American colony. Faster ships were bringing a steady stream of English newspapers, magazines and professional journals to the province, where eager readers could follow the various reform debates. But England was not the only country whose legal system was of interest in the colony: law in the republic to the south – particularly in the bordering states – was beginning to influence attitudes here. Interested Upper Canadians, many with American business or personal connections, learned that, among other reforms, New York, Vermont, and Massachusetts now gave married women certain rights to their separate property.

The people of Upper Canada had a unique vantage point in forming their opinions on issues of the day. Their sympathies might sometimes be divided between two separate, even opposing, political and social systems; they might feel the confusion of sharing geography and family ties with one while remaining closer philosophically and politically to the other. But, from that same perspective, they also had the opportunity to grasp the weaknesses of each system because it was underlined by the strengths of the other.

The result would influence the development of that staple of Canadian political behaviour, the compromise. Without self-consciously choosing, the people of the province were fashioning a society that was neither English nor American; instead, it contained elements of both, altered to meet their specific needs and attitudes. The progress of family law in mid-nineteenth-century Upper Canada – different from that in either England or the United States – was a prime example of that process.

In England the fight to gain access to separate property for married women was at a virtual standstill. Ironically, one of the most influential enemies of reform was the woman sitting on the throne of England, her implacable hatred of women's rights well known to all her subjects.

Referring to herself in the third person, as she usually did when speaking for public consumption, Victoria said in a letter to Sir Theodore Martin, the royal biographer:

> The Queen is most anxious to enlist every one who can speak or write to join in checking this mad, wicked folly of "Women's Rights," with all its attendant horrors, on which her poor feeble sex is bent, forgetting every sense of womanly feeling and propriety. Lady Amberley ought to get a *good whipping*. [The emphasis is hers.] It is a subject which makes the Queen so furious that she cannot contain herself . . . Woman would become the most hateful, heathen, and disgusting of human creatures were she allowed to unsex herself . . .

However vehemently opposed Victoria was to "women's rights," her personal vision of motherhood was, if anything, even grimmer. In a letter to the Empress Eugénie, her daughter, she said:

> Though I admit the comfort and blessing good and amiable children are – although they are also an awful plague and anxiety for which they show one so little gratitude very often! What made me so miserable was – to have the first two years of my married life utterly spoilt by this occupation! . . . What you say of the pride of giving life to an immortal soul is very fine, dear, but I own I cannot enter into that; I think much more of our being like a cow or a dog at such moments; when our poor nature becomes so very animal and unecstatic . . . Think of me who at that first time, very unreasonable, and perfectly furious as I was to be caught, having to have drawing rooms and levees and made to sit down – and be stared at and take every sort of precaution.

However, it had been clear for some time that Victoria's views had little impact on her North American subjects. They followed news of her voluminous family with seemingly insatiable interest and they were cordial – even adoring – when her offspring came to visit. (The Prince of Wales' 1860 trip to Canada was widely talked of as the most important event of the century.) Nonetheless, on social issues, they often found more in common with their U.S. neighbours than with English royalty.

For example, a publicly funded, universal education system like New York's was more suited to Upper Canada than was England's casual and inadequate schooling of the poor. Thus, when Egerton Ryerson, school superintendent for Canada West and the father of the province's education system, was searching for a model, he included many elements of the New York law in his Education Act of 1846. It established the principles of public responsibility and financing for schools and (against Ryerson's strong opposition) provided for the education of females as well as males.

There were other issues on which a more enlightened attitude – like that in some of the American states – was becoming evident in Upper Canada. In a country where the family worked together, often at heavy manual labour, it seemed unrealistic to suggest that children were chattels of their father while their mother was entitled to "no power but only reverence and respect." Although it was 1855 before Upper Canada adopted legislation to equal Lord Talfourd's Act, at least one major court decision, made several years earlier, is evidence that some senior members of the judiciary were uneasy about the weakness in the law of the time.

In 1846 (in a case that, technically, was for possession, not custody) Richard Snooks asked the court to order his father-in-law to hand over Snooks' wife Elizabeth to him and to order Elizabeth to hand over their seven-month-old daughter. Evidence showed that Snooks was often "intoxicated from the effects of strong drink" and, at such times, beat both mother and child.

The husband's lawyer argued that

> The guardianship of the children is properly with the father; and if it were not so, but the mother were allowed to remove them from him at her will and pleasure, there would perhaps be more frequent separations between husband and wife; but the knowledge when she leaves her husband, she must also lose the society of her children, must frequently have the effect of inducing her to remain with him, when she would leave his home if the law were otherwise.

Children, in other words, were hostages designed by nature to keep families together.

Eventually the case went to the Court of Appeal; in his decision the provincial Chief Justice of the day, John Beverley Robinson, was not swayed by Snooks' reasoning. Solidly conservative, a protégé of Bishop Strachan, Robinson believed firmly in the essential wisdom of English law. He had been on business in London in 1839 when Talfourd presented his Infants Act to Parliament; Robinson knew that it had no force in Upper Canada, but it influenced his thinking when he ruled that the baby's "health if not its life might be endangered by depriving it of that care and of the natural food which the mother supplies to it." Neither Elizabeth nor Baby Snooks was required to return to Richard.

In 1855, when Upper Canada finally passed an Infants Custody Act, it was actually an improvement on Talfourd's legislation. Children would be allowed to remain in the custody of their mothers until they were twelve years old, instead of being removed when they were seven. Furthermore, the provincial act, unlike that of England, gave courts the right to order maintenance payments for children in their mother's care.

England's Parliament was moving on another front: in 1857 it took the last major step in making divorce a civil matter; persuaded by Caroline Norton and the reformers, members finally passed Cranworth's bill, the first Matrimonial Causes Act. This legislation relieved the Ecclesiastical Courts of all but minor responsibility for dissolution of marriage and established Matrimonial Causes Courts to deal with separation and divorce. (Upper Canada remained unaffected by the changes: the Ecclesiastical Courts had never been established here and divorces were still being obtained from Parliament.)

Under the Act, a man could, if he wished, sue his wife's lover for criminal conversation, but the success of that suit was not a prerequisite to a divorce action. However, grounds for dissolving the marriage continued the practice of discriminating against wives: they had to prove that their spouses had committed two marital offenses, one of which was adultery; husbands had only to prove adultery. However, the Act did make one small improvement in the situation of married women: if they were separated or divorced, it conferred single status on them in property matters.

Surprisingly, Upper Canada was about to enact a much more liberal law – an Act that, with one significant exception, gave married women many of the rights to separate property they had sought for so long.

As extraordinary as the law itself is the fact that, even now, its existence is virtually unknown; the most commonly accepted version of the history of this seminal legislation is that it was passed in England in 1882 and copied in the province of Ontario in 1884. In fact, the opposite is true: the law giving married women separate property rights was passed first in Upper Canada in 1859, and then (after advice from at least one Canadian Parliamentarian) was passed in England in 1870. Because of the errors in dating and placing the event, Canadians mislaid a small but vital part of their social history – the story of how the still-fragile colony took one of the first important steps toward equality in marriage.

Despite the fact that the law was known and applied in its time (Parliamentary debate about the bill was fully reported and legal commentaries appeared in the professional journals of the day), the following is the first significant description, albeit incomplete, of this key Act and its passage.

It is a story without a tidy beginning or a straight line that snugly attaches cause to effect; clearly, however, the law in one or two of the nearby American states played a part in what was about to happen and it is entirely possible that awareness of Caroline Norton's much-publicized travails was also a factor in the fight to obtain property rights for married women.

It all began quietly enough in Kingston on April 2, 1856, when the Legislative Council, Upper House of Parliament, passed a bill urging adoption of *An Act to Secure to Married Women Certain Separate Rights of Property*. The next day the bill was sent to the Assembly to be read the first time; on second reading, it was referred to a Select Committee of the Legislature whose members included a future Canadian Prime Minister and two future Premiers of the province of Ontario: John Alexander Macdonald, John Sandfield Macdonald, and Oliver Mowat. Whatever the findings of the committee, the bill did not get to third reading.

Although the first attempt to legislate some property rights for married women was a failure, the issue was far from dead. In 1857 a similar bill was proposed in the Legislative Assembly on a motion by the Honourable Malcolm Cameron. Cameron was a hot-tempered and erratic reformer, sometime friend and ally (and sometime enemy and opponent) of John A., of the Honourable George Brown, and of the cause of annexation to the United States – a man whose only constancy was his devotion to the temperance movement.

Cameron was not alone in his interest in the rights of married women: two days after his motion, leave was given to bring in another bill, A Bill to Secure to Married Women the Right of Holding Property; it was withdrawn a few weeks later, leaving the field clear for Cameron's proposed legislation. Nevertheless, that, too, was read twice, referred to a Select Committee, then allowed to die without being brought to a vote.

Records of proceedings show that one lone petition in favour of property rights had been received by the Legislature in 1856, from "Mrs. Hawley and others"; in the spring of 1857, however, there was concerted public support for the legislation, and several petitions were brought forward "praying for the passing of an Act making the personal property of the wife, previous to marriage, free from the control of her husband, and to enable the wife to hold separate property." Petitions came from every part of the province: among the first were those from Elizabeth Dunlap and from Elizabeth Hawley – presumably the same Mrs. Hawley – of St. Catharines, but most carried men's names ("William Barber and others, of Esquesing, County of Halton"; "James Strang and others, of the Town of Galt"; "John Thompson, junior, and others, of the Township of Leeds, County of Megantic"; there were also petitions from Middlesex, Norfolk, Durham, Halton, Bruce, and Lincoln counties; and from two ministers, Duncan Cameron of Glengarry and Thomas Wightman of York Mills.)

Even the Canadian legal profession was becoming aware of the serious deficiencies in the law and of the work being done by England's Law Amendment Committee to correct them. The *Upper Canada Law Journal and Local Courts' Gazetteer* of 1857, under the heading "Contemporary Literature," reprinted an article from the *Law Magazine and Law Review* of May, 1857. It said that

> . . . few subjects . . . have excited more lively and a more general interest than the glaring imperfections of the law respecting married women. . . . friends of law amendment (have) directed their attention to the necessity of singling out the more gross instances of injustice – it may be said oppression.

The article described "the great petition of above 2,000 women" and said that "it plainly appeared from the public men, of various parties . . . that immediate attention must be given to the strongly expressed wishes of the community."

It singled out as an especially "hard case" the wife who

> . . . earning by her skill and industry that which she has by law no right to call her own, and which may, at any moment, be carried off by the man who has deserted her, or who, continuing to live with her, yet leads an idle and dissolute life supported by her gains, while he leaves her and her child in want.

The report showed awareness that some American states and France had outpaced Britain in passing laws related to the property of married women: it told the story of a French milliner who, on the urging of a client, settled in London and opened a hugely successful business. Her husband followed her to England, collected all the money she was owed, and returned "to continue his dissolute life in Paris. 'Oh, Madam,' she said to her patroness, 'how can you bear to live in so barbarous a country?' It is needless to add that this outrage on all justice and all feeling would have been impossible in Paris."

For a brief period in 1857 it seemed as if the large number of lawyers in the Legislature were sympathetic to the tenor of their *Law Journal's* report and might pass a new version of the legislation. The Assembly amended and passed a bill it had received from the Legislative Council – the first time the matter of property rights had gotten as far as third reading and a vote. The Upper House, however, was apparently unhappy with the changes and left the proposed law to die on the Order Paper at the end of the session.

There is no obvious explanation of why the legislation was brought forward yet again the following year – just as there must have been no reason to believe that, this time, it would succeed. On February 1, 1859, when James Morris moved first reading of a married women's property act in the Legislative Council, it could hardly have found more illustrious sponsorship. A successful Brockville banker, Morris had been appointed Postmaster-General in 1851, when the British post turned service over to the colony, and he had arranged for Sandford Fleming to design and engrave our first postage stamps. Morris had been speaker of the Legislative Council on several occasions and enjoyed a reputation as a highly principled reformer and a thoroughly decent man. Perhaps it made a

A young and vigorous John A. Macdonald, a nation still ahead of him.

difference – or perhaps members were just weary of having to deal annually with the matter.

The motion for first reading in the Assembly came from Malcolm Cameron, who moved "That the Bill from the Legislative Council, intituled, 'An Act to secure to married women certain separate rights of property' be now read the first time. The Bill was accordingly read the first time; and ordered to be read a second time on Wednesday next."

On March 10, "Wednesday next," it came up again when, according to *The Globe:*

> . . . Mr. Cameron . . . [said] this Bill was of great importance and it was astonishing that its provisions had not become law in Canada long ago. A similar law had for a great period been in successful operation in the different States of the Union, and in the Eastern Provinces. The disabilities which it was the purpose of this Bill to get rid of were in fact a relic of barbarism quite unsuitable to the present day. The object . . . was to relieve married women from imposition and injustice on the part of their worthless, drunken husbands, who had, under the existing law, all control over their wives' property. From this state of things the greatest possible hardships had arisen.

According to the report, the Attorney General West (John A. Macdonald)

> . . . was in favour of the principle of the Bill, though he was . . . apprehensive that the credit and standing of the husband would be thereby placed in jeopardy, and that great difficulty would arise in determining what property belonged to the husband and what to

John Sandfield Macdonald.

> the wife – that there was difficulties in the way, in fact, in compelling a bad husband to do his duty. (A laugh.) But while the Attorney General was unwilling to interfere by law with the right of the husband, he was not unwilling to be appointed a member of the committee to consider the Bill.

The new Select Committee, which also included Cameron, Mowat, and John Sandfield Macdonald, was ordered to study the problem and "to report thereon with all speed; with power to send for persons, papers, and records." It certainly worked "with all speed": a week later it reported through Cameron "That the Committee had gone through the Bill, and directed him to report the same without any Amendment."

Because there were no verbatim reports from the Legislature, *The Globe* often carried detailed third-person descriptions of proceedings; according to the March 24 edition, one opposition member, a Mr. Foley, said he

> . . . could scarcely refrain from speaking with indignation of this Bill, and he protested against its introduction as a subversion of rights already existing, and an invasion of rights vested in married women for their protection. It is likely that the Bill would pass. (Cries of "no, no.") His hon. friend (Mr. Notman) had said it was a most outrageous Bill; but he forgot that it affected Upper Canada alone. The fact of a Bill relating to Upper Canada alone seemed to be

James Morris, who introduced the first act for the separate property of married women in the Legislative Council.

The Honourable John Rose.

> sufficient to ensure for it the approbation of the majority of Lower Canadians, no matter how obnoxious or outrageous it might be.

Perhaps the rancorous debate changed Mowat's mind; he discarded the Select Committee recommendation that the legislation be adopted without amendments and, said *The Globe,* moved that "the words of the first clause which gave to a married woman all her personal earnings be omitted." On April 25 the amended bill finally passed both houses of Parliament. The following week, the House also approved related legislation, an Act that gave married women certain rights to sell property they had inherited. On May 4, both acts were given Royal Assent and became law.

The provisions of the separate property legislation dealt almost exclusively with property that the wife owned before marriage but that had not been covered by marriage settlement or prenuptial agreement. It allowed her to "have, hold and enjoy" all that property (real estate as well as her possessions) in exactly the same way as if she had remained single. Moreover, she could be sued to the value of her separate property if she did not fulfill a contract she had entered into before marriage.

However, the Act still restricted her separate property rights after the wedding: they applied only to property that was *bequeathed* to her; although she could now make a will, her belongings could be left only to her husband and children. She could look to the courts for protection against her husband if he had deserted her or was in prison and, while under court protection, keep her own earnings and those of her children who were younger than twenty-one. In all other circumstances, her earnings belonged to her husband – a considerable problem in a period when more and more "wealth" existed in that form.

However timidly, after four years of consideration and eight centuries of law, a Legislature of 130 men – nominal rulers of a tiny society clinging to the margins of a wilderness – had declared that a wife was no longer her husband's "horse, his ox, his ass, his any thing."

Nine years after the passage of the Act, a Special Committee of the British Parliament was formed to study the advisability of adopting similar legislation in the Mother Country; it asked for advice from John Rose, who had been a Member of the Parliament of the Canadas that passed the first Married Women's Separate Property Act in 1859. In 1868, when he went to London to describe the legislation, Rose was Finance Minister in the First Parliament of the Dominion of Canada; his testimony to the committee, although sketchy, is one of the few firsthand descriptions from a politician directly involved in the event.

"I little doubt but that the Bill was a copy, more or less close, of the same legislation in some of the United States . . . " Rose said. "Wherever its provisions have been invoked it has been found to work beneficially." He made special mention of the wife whose spouse tried to deprive her of property that belonged to her under the law; she could "obtain permission to sue her husband, and recover from him, as if from a stranger, any property which he either dissipated or made away with."

Rose, whose attitude toward the British legislators was, at best, anxiously avuncular, was asked by Lord Eversley, the committee chairman, "The cases in which women earn anything themselves among the lower classes are not very common with you, are they?" Rose agreed, possibly trying to justify the failure to include wages in separate property. (That he was wrong is evident from a study of female employment, published in the Toronto *Globe* in the year that Rose appeared before the committee. The largest city in the province had a population of 50,000, slightly more than half of whom were female. Of those, nearly *20 percent* were self-supporting, the majority working as servants or in the clothing industry.)

There is no suggestion that, when they passed the original Act in 1859, Rose or his colleagues understood the full meaning of what they were doing; surely they might have paused at the idea that they were changing certain of the most basic assumptions on which their society operated. The law that permitted a woman to consider an act by her husband "as if from a stranger" could never be anything other than the first step in an inexorable march to equality. It can even be argued that the ensuing suffrage battles, culminating in success seventy years later, had now become inevitable. (Many of the changes in family law, right up to the present, stem from the concepts embodied in the Married Women's Separate Property Act of 1859.) If the law said that a woman could *have* something separate, it must eventually acknowledge that, married or not, she *was* something separate.

Rose finished his meeting with the committee by saying that he could "see no reason why the [same system regarding married women's property] . . . should not work as well with the same classes here as those which it affects in Canada and in the United States." Apparently the British Parliament agreed with this self-satisfied appraisal and in 1870 it passed an Act that followed the provisions of the provincial legislation – but included wages in the definition of a wife's separate property.

In 1872 the Ontario Legislature followed England's lead in the matter of wages. In making changes to its original Act, it also copied the other major stipulation of the English law: husbands would no longer be held responsible for any of the debts their wives incurred before marriage.

It rapidly became clear that a howling mistake had been made in England and copied in Canada: if a husband was not responsible for his wife's prenuptial debts and, as a married woman she was responsible only for contracts – not debts – incurred before marriage, tradesmen had no way of collecting their bills. A number of young English brides-to-be headed straight for the poshest shops in London and Paris, where the best was barely good enough to meet their exacting standards. Worth, the most popular couturier of the day, was swamped with orders for expensive trousseaux. When bills were rendered, however, the well-bred ladies with the sumptuous tastes often turned out to have threadbare scruples that allowed them to reject the accounts they owed.

While there were fewer fleecing opportunities in Ontario, the offending clause was deleted in 1877, following by three years a similar move in the British Parliament.

On July 1, 1884, the Legislature of Ontario passed another Act that included improvement to its pioneer legislation twenty-five years earlier and to the amendments made both in England and in Ontario during the 1870s. Under the revised Act, a married woman had the right to all property she acquired, either before or during the marriage; the right to dispose of that property in any way she saw fit; the right to bequeath it to whomever she wished and to act as the administrator or executor of an estate; the right to enter into contracts to the extent of her property and to be sued, separate from her husband, to the same extent. Moreover, she had the right to sue her husband if he misused or damaged her property and, if a court case resulted, she could testify against him. (She did not have the right, however, to sue him for an *action in tort* – a wrong he committed against her; the law, while well-meaning, had the effect of punishing a man for breaking his wife's watch – but not her leg.)

It made a husband responsible for all his wife's prenuptial debts and contracts, but only to the value of property that had been hers and was now his. If there were disputes about what property belonged to which spouse, either could apply to a court for a ruling on the matter. All the provisions of the legislation had been copied from England, where the Married Women's Property Act, passed in the autumn of 1882, had come into effect on January 1, 1883.

London, January 1, 1883: although the Act was now law, the skies over England did not rain blood. An editorial in *The Times* declared:

> Today several Acts of great importance . . . come into operation. Without denying their significance, we may truly say that all yield in practical consequence to the Married Women's Property Act of 1882, which . . . in fact revolutionizes the law upon a vital subject [that] concerns every husband and wife.

With minor alterations, both the British and Ontario acts would remain the law for more than ninety years.

Caroline Sheridan Norton did not live to share the triumph that owed so much to her; even at the end, her life was heavy with every sadness and frustration. Perhaps the bitterest blow occurred in 1859 when, once again, she and George stood at the graveside of a son: Fletcher, Caroline's adored eldest, dead at thirty of tuberculosis.

Sixteen years later – still legally her husband – the wretched Norton died, adding to Caroline's devastation; her life's tormentor, object of the bright-burning rage that had always sustained her, had outwitted her by deserting the field of battle. She was said to have complained that George had not even lived long enough to make her Lady Grantley. (When the bearer of the Norton family title died less than a year later, Caroline's sister-in-law was similarly disparaging about *her* husband. She would be buried anywhere but with Grantley, she said. Having lived all her life with the Nortons, "nothing would induce" her to be buried with them.)

Caroline's remaining child, Brinsley, was by then an invalid who spent much of his time in the salubrious Italian climate, leaving her with the responsibility for raising his son and daughter.

In 1877, her own woman to the end, Caroline managed to set the dovecotes fluttering one last time. She married the widowed Sir William Stirling-Maxwell of Keir, father of two small children, an unflappable, charming man ten years her junior. In reality the marriage was simply a generous gesture designed to provide Caroline with the peace and comfort that circumstances, and her own temperament, had always denied her.

Sir William's gift was of short duration: in June, 1877, three months after the wedding, Caroline died. Brinsley, now Lord Grantley, was too ill to attend his mother's funeral; within three weeks he followed her to the grave. Six months later, the gallant Stirling-Maxwell was dead.

Caroline Sheridan Norton once said that she had "learned the English law, piecemeal, by suffering under it." Learned – and changed it. And, in doing so, became a force for change in a province she never saw.

Certainty and joy long gone, Caroline Norton's face still radiates strength of character, not long before her death in June, 1877.

The Prince of Wales (light trousers, foot on a rock) was still 41 years away from the throne when he made this 1860 visit to Niagara Falls.

Kelso, Hoodless and the Childsavers

Every age assumes that *it*, more than any other, has witnessed dizzying change; with mixed pride and irritation people measure their era's technology, society, economy, against the past and inevitably conclude that life has been altered with never-before speed and impact. Few periods, however, actually experienced the kind of basic shifts that occurred in Ontario in the half-century between Confederation and the end of World War I.

As Upper Canada prepared to give way to the new province of Ontario in the new Dominion of Canada, all but a few of the first-generation Loyalists were dead. In 1859, with foresight that was rare in its day, the government had commissioned George Coventry to set down the old people's memories. The result, *The Loyalist Narratives*, remains a tribute to, and an authentic voice of, the band of men and women who had come here to shape the future.

By 1867 John Strachan, the stalwart young Scot who had arrived in the final days of the eighteenth century, was one of those whose memories reached across the years to the earliest Cartwrights and their friends. The bishop was now heavy with honours, a lonely old man who had survived most of the members of his family. On July 1, the province stepped into Confederation. On November 1, his life having spanned its entire history, Bishop Strachan died in Toronto, aged ninety.

The name of the new province was taken from the lake – known at different times as St. Louis, Frontenac, Tadenac, and finally as Lake Ontario – that hems the southeastern edge of the province. Although it is not known precisely which Indian language gave us "Lake Ontario," in various native tongues it refers to clear or bright or sparkling waters.

The Ontario of 1867 was prosperous and sophisticated. Seven years earlier the popular young Prince of Wales had made a visit to the province, the first ever by a member of the Royal Family. His arrival in Toronto was greeted with particular enthusiasm: an arch of lattice and bunting, topped by crowns and adorned with fresh flowers, stood at the foot of John Street, a graceful focus for the thousands who cheered the boat bringing the Prince from Niagara-on-the-Lake.

Now the thriving cities with their gas lamps and bustling stores were testimony to a hard-working people who feared God and admired industriousness. In the larger centres the

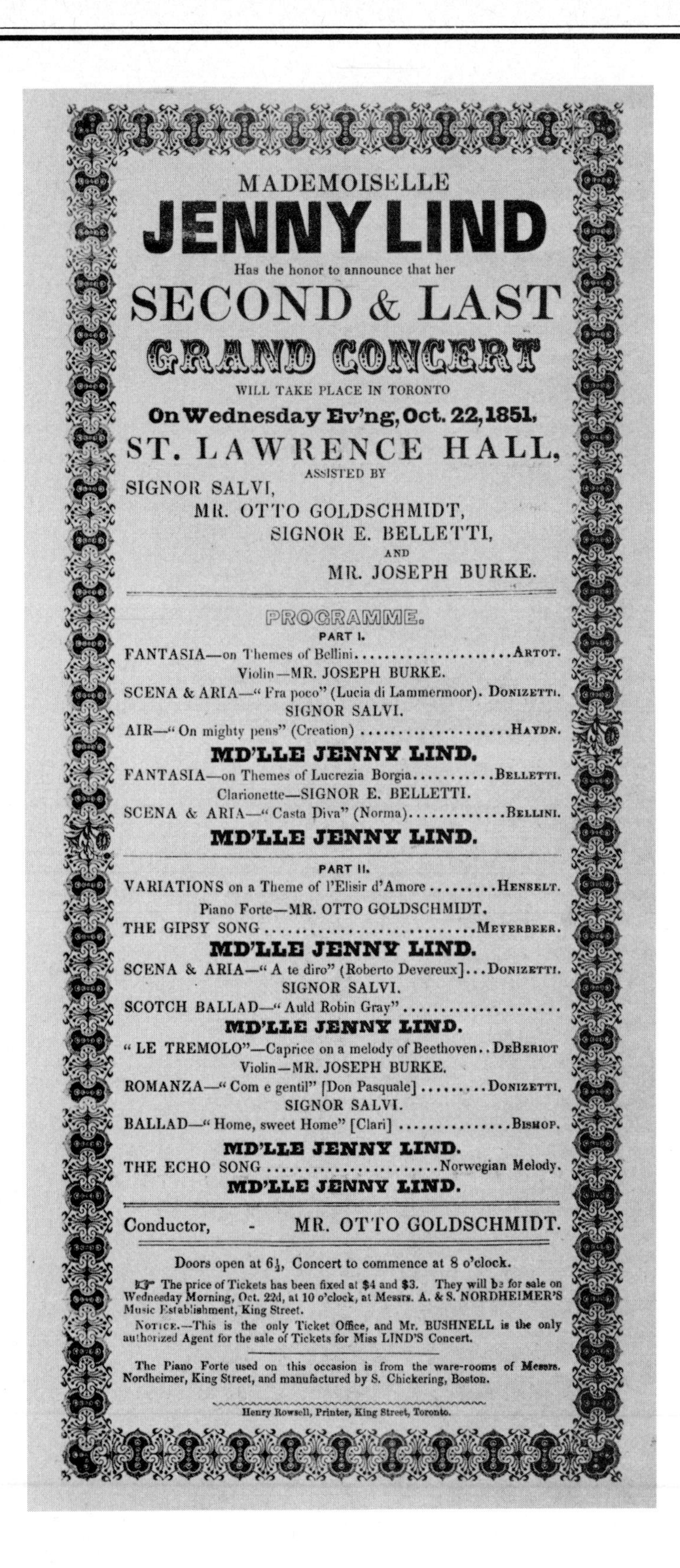

An international diva visits Upper Canada.

luxuries of the world were available: the most fragile English china, lushest Oriental silks, costliest imported wines, most ornate jewelry. Culture was almost as lively as commerce: even a decade and a half earlier, three concerts by Jenny Lind, the "Swedish Nightingale," had been greeted with feverish enthusiasm unequalled to this day. But more than Mammon and the Muses were satisfied: politicians and boosters called Toronto "the City of Churches," in deference to its 102 houses of worship. (Its 140 brothels were not deemed to be similarly noteworthy; however, a song of the times did pay tribute to its "nineteen taverns in a row.")

Whatever the province *was*, good or bad, a picture of what people *wanted* it to be was not to be found in either its busiest streets or its shabbiest laneways. Just as the first statute had defined the Upper Canada its leaders envisioned, the law of Ontario was still the most accurate measure of what its citizenry expected of it. Legislation was beginning to outline a society ready to change even its basic assumptions and ways of thinking. The province was notably ahead in certain areas (married women's property rights, child support, suffrage), markedly lagging in others (maternal custody, divorce).

Since each of Canada's four constituent provinces – Nova Scotia, New Brunswick, Quebec, and Ontario – had a complete, functioning legal system, the advent of Confederation made it necessary to restructure that system. The provisions of the British North America Act (and the ways those provisions have been applied by federal and provincial governments) have produced a court structure that is sometimes coherent, sometimes needlessly complex. The field of family law abounds in excellent examples of the complications.

The first complication stems from the decision to give control of different aspects of family law to the federal and provincial governments: Ottawa is responsible for the rules that determine whether a marriage is valid, but the provinces issue marriage licenses and (*pace* Cartwright and Simcoe) define who has the right to perform the ceremony. In exercising their powers, the provinces, of course, also exercise some say about whether or not a marriage is valid.

The laws affecting custody, the support of a spouse, and the division of property are all left to the provinces; that provincial power, however, is not clear-cut because the federal government can make overriding laws on the same issues as they apply *at the time of the divorce*.

The provinces, which have the right to pass laws relating to civil rights, decide whether a child's behaviour is a matter of concern according to the laws governing child welfare; but Ottawa, which is responsible for criminal law, determines when that same behaviour by that same child constitutes the "crime" known as juvenile delinquency. (The Young Offenders' Act, a federal law that came into operation in 1985 will help to clarify such cases.)

If the first complication is the division of legal jurisdiction, the second is the division of decision-making among the various courts. In Ontario, at the lower-court level, the system is dense with overlapping jurisdictions: a parent accused of sexual abuse will face one part of the Family Court, while the question of the child's welfare will be dealt with in another; cases involving support and custody can be dealt with in any one of *three* courts. (It might have been even worse if the federal government had duplicated the United States, where totally separate federal and state courts are blamed for some of the confusion and expense of that system. In this country the Federal Court of Canada deals only with certain federal matters, not including family law.)

Fortunately, the appeal system in Canada is coherent and straightforward: since the BNA Act gave responsibility for the administration of justice to the provinces, each used it to establish a Court of Appeal, the last court before cases are taken to the one, final appeal body for all laws, the federally established Supreme Court of Canada. (Originally, it was possible to take appeals one step further, to Britain's Privy Council. It took eighty-two years, until 1949, before the Supreme Court of Canada was given final say over Canadian law.)

The third complication is the federal government's exclusive power to appoint senior court judges, the only judges permitted to hear certain cases (property questions, the division of assets, the granting of the actual divorce). According to the British North America Act, such matters cannot be referred to provincially appointed judges. As a result, a Family Court judge in Ontario can grant support and custody but cannot decide who owns the family home, who will have the exclusive right to live in it, or declare that the spouses are divorced from each other. (In 1867, it was thought that, since the federal government would have little reason to control judicial decisions, federally appointed judges sitting in the higher courts of each province would preserve the bench's independence from provincial governments.) Clearly, the Fathers of Confederation could not have imagined the hair-splitting confusion that would result from their design of the justice system. Those problems lay in the future.

In 1867 there were other, more immediate difficulties. Orphans and children dependent on charity were still being apprenticed to employers who might, or might not, treat them humanely. The law, made even stricter in the early 1870s, denied parents the right to withdraw their offspring from apprenticing arrangements; it stressed the rights of the master and responsibilities of the apprentice, rather than the other way around.

Delinquent children roamed the streets in gangs, stealing, setting fires, drinking, accosting pedestrians; there were hundreds of other "street urchins" – destitute kids who supported themselves (and, often, their families) by working as bootblacks and newsboys, frequently sleeping on the streets, supplementing income with petty thievery and bootlegging. Nearly 8 percent of the male population in provincial jails comprised boys less than sixteen years old. A newspaper article emphasized the similarities between the slums of Toronto and Dickens's London under the headline "Oliver Twist Again."

Educational opportunities for women were restricted and universities routinely denied them admission. Although the law offered a wife protection against her husband's abuse (he could be charged with assault and, if convicted, be required to pay alimony, should she choose to not to live with

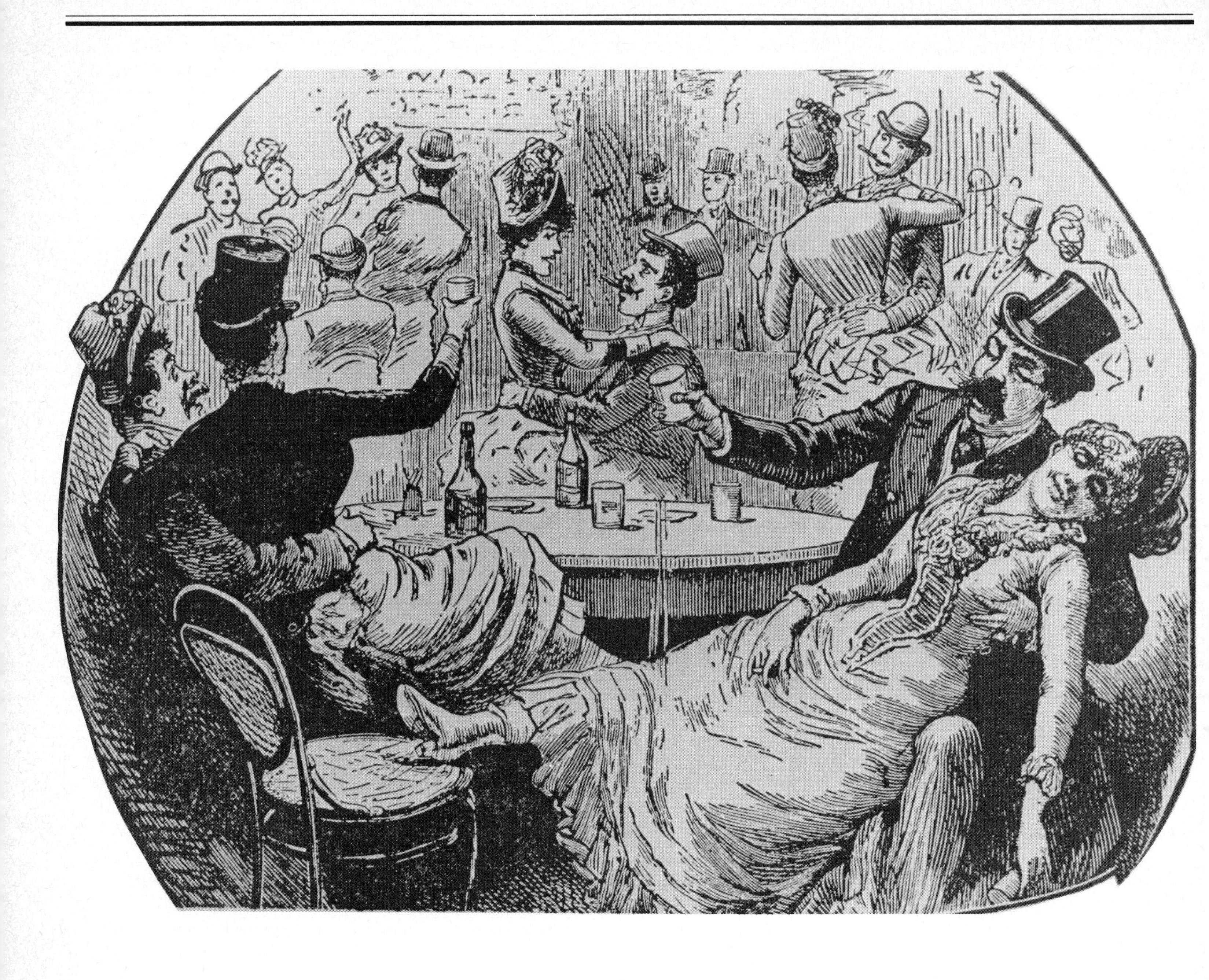

The far-from-genteel underside of the "Victorian" era: an 1880s cartoon entitled "Drinking With Tarts."

him), many women submitted to domestic violence in the mistaken belief that it was their duty to do so and because of their economic dependence on marriage. Only females who owned property could vote for school trustees, but none could vote in any other kind of election. Pornography by mail order was readily available; prostitution was among the few occupations open to poor, uneducated girls.

Drinking was a seemingly insoluble problem: the year after Confederation a report by Toronto's chief of police showed that 1,701 males and 828 females – 5 percent of the city's population – had been arrested as drunk and disorderly. In the 1870s the city had 120 taverns – which meant that, leaving aside children and drys, each needed only sixty customers in order to thrive. The growing anxiety about drunkenness would lead to the formation of a temperance movement with strong suffragist goals, a result of the belief – stronger in Canada than elsewhere – that the success of their cause depended on giving women the power of the ballot. As a result, the histories of the prohibition and suffrage movements are intertwined here as they are in no other country.

Like so much else in family law, the story of change in the fifty years after Confederation is a complex one, filled with the subtleties that human beings bring to all their most important behaviour. It was rooted in a major movement – the shift in much of the religious thinking of the time toward a social interpretation of the Gospel – and became visible in a thick sheaf of legislation asserting society's right to intervene in previously private domestic behaviour.

These changes marked the tacit recognition that the tightly enclosed pod of the family had been broken open by the Industrial Revolution and that not all husbands loved their wives "as Christ loved His church." The Act to Secure to Married Women Certain Separate Rights of Property was the first major acknowledgement of that fact; now the law was about to further abandon its view of the husband as a surrogate god and his wife and children as a choir designed only to sing his praises and tend to his wants.

Unhappily, it would engender another set of problems as the unrealistic ideal of the all-wise, all-powerful husband/father was discarded in favour of another, equally unrealistic, image: the perfect family. One speaker, typical of the entire period, described the family as the place that provided the foundations of

> . . . rectitude, industry and all virtues . . . not in the church, much as I revere it, highly as I esteem it, not by the government, not by the school except as it is an auxiliary of the parent, but in family life with all the seeds of our highest culture must be sown and there must their first fruits be gathered.

According to this view, divorce, women in the work force, alcohol abuse, unsanitary living conditions, were all threats to the ideal. Mommy was pious, pure, sexually submissive, and totally absorbed in meeting the needs of her husband and children. Daddy was strong, firm, kind, and industrious. But what exactly was their child?

Originally he had been a sinner awaiting salvation, a miniature savage needing civilization. The consequence of that view, of course, was that society saw no need to improve his life on earth: the most pressing need, after all, was to fill his soul, not his stomach. By the 1860s, however, that attitude was being rejected even by some churchmen: the Reverend Alexander Sutherland, a leading Canadian Methodist, felt that, although children might be "fallen" by nature, they could be saved from eternal damnation by atoning for original sin. In *this* world, salvation lay in proper moral training.

The ideal of the child and how he was influenced by his family was expressed by James L. Hughes, the Superintendent of Education for Toronto in the early years of the twentieth century. Hughes was a reformer, the author of seven volumes of verse, editor of a book of Robbie Burns's poetry, a devout Methodist, and a spirited feminist. He wrote that:

> . . . every child has in its nature an element of divinity which should be fostered . . . the natural tendency of childhood is toward the right if supplied with right conditions for growth of its bent; that training should be given at birth but never should interfere with its spontaneity . . . the first germs of religious growth are found in community, love, reverence, filial and fraternal relationships as revealed by the experiences of the pure family.

The underlying assumption of the existence of "the pure family" is that environment plays the most important role in shaping character; it was exactly that interpretation which gave the impetus to several decades of provincial legislation for children and their families, as well as to the organization of services for their benefit. The new laws differed from those of earlier days

Adelaide Hunter Hoodless.

which had emphasized the utility of children as free or nearly free labour (the 1799 Act to Provide for the Education and Support of Orphan Children and other apprenticeship statutes, for example). In taking a more realistic attitude toward children's emotional and material needs, the law also moved forward from previous attempts to provide, as meagrely as possible, for children whose circumstances (orphanhood, neglect, illegitimacy) made them community charges.

The increased industrialization of society helped to sharpen and focus worry about the environment and its effects, especially on children. A Dominion Commission on Mills and Factories reporting in 1882 showed how well-founded these concerns actually were. According to the commission, factory workers in the late 1870s and early 1880s laboured for an average of sixty hours weekly, including a seven-hour daily stretch unbroken by rest or meal periods; the lack of protection against dangerous or badly placed machinery was standard; steam boilers, situated near production lines, were often tended by children who were under eleven years of age; fire regulations were nonexistent; toilet facilities were inadequate; poor ventilation was a serious health hazard, especially in factories where cloth was bleached and dyed in moist, stale air, which was ideal for breeding tuberculosis.

Thirty-five percent of the manufacturing labour force was made up of women and children. (Even those women fortunate enough to enter higher-status occupations were confined to roles that emphasized hard work and obedience. When the province's first nursing school opened in St. Catharines in 1874, its motto was a meek "I see and am silent.") Of the children employed in manufacturing, a significant number were between the ages of five and fourteen – and children as young as *two* had been used.

There was, as well, a growing awareness of the impact of the city on society and a conviction that it, too, represented a hazard, especially to children. Cities tended to act as magnets for the poor who, in earlier times, had been less visibly distributed amongst the small towns and rural communities of Upper Canada. Now they lived in areas that were readily definable as slums, with problems of crowding, unemployment, crime, drunkenness, neglect, inadequate housing, poor standards of sanitation and health, and prostitution. But cities posed other dangers, even outside slum areas.

Toronto, the province's largest metropolis (1891 population: 144,023), was the favoured Sodom of reformers, a classic example of growth uprooting decency, with a resultant loss of morality and rectitude. The move to permit streetcars to run on Sundays was just such a battle: *The World*, a leading supporter of the idea, published verse intended to show that the cars would increase church attendance. "I had a dream the other night/ When everything was calm and still,/ I saw the cars one Sunday bright/ To church go streaming down the hill . . ." *Grip*, the satirical weekly, showed that the opposite view could lend itself to equally dreadful poesy: "I don't go for Sunday cars,/ Sunday papers, Sunday bars . . . "

The appearance of mechanized trolleys on city streets had not fazed the hordes of Torontonians who continued to use bicycles as their major means of transportation: in 1895 there were ninety stores selling bikes and their manufacture was a major industry employing more than 500 men. The cycling hordes did present some problems: collisions with pedestrians were so common that in 1895 a legislative committee investigated the problem – and discovered that all the victims were lawyers. (One wag suggested that bicyclists were engaged in useful work, while another said it meant only that "a bicycle cannot go astray in Toronto without knocking down a lawyer.")

There was a darker side to the streetcar story: it involved contracts in which public spending favoured personal gain, civic politicians who had been purchased by the job lot, a city hall ripe with the stench of corruption. A *Globe* editorial despaired: "When the Toronto historian of the distant future begins his chapter on the city . . . he may refer to the period as the boodle era, and if he is loyal he will weep copiously while he writes."

Goldwin Smith, the influential journalist and historian (a proponent of Sunday cars), described what was happening – and what could be expected – in an increasingly urbanized Canada:

> The people cannot afford to be so well housed in the city as they are in the village; their children grow

> up in worse air, physical and moral, and though they have more of a crowd and bustle they have really less of social life, because in the village they all know their next door neighbour. In the cities the people will be brought under political influences different from those of the country, and a change of political character with corresponding consequences to the commonwealth can hardly fail to ensue.

In time Ontario would have cause to be grateful not only that Smith identified the problems of urban life but that, given the opportunity, he would respond generously to alleviate some of them.

The period seems rich in strong-minded men and women determined to change society; but no picture of the province at the turn of the century is complete without reference to the remarkable matron whose crusades altered health, education, nutrition, and the lives of women throughout Ontario and – even today – throughout the world.

On February 26, 1910, the eve of her fifty-third birthday, Adelaide Hunter Hoodless was, as usual, speaking to a packed meeting, this time to members of the Federation of Women's Clubs gathered at Massey Hall.

She was looking forward to telling them about a university course she wanted set up for the advanced training of household science teachers. Certainly, no one listening could have been surprised that she was urging them to rally around yet another good work: for more than twenty years they had all heard, and heeded, her pleas for dozens of causes that she had energetically and effectively espoused. She had been one of them from the time of her birth, the youngest of twelve children, in the lush countryside of southwestern Ontario, near the village of St. George. It was an area in which people held political and religious beliefs with at least equal fervour. As a young woman engaged to John Hoodless, a prosperous furniture dealer, she asked her minister for advice since "... I am a strong Presbyterian and a Whig, planning to marry a man who is not only an Anglican but a Tory." "My dear," the clergyman answered, "you can be a good Christian in any church, but stick to your politics." As a result, the Hoodlesses, who could be found worshipping together at the Anglican church in Hamilton, occupied separate pews politically.

Mrs. Hoodless, however independent-minded, might have remained the busy young housewife and mother of four small children had her baby, John Harold, lived. But in 1889, aged eighteen months, he died and in the succeeding months his grieving mother found a new direction for her life. The loss of an infant, more than a century after the Simcoes buried their Katherine, was still a commonplace in Ontario. One child in every five died and the tiny gravestones with their inscriptions of anguished submission – "an angel returned to the Lord," "safe in his loving Father's arms" – were part of every family's plot.

But Adelaide Hunter Hoodless had little interest in meek resignation; she was determined to find out why her John and so many other babies still died in infancy. When she finally learned the cause of John's death – impure milk delivered to her home – she held herself responsible. Rather than give in to guilt and despair, however, she determined that other women would have the education necessary to prevent such needless waste of life.

> Apart from my family duties, the education of mothers has been my life work [she would say later] with a special attention to sanitation – a better understanding of the economic and hygienic value of foods and fuels and a more scientific care of children with a view to raising the general standard of the life of farm people.

An ambitious goal. Nonetheless, by the time she stepped onto the Massey Hall stage, Adelaide Hunter Hoodless had founded or helped to found the YWCA, the Victorian Order of Nurses, Macdonald Institute (now part of the University of Guelph), and McGill University's affiliate, the School of Household Science. When Lady Aberdeen, wife of the Governor General, moved beyond the tea-pouring limitations of most vice-regal spouses to found the National Council of Women in 1887 (dedicated to "applying the golden rule to society, custom and law"), Hoodless was named the organization's first treasurer.

Today, however, Adelaide Hunter Hoodless is best remembered for an organization she first suggested in 1897, in a speech given to a meeting at Squire's Hall in Stoney Creek: "rural universities" that would teach homemaking skills, mostly to farm women. This was the foundation of the Women's Institute, which by the 1930s would blossom into more than 3,300 chapters in 108 countries – to this day the largest, most influential organization of rural women in the world.

On that February night in 1910 Mrs. Hoodless was as determined as ever to keep pushing for better health and

John Joseph Kelso and some of his young charges.

education standards. According to a friend who was in the Massey Hall audience:

> . . . she gave an inspired speech, which resulted in the subsequent founding of the Lillian Massey School of Household Science in Toronto. Halfway through her talk, while her audience was enthusiastically applauding, Adelaide Hoodless, smiling, sipped some water. Suddenly the crash of glass was heard, and she fell to the floor, lifeless.

Thanks to Hoodless and her fellow pioneers, more children were now living through infancy and beyond. In the year of baby John's death, fewer than two-thirds of Ontario's children survived to age five; a quarter-century later, as the glass slipped from Adelaide Hunter Hoodless's dying grasp, nearly 85 percent of babies born in the province were alive on their fifth birthdays.

The fight to make those additional years worth living would fall to other reformers, men and women who believed that their task was to alleviate the problems of urban, industrial society of turn-of-the-century Ontario – especially as those problems touched the lives of children. None, however, would be as energetic or single-minded in that work as a remarkable young Irish immigrant named John Joseph Kelso. In time he would give up a flourishing career in journalism – which had been his childhood ambition – to become the driving force of Ontario's child-saving movement. In doing so, he would profoundly alter the law affecting children and their families.

Kelso was ten years old, the youngest of nine children of a previously well-to-do starch manufacturer who immigrated to Toronto in 1874 after the family business failed. Their circumstances had been so reduced that the youngster searched the streets for wood scraps to be used at home for heat. By the time he was fourteen, Kelso had been a boy labourer in an iron foundry, sold stationery on Front Street, run messages for Dominion Telegraph, and sold drygoods for Timothy Eaton. One day, as he sat at Union Station eating his lunch, he watched the stir created by the arrival of the Honourable George Brown, famed editor of *The Globe*; that incident, he later said, made him decide on a career as a newspaperman.

Each night he read the Bible and Shakespeare and, like a hero in a Horatio Alger novel, Kelso's persistence was rewarded. It brought him to the attention of soldier-politician Sir Sam Hughes, who tutored the ambitious youngster privately. In 1884 Kelso enrolled at Jarvis Collegiate High School – although, at twenty, he was several years older than his classmates – and completed the course in one year. Still determined to become a reporter, he took a job as a printer's devil at *The World* and, without pay, wrote articles in his spare time. He eventually got a promotion to the writing staff, where his pieces exposing the city's slum conditions included the Oliver Twist article.

The idea that children needed protection – especially poor children living in the city – was beginning to take hold. In 1886 the province passed An Act Regarding Infant Boarding Homes; modelled on British legislation, and tightened over the years, it required Ontario's municipalities to inspect places where small babies were being dumped, usually by their mothers. At a time when there were few support services for poor, deserted, or unmarried women who worked, the boarding establishments thrived – unlike their charges, who often died.

One cold February night in 1887 John Kelso moved from reporting the news to making it: in a speech to the Canadian Institute, he urged the establishment of a society that would prevent cruelty to children and animals; its basic premise was that education was needed to make people more humane. The idea was enthusiastically taken up by some of Toronto's most influential citizens and led to the formation of the Toronto Humane Society. Although the name now conjures up lost kittens and puppies, it was meant to emphasize "the development of the humane spirit in all affairs of life."

The society's board showed Kelso's sure grasp of how to attract power and influence a cause: he had the inglorious but important job of secretary, while Ontario's Lieutenant-Governor (and son of the former Chief Justice) John Beverley Robinson agreed to act as patron and Toronto Mayor W. H. Howland as honorary president; as a signal of the esteem in which he was held in the child-saving movement, Kelso was also appointed secretary of the American Humane Society.

In 1889, after representations from Kelso and the society, Toronto City Council proposed a bylaw licensing newsboys; it prohibited girls of any age and boys under eight from selling newspapers on street corners. Because many families needed the income generated by their children and because newspapers depended on them for circulation, the law was vigorously opposed.

Traditionally, newspapers had supported various schemes to help children; this time, however, a different ox – their own – was being gored and Kelso's bosses at *The World*, as well as his erstwhile hero, George Brown, were furious. Kelso was accused of being "The Newsboy's Enemy" and nicknamed "Tagger K," a reference to the tags that licensed newsboys would be required to wear. Caricatures pictured him as a dog catcher chasing child newsies, and *The Telegram* published editorials of gloriously empurpled rage: "A Board that will pass such an obnoxious, senseless, absurd, degrading and uncalled for set of resolutions," it stormed, "is capable of meddling in almost anything." It took another eight years for Toronto politicians to brave such denunciations and pass the legislation.

Despite Kelso's part in the newsboys' battle, he was offered a job at *The Globe* in 1889 and continued his slum exposés during his four-year stint at the paper. In addition, clearly in his element, he was busily rounding up community support for other causes. He persuaded the Toronto Trades and Labour Council to endorse a scheme under which the province would build free public

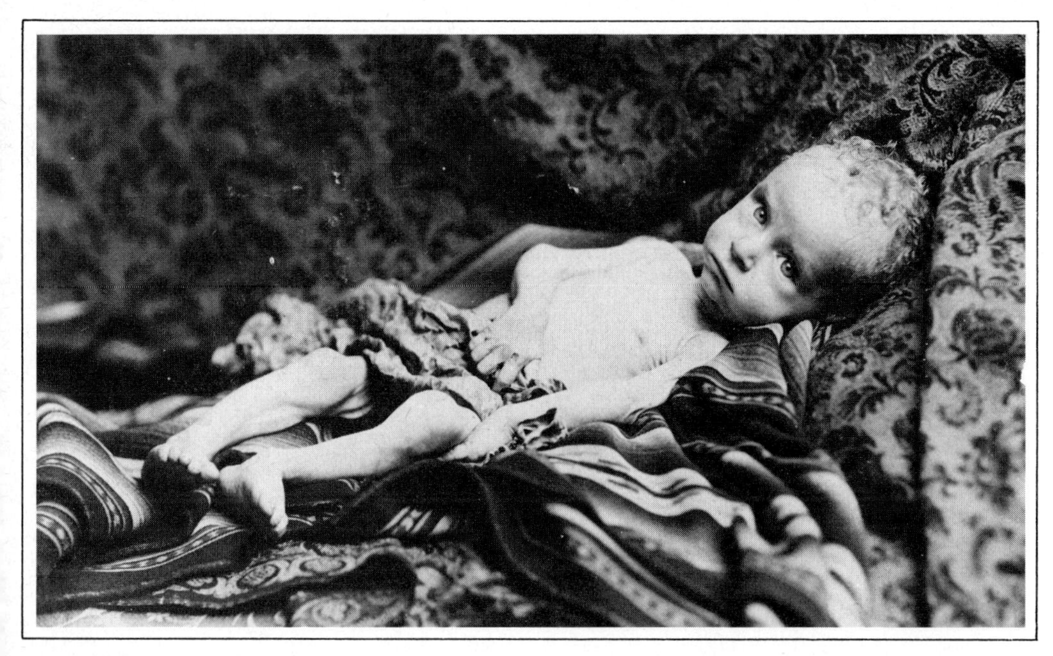

The Children's Aid Society cared for children who were starving or simply unwanted.

playgrounds, using a legacy tax as capital. Kelso obtained the support of the Toronto Public School Board, which lobbied Ontario's Minister of Education; eventually, Jesse Ketchum Park in North Toronto was made into a permanent children's playground.

J. J. Kelso was far from satisfied. Next on his list was formation of an organization that would push for the preservation of public places of exceptional beauty, interest, or recreational value – and that would adorn them with statues of famous Canadians. It also pushed for establishment of a Provincial Museum of Science, Art, and History, an art museum, and a concert hall. To a man like Kelso, with his passionate belief in the importance of environment on human behaviour, unchecked urban development invited disaster; it destroyed places of beauty, robbed people of their cultural heritage, limited their access to recreation, and, as a result, deformed their character. A pioneer in stressing the spiritual quality of urban life, the Ontario Public Places Association (secretary: J. J. Kelso) was short-lived, disbanding after the failure of its plan to turn the grounds of Upper Canada College into a public recreational park.

Nonetheless, it had at least one major, although indirect, success – thanks to Goldwin Smith, who was a friend and colleague of Kelso in the child-saving groups, the Public Places Association, and other causes. He and other PPA members had talked enthusiastically about their ideas with Smith's wife, Harriette; she was the owner of The Grange, known to be one of the most beautiful private homes in Toronto from the time it was built in 1818. The Grange had been the original family residence of D'Arcy Boulton, Jr., member of the distinguished family of lawyers and parliamentarians (his brother Henry had been the Attorney General responsible for passage of the 1829 Marriage Act).

Unfortunately the Boulton men, while socially and politically shrewd, were so financially inept that, to avoid creditors, The Grange had been passed from daughter-in-law to daughter-in-law rather than from son to son. That was how Harriette, an American heiress who had been widowed by a third-generation Boulton, came into possession of the mansion and the charming park in which it stood. After her marriage to Goldwin Smith, she had written a will leaving him The Grange. Now Kelso and the selfless Smith were urging her to bequeath it instead to a group of prominent Torontonians who were sponsoring art exhibitions and looking desperately for a permanent building to use as a municipal art museum. According to the altered terms of the will, Smith was to have only lifetime rights to the mansion after Harriette's death. Goldwin (brilliant historian, biographer of Jane Austen,

Harriette Mann Dixon, not long after she married into the financially troubled Boulton family, and husband William Henry Boulton, Mayor of Toronto. (detail)

public-spirited citizen) outlived Harriette by only nine months and, with his passing in 1910, a portion of the dream of the Public Places Association was translated into reality as the core of the Art Gallery of Toronto (later, the Art Gallery of Ontario).

Undaunted by the association's failures, Kelso had decided to provide rural excursions for urban children. He argued that they "might benefit from life-long impressions gained from contact with nature, and association with good men and women who wish to be of service." To that end, Kelso founded the Fresh Air Fund; the first group of 400 children met at Lorne Park on June 27, 1888, and marched down Yonge Street, accompanied by a fife band, to meet the boat taking them for the day's outing. An organizational debt of $22 was incurred, but this amount, and more, was raised at the fund's first meeting.

In the next five years more than 30,000 youngsters embarked on Fresh Air trips. Remembering a visit to Toronto in 1890, Mr. (later Sir) John Kirk of the Shaftesbury Society and Ragged School Union in England wrote:

> . . . I confess that my experience of the working of the Fresh Air Fund in Toronto, under Mr. Kelso, came to me as an inspiration . . . I realized that the press were able and willing to do great things for the child, and with the funds provided, those specially interested and working amongst the slum children could get them out of congested districts into the fresh air . . . [The English Fund] may be said in its particular form to have received its inception on board the splendid steamer sailing around Toronto . . . [and] has been the means of giving a day's holiday in the country to no less than a million and a half children from the crowded courts and alleys of the thirty-six biggest cities of the United Kingdom.

That must have been particularly gratifying to Kelso, who had used parallels to the fictional (but far from imaginary) story of an English slum child, Oliver Twist, to goad his fellow citizens into action. In time the Fresh Air Fund became a favourite cause of Joseph Atkinson, Kelso's friend and fellow-reporter at *The World* and *The Globe*. "Holy Joe" eventually bought *The Toronto Star* – the newspaper that to this day sponsors both the Fresh Air Fund and its winter offshoot, the Santa Claus Fund.

John Kelso's idea of one-day holidays may have been naïve – annual trips, later expanded to longer camping expeditions, would hardly impress youngsters who spent the rest of their time in slums – but he was no fool. To Kelso the Fresh Air Fund was simply another necessary step on the long road of reform. In 1891 he was ready to move again: a provincial commission investigating prisons and asylums had concluded that there was a "lack of provision for the reformation or preservation of children in their own homes" – an opinion that Kelso shared. He sensed that the time was ripe for the "organization of a children's aid society to wisely direct the trend of the legislation that was sure to follow." Once again he looked to influential friends to transform the idea into reality.

The goals of such a society would reflect what Kelso (a devout Presbyterian) and the others had pursued for years: compulsory education, religiously oriented kindergarten schools for underprivileged children, establishment of a temporary home for youthful offenders and a separate trial procedure for them, a juvenile probation system, industrial homes to give life and work skills to homeless youngsters, more playgrounds and fresh-air excursions, clubs to keep boys off the street. Speaking to a public meeting just before Christmas, 1891, Kelso outlined plans for an agency to implement such an ambitious program; on that night the Toronto Children's Aid Society was formed.

On May 17, 1892, the CAS opened the doors of its first temporary shelter at 18 Centre Street. It accepted children who had been abandoned, or whose parents needed temporary relief from their responsibilities; neglected or deserted children; juveniles awaiting trial or those who had been convicted of crimes. The society's first president: John Joseph Kelso. A year later he resigned and, in keeping with his understanding of the need to fill boards with the powerful and the wealthy, turned over the presidency to J. K. Macdonald, president and founder of the Confederation Life Association.

Kelso's ideas about the care of children showed a rare, innate understanding of their needs, well in advance of many

Goldwin Smith on the lawn of The Grange, 1905.

Name tags firmly pinned on pinafores and jackets, a Fresh Air Fund Party is ready to go.

of his colleagues. In an undated pamphlet entitled *Can Slums be Abolished or Must We Continue to Pay the Penalty?*, he said:

> The best work is not that which, recognizing the imperiled condition of the child marches it away to a place of safety – but the directing of all forces to the removal of the danger so that the child may remain in its natural environment, with all the thorns removed from its path. Prevention – that is, the prevention which purifies the home life and restores maternal care and affection, is the very highest form of child-saving work, and the ideal toward which all efforts should tend.

To a degree that modern complexity renders unlikely, he worked most of his adult life – with considerable success – in that cause.

Kelso remained the key figure in the welfare of Ontario's children for the next quarter-century. His appointment, in 1893, as Ontario's first Superintendent of Neglected Children was proof of government determination to involve itself in the quality of care that families and organizations gave to children for whom they were responsible. This new job placed Kelso in frequent conflict with the Children's Aid Society board, whose management of the organization was, in his opinion, sometimes inadequate. If they ever expected deferential treatment from him, Kelso's erstwhile colleagues soon learned that his fierce loyalty belonged to only one group: needy children. Kelso's role now meant that he had access to legislative decisions; whatever his part in shaping any one act, it is clear from the over-all direction of the law that his concerns about youngsters were widely shared within government.

Nor was the government's attitude entirely new: the mid-nineteenth-century ferment affecting marriage and property had also influenced legislation dealing with needy or troubled children. In 1857 two bills had been passed by the Legislature: one, An Act for Establishing Prisons for Young Offenders, provided for construction of "reformatory prisons" in both Canadas. The other, An Act for the More Speedy Trial and Punishment of Young Offenders, encouraged the courts to try children quickly in order "to avoid the evils of their long imprisonment previously to trial."

Under 1894 amendments to the Criminal Code of Canada, children younger than sixteen were kept in custody separate from adults both before and after trial; the proceeding itself was not publicized and took place in a separate court. That type of court already existed, according to Toronto Police Court Magistrate Colonel G. T. Denison:

> In 1892, we instituted the Children's Court. It was not really [separate] . . . but we set aside a small room in the lower part of City Hall . . . I was accustomed to go down to that room to try all charges against children, in order to keep them out of the public court.

As Superintendent of Neglected and Dependent Children, Kelso was given responsibility for supervising children's aid societies. In reacting to his enthusiasm for probation as a method of helping young offenders, some CAS staff members would later be assigned to work as juvenile probation officers, reporting periodically to the courts "concerning the progress and welfare of the child."

(All this activity for social betterment, however praiseworthy, should be seen in the context of a time when reforms in one area still left plenty of room for improvement in others. For example, when W. L. Scott, president of the Ottawa Children's Aid and a judge of the Supreme Court of Ontario, came back from an American corrections conference in 1908, he appointed two women, one a French Catholic and the other an English Protestant, as probation officers; he later explained that the decision to use women was not simply a response to the belief that "women, intended by nature for motherhood, are better fitted for the work than men" but because "a better class of women than men can frequently be got for the money available.")

By the early years of the new century, the most senior government officials recognized the shortcomings of the various institutions for delinquent children. Kelso later recalled that, in 1909,

> I successfully waylaid or intercepted some forty boys, all under sentence to the Reformatory, and all were spirited away to situations and foster homes before they reached their legal destination. The Attorney-General one day asked me, "Look here, Kelso, where do you get the law for all this?" "Law," I replied, "there isn't any law that I know of, but don't you think it is the best thing for the boy?" He agreed that it was, and kindly consented to shut his eyes to what was going on.

Industrial schools, which had been established in 1874 to "teach and train" offenders under fourteen, were equally unsatisfactory; in Judge Scott's words: "What wise parents would place a naughty child with other naughty children in order to make him better?"

Clearly, the fight for better treatment of children in trouble with the law was

Crumbling plaster, an aching back – but the steps have to be cleaned.

far from over. Kelso and Scott were among the authors of a proposed bill that would define the offense of "delinquency" as the violation by a child under sixteen of any federal or provincial statute or of any municipal bylaw. It would also include children who could be placed in schools or reformatories because of their behaviour (truancy, promiscuity), even if the behaviour itself was not illegal.

The stated intention of the legislation was that

> . . . the care and custody and discipline of a juvenile delinquent shall approximate as nearly as may be that which should be given by its parents, and that as far as practicable every juvenile delinquent shall be treated, not as a criminal, but as a misdirected and misguided child, and one needing aid, encouragement, help and assistance.

There was far from unanimous praise for this legislation, and some child-savers who were sympathetic to its underlying ideals were nonetheless concerned that it might be abused. An even larger, more vociferous group, including Denison and other police magistrates, were choleric at the very idea of the proposals. Their reaction makes it clear that arguments about how to treat the young are themselves anything *but* young.

One especially intemperate effusion described the proposed legislation as "propaganda" advocated by "superficial and sentimental faddists" who

> . . . work upon the sympathies of philanthropic men and women for the purpose of introducing a jelly-fish and abortive system of law enforcement, whereby the judge or magistrate is expected to come down to the level of the incorrigible street arab and assume an attitude absolutely repulsive to British Subjects. The idea seems to be that by profuse use of slang phraseology he should place himself in a position to kiss and coddle a class of perverts and delinquents who require the most rigid disciplinary and corrective methods to ensure the possibility of their reformation. I would go further to affirm from extensive and practical experience that this kissing and coddling, if indiscriminately applied, even to the best class of children, would have a disastrous effect, both physically, mentally, morally and spiritually.

Scott and Kelso may have been good, but they were *not* goody-goodies. Scott described the author of the statement as a "person of very limited intelligence"; Kelso called him "self-opinionated" and "opposed to those who failed to treat him with deference." Scott's father, a Senator who was also a Cabinet member, inserted a reference to the proposed law in the 1906 Speech from the Throne; but he had tactlessly neglected to discuss the issue with the Minister of Justice, who was so incensed that the bill was withdrawn and did not come before the House of Commons until 1908.

The work of Kelso, Scott, and the others would eventually encompass many programs for troubled children and would be carried on by educators, psychologists, doctors, and members of several professions; it would involve provincial ministries of education, welfare, health, and, for some seventy years, corrections. Of all the events of the child-saving movement, it was the successful battle for separate juvenile court facilities, first permitted by the 1908 legislation, that would most directly affect the administration of family law in Ontario.

The Act applied only in those provinces which chose to proclaim it and only after they had established juvenile courts. The province of Ontario finally moved in 1910, but the court's operation was hampered by meagre funding and by the low esteem in which it was held, especially within the legal profession. The concept that a juvenile delinquent should be treated "not as a criminal, but as a misdirected and misguided child . . . needing aid, encouragement" was a new one and it made some of the ensuing difficulties inevitable. The court atmosphere was informal; there were no juries; cases could be handled without the involvement of lawyers; publicity was forbidden. Furthermore, if the "defendant" was not a criminal but a "misdirected and misguided child," it seemed reasonable to discount the importance of legal training in those chosen to hear such cases. To further complicate matters, juvenile courts and the Act itself had been introduced into Ontario on a piecemeal basis, county by county, in those counties that asked for them and were prepared to pay a portion of their cost. As a result, juvenile courts were not established everywhere in the province until the 1960s.

Learning to strip cane was essential: most students at the Brantford School for the Blind could expect to spend their lives weaving cane chair seats.

In the name of "common sense" (and in order to keep costs down) juvenile court judges were frequently chosen from amongst people with no legal training. There were other contentious issues that centred on the court itself and on the treatment of juveniles. For example, some people wondered if there would be abuses of justice in courts presided over by magistrates with little or no knowledge of the law. Might that, especially in a court closed to outside scrutiny, leave the juvenile without any kind of protection against poor decisions, harsh sentencing, unreasonable treatment?

Was there justice in the way the law was applied to children? The school truant, for example, could be incarcerated for the kind of chronic absenteeism that would cause an adult no stiffer penalty than the loss of his job. And what of the double injustice done to the female juvenile accused of "promiscuity"? She was being punished for her (usually unpaid) sexual activity, while her professional sister was liable to prosecution on the grounds that she accepted money – and both were being sentenced while their partners went free.

Was it possible that the courts, in the service of a noble cause, were subverting the tenets of British justice when dealing with children – the very group most in need of protection against abuse?

Nor were these the only difficulties facing the juvenile court. One of the most persistent and longest-lasting – there are traces of it even today – was the patronizing attitude of the legal profession itself toward the law affecting children and families. Separation, access, custody, the fight over support – these were distasteful cases, the bottom of any lawyer's practice – filled with the rage of wounded and vengeful spouses, the messiness of people's everyday lives.

Juvenile delinquency cases were even worse. They were heard in a court that did not need lawyers and in a courtroom often presided over by a layman; the atmosphere of the courts reeked of low-status law where unappealing people with seemingly unlimited needs and limited funds required enormous amounts of attention. Battalions of sullen Artful Dodgers, their histories filled with drunken parents, poverty, indifference, the furthest reaches of despair and cruelty, are not the clients on whom luminous legal careers are built. For many lawyers, any practice in juvenile court was better than chasing ambulances – but only just.

Nonetheless, the power of the juvenile court was expanded over the years: in 1934 family matters (maintenance of deserted wives and children, for example) were gradually transferred to juvenile court judges. In 1960 diagnostic facilities were added to the larger courts to aid them in assessing the needs of children and families. In 1970 family courts were given jurisdiction over cases of child welfare, enforcement of alimony and maintenance orders made by other courts, paternity suits and actions that had been brought under a variety of family law statutes.

But the greatest improvements to the operations and reputation of juvenile courts did not take place until 1968, the beginning of a period that has seen the most extensive legal overhaul ever to take place in Ontario. For the first time the provincial government passed legislation under which it assumed the total costs of financing the juvenile courts and reorganized them as the Provincial Court (Family Division), with uniform powers and responsibilities. The same law also restricted judicial appointments to those people with legal training, a necessary step at a time when the law was moving in new directions and the issues being tried before the court were more complex.

(One of the most important side effects of the rewriting of family law – and one least understood by the families who are most affected by it – is that the new body of legislation attracted many of the brightest, most interesting young lawyers to its practice. In part, this is because the women's movement of the late 1960s brought waves of females to the legal profession in unprecedented numbers; they understood, often from experience, the importance of family law and they took it seriously. Moreover, their entry into the field coincided with that period of vast social change which emphasized the importance of individual needs and rights – the very stuff of family law. Suddenly it became a legitimate specialty, challenging enough for even the brainiest, or most ambitious, lawyers of either gender.

(Another aspect of reform has been the appointment of a new generation of judges: many of them, like the lawyers who appear in their courts, are talented men and women with extensive experience in family law. The implications of the Charter of Rights and Freedoms for all Canadians make this upgrading of talent on both sides of the bench vitally necessary to the operations of courts and of the society they represent. For more on changes to family law in the past decade, see Chapters 8 and 9.)

In their early days the juvenile courts restricted themselves to the child who was in trouble with the law; fortunately, however, attempts to improve his lot did not diminish the drive for better legislation to deal with other needs of other children. One of the key changes occurred in 1887, when the provincial government decided to build on existing legislation, passed in 1855 and based on England's Talfourd Act. For the first time a judge had to make custody and access decisions "having regard to the welfare of the infant"; he was also required to take into account the conduct of both parents (rather than just the mother's conduct) as well as the wishes of both parents (rather than just the father's wishes).

Despite these and other improvements, the double standard continued to be underwritten by custody and access laws: until 1911, a mother was not entitled to custody of her children if she had committed adultery, although this sanction was not applied to the adulterous father. Under the same legislation, a mother gained the right to consent to the marriage of a minor child – but only if the father was dead; for the first time, the law also established a minimum marriage age – fourteen – except in cases "where marriage is shown to be necessary to prevent illegitimacy of offspring."

Not until the beginning of World War I did court decisions slowly expand maternal rights: according to the judgement in one case, when a mother had custody of her child, "the father's right to make any decision regarding the child's upbringing and conduct were severed almost completely." The law now allowed her to appoint a guardian to act alone or jointly with a guardian appointed by the child's father; if the father had died without appointing one, she had the right to do so. Clearly, we were moving a long way from the seventeenth-century concept of the father as the only parent with power over the life of the child.

The erosion of the husband's power had begun in other areas as well: an 1891 decision had held that he could no

After long public service and not-always-private tragedy, Sir John A. was, in truth, "the Old Man."

longer "personally chastise" (i.e., beat) his wife or imprison her. In 1909 a Criminal Code of Canada amendment set the maximum sentence for abduction of a woman at ten years. (The need for caution against overestimating the law's respect for women as women was still valid, however: the maximum sentence for abducting a woman *with property* was set at fourteen years.)

Innovative family laws were part of a pattern of change that spanned the last years of the old century and the first ones of the new. Sometimes the change was largely symbolic (Belva A. Lockwood's run for the American presidency in the 1884 elections; the abolition, in 1909, of the *Jury of Matrons*, the only kind of jury on which a woman could sit – a bizarre relic of nineteenth-century Upper Canada, where it was convened only to decide whether a woman who had been sentenced to death was pregnant – in which case she could not be hanged until after she had given birth, although in practice, her sentence was usually commuted to life imprisonment.) At other times the changes were plainly indicative of a basic shift in society (the revelation in the 1891 census that one of every eight persons who worked for pay was female).

There were new attitudes toward education that were also significant: according to an Act passed in 1891, children aged eight to fourteen were required to attend school during the entire period that it was in session (rather than, as previously, only for a minimum of four months of each academic year).

The doors of higher education were still closed to women, but Clara Brett

The genuine affection for the dour Widow of Windsor and her family would soon be tested in war.

Martin was determined to pursue a legal career. Rejected by the Law Society of Upper Canada for admission as a student in 1891, she turned for help to her influential grandfather and, thanks in part to his persistence, Ontario passed an Act in 1892 authorizing women to become solicitors. When the Benchers of the Law Society nonetheless continued to balk, Premier (and Attorney General) Oliver Mowat intervened and Martin was permitted to study to become a solicitor. In 1895 Martin applied to be called to the Bar (i.e., to become a barrister) and was refused; that year the Legislature passed another Act, this one authorizing the Law Society to call women to the Bar but, once again, the Benchers refused. Arthur Hardy (by then Premier and Attorney General) pressured the Law Society and Clara Brett Martin was called to the Bar in February, 1897, the first member of her sex practicing at the bar anywhere in the British Empire.

A major shift was about to take place in the political life of the Dominion. In March of 1891 Sir John A. Macdonald, staking his reputation on his belief that Canadians would respond to appeals to their nationalism, warned that commercial union with the Americans, as promoted by the Liberal opposition, was just the prelude to a complete U.S. takeover; he won – narrowly – thanks in part to ham-handed American financial contributions to the other side.

Six weeks later, while conferring on international problems with Lord Stanley, the Governor-General, Macdonald suffered a slight stroke but carried on, both inside and outside the House, for the next ten days. In the following week he was felled by a second stroke, his condition listed as "hopeless," his command of language and men reduced to pressing his wife's hand to indicate what he wanted. On June 6 the "Old Man" was "borne on and outward, past care and planning, past England and Canada, past life and into death."

Macdonald's belief that Canadians were nationalists with strong ties to England would long survive the man himself – often given new energy by the bullying tone that successive U.S. governments adopted when dealing with Canada. In 1898 one such dispute between the two countries – this time over the Alaska-British Columbia border – was so acrimonious that it was eventually turned over for arbitration to a joint Anglo-American committee. (The committee's report, in 1903, was considered an attempt by the English to placate the United States government at Canada's expense; it temporarily soured Canadian attitudes toward both countries.) However, support for the "Mother Country" was still strong in 1901 when more than 8,000 Canadians volunteered to serve in the Boer War raging in South Africa – under British command and on British pay.

On January 1, 1901, the twentieth century began (accompanied by the usual controversy about whether it actually dated from the previous year; the argument that calendars are calculated from one to ten, rather than from zero to nine, seemed to establish the later date as the correct one). On the tenth day of the new century the death of Queen Victoria – nanny to an Empire for sixty-four years – emphasized, with almost theatrical symmetry, that one era had ended and another was beginning.

Further evidence of change, closer to home, was contained in the data collected for the 1901 census: 43 percent of Ontarians lived in cities, an increase of 10 percent in twenty years. (And twenty years after that, in 1921, the province's population would divide evenly between city and rural dwellers for the first time and, thereafter, become increasingly urban.)

The Industrial Revolution, of course, had made that shift inevitable. Today's antique hunter bent on bagging a prime specimen of dry sink, *circa* 1880, has the luxury of contemplating the integrity of its workmanship, its echoes of a bygone age; to its original owner, however, that sink was just another inefficient object in a life filled with them. The factory, on the other hand, produced less expensive goods *and* provided opportunities for family members to labour to earn the money to buy the machines to escape the labour of the farm or cottage.

From the earliest days of industrialization, both men and women yearned for mechanized conveniences that promised to ease their ceaseless workload. (One of the first was advertised in the 1850s in a Sarnia newspaper as an "anti-friction washing machine" that would save labour and soap without damaging material. "The clothes," said the ad, "are placed in a Frame, made for their reception, and submitted to the action of 200 FLOATING BALLS, which action in a few minutes will make the dirtiest clothes perfectly clean." There is no evidence that, even at $8, this incomprehensible labour saver was a success.)

Governments had already begun to enact laws protecting workers from the near-slavery in shops and factories. In 1884, for example, the year of the major consolidation of the Act to Secure Certain Property Rights to Married Women – a move to save one member of the family from exploiting others – the province had passed An Act for the Protection of Persons Employed in Factories – a move to minimize opportunities for one group to exploit another in the workplace.

Its provisions, and those of the bills passed in the years up to the end of World War I, reveal the extent to which labour legislation was rooted in the child- saving movement. In fact, the major purpose of such laws, in addition to establishing certain safety and health measures, was to regulate the times of the day and the maximum number of hours daily that women and children could work in factories and shops.

According to the 1884 Act, no girl under fourteen or boy under twelve could work in a factory without a parent's written permission; children and women could not do factory work for more than ten hours daily or sixty hours weekly, unless special permission were granted by a labour inspector; separate "privies" were required for males and females. (An exception to the rules, passed in 1887, stressed the continuing importance of agriculture to Ontario's economy: in June, July, and August, boys under twelve and girls under fourteen were permitted to harvest and prepare food for canning. Later legislation, forbidding factories to hire any children under fourteen continued

The Pageant at Massey Hall, following Eaton's 1914 parade.

to exempt those involved in summertime food preparation. It was not until 1914 that a limit of eight hours daily was set for children in canning factories and not until 1918, as veterans began returning to the labour force, that employment of children in those factories was abolished.)

By 1888 the government had begun to regulate conditions of labour in the retail and wholesale trades as well: initially, boys under fourteeen and girls under sixteen were permitted to work no more than seventy-four hours a week. Later amendments prohibited the hiring of any person under the age of ten and stipulated that a child, young girl, or woman could not begin work earlier than seven in the morning and finish later than six in the evening – except on Saturdays, when she was permitted to remain on the job until 10 P.M.

Successive laws regulated standards of safety and hygiene, including rules for guarding dangerous machinery, providing proper ventilation, and relieving overcrowding. By 1904 women were required to wear their hair "rolled or plaited or fastened securely to the head or confined to a close-fitting cap"; while the intent of the legislation was to minimize the danger inherent in the long hairstyles of the time, it was strongly resisted by the women themselves.

Part of the problem lay in the character of John Dryden who, as Ontario's Minister of Agriculture, had been given responsibility for labour legislation. A harsh- tongued anti-feminist, Dryden was guaranteed to raise the hair – long or short – on most women's heads. A mixture of suffrage and racism (both soon to be key social issues) was evident in the response by one indignant worker, interviewed by *The Toronto Star* on March 17, 1904: "If I have to wear my hair plastered down like a Chinaman, I won't do it," she said. "I might resign . . . I think Mr. Dryden might have consulted us before drafting that bill. I wish women had votes."

To men like Dryden, that hardly seemed necessary in the pleasant years of the twentieth century's first decade. Problems there might be – but no problems so large that they could not be settled amongst decent men. By an act of 1897 all males aged twenty-one or over who were able to meet certain citizenship and residency requirements could vote in provincial and federal elections. The municipal ballot was open to males or unmarried females who fulfilled certain property qualifications; generously, the property belonging to a man's wife could be treated as his when considering his eligibility to vote. Only those involved in the "mad, wicked folly of Women's Rights" that had so exercised the late Queen would gracelessly notice the anomaly by which a male's property did not count similarly in his wife's favour.

But not every moment of life was filled with unhappiness and injustice; in summer families picnicked or spent the day at the "Ex," applauding candidates in swimsuit competitions or pretty baby contests. Once cold weather arrived, the most exciting event, other than Christmas itself, was Eaton's Santa Claus Parade; started in 1905, it was soon a major outing for anyone in and near Toronto.

That first year Santa arrived at Union Station, circled several downtown blocks and entered Eaton's store. By 1910 the fun was spread over two days: on Friday the six or seven people who made up the entire "parade" left Newmarket and, as they proceeded down the muddy farm roads, waved at the excited kids dressed in their Sunday best. According to one man who took part:

> As night fell, we stopped at the home of a farmer for supper. We all went upstairs and Santa took off his costume; then we assembled for a large meal, for the cold had given us hearty appetites. One of the farmer's children was worried about Santa, whom he thought was upstairs without his supper. We finally consoled the lad by taking Santa his meal, and then had a dreadful time hiding the food in newspapers so the little fellow wouldn't see it.

In 1913 – remembered grimly as The Year of the Reindeer – explorer and naturalist Sir Wilfred Grenfell, a friend of Timothy Eaton, offered some of the beasts for use in the parade, which was even then becoming famous. The animals were brought from their Greenland home and bedded at the Davisville Hotel, where a subway station now stands.

There may have been no Dashers, no Dancers, and no Prancers amongst the animals, but there certainly were any number of Vixens. Unnerved by the heat, crowds and noise, the animals, normally gentle vegetarians, began to take an unhealthy mealtime interest in their keepers. Aside from alarming the children ("Look, Mummy, Santa's reindeer are trying to eat the man"), the reindeer were an up-close disappointment, so tiny that it was hard to imagine them hauling a trike around the block – let alone a sleigh full of toys around the world.

Nor were Eaton's horses – which originally pulled the floats – always easy to deal with. One veteran of the time remembers a horse that would

> . . . go a hundred yards or so, then stop dead. Nothing I tried would budge him. Finally, I caught on: he was waiting for someone to yell "Eaton's" – the way we did at each house on the route. After that, whenever he stopped, I'd whisper softly in his ear, "Eaton's" – he'd recognize his signal and gallop the next hundred yards.

For several years the parade included a reception, in three shifts, held at Massey Hall for more than 9,000 children and adults. Presented until 1915, and revived once in 1919, the event included a singsong, favours and a "London-style pantomime"; it finally had to be abandoned when the crowds became too large to handle, even in three shifts.

The memory of such innocent merriment would prove durable – and it would need to be. The rosy time was very short: the French called it *La Belle Epoque* – and the creamy shoulders, *décolletage*, and erotically emphatic lines decreed by fashion made it indeed lovely. But the English proved closer to the mark when they named it for their popular, debauched sovereign, Edward VII – the age barely outlasted his death of heart disease in May of 1910.

In the view of one biographer, Edward "was more than a figurehead, and his removal opened up the unease of many people at the latent violence of a society growing increasingly complex and estranged from traditional reassurance."

Edward had roused similarly strong feelings during his lifetime. Some of his subjects adored him; other people, at home and abroad, were openly contemptuous: a 1903 cartoon, published on the eve of Edward's visit to Paris, was captioned *L'Impudique Albion*; it

Of the mourners at the funeral of Edward VII, one was already a king and one an emperor; the two teen-agers would become kings. Of the four, one declared war, one rejected his crown, and two were passionately devoted to safeguarding the monarchy.

pictured France's symbolic *Marianne* bent over, the King's face sketched obscenely on her buttocks. As a young man, Edward had borne his mother's unyielding hatred (her beloved Albert had taken ill after a particularly trying scrape in which the Prince of Wales had been involved and the Queen melodramatically held her son responsible for his father's death).

On that spring day of 1910, as Edward's coffin was carried through the streets of London, the cortege of mourners was led by four cousins, each of whom would be a king, his life inextricably interwoven with the others over the next thirty years. There was the solemn King George, heartsick at the loss of "the best friend and best of fathers"; behind him walked David, his eldest son and now heir to the throne; to David's left was his younger brother, "Bertie," whose frail angularity hid an indomitable will that would become evident – and cherished – two wars later; to the new monarch's right was Emperor Wilhelm, the nephew whom Edward had never liked – at least in part because Victoria had doted on him.

A half-century earlier, on the occasion of Wilhelm's birth, she had written to her eldest daughter, the infant's mother, "God be praised for all his mercies . . . Our joy, our gratitude know no bounds . . . people here are all in ecstasies – such pleasure, such delight . . ."

Even if Victoria was correct and not simply assuming that her subjects felt exactly as she did in all matters, events would prove soon enough that the Prince's existence was hardly cause for celebration. In 1888 the "dear little darling," then twenty-nine years old – naturally bright but poorly educated, a compelling speaker but a superficial thinker who subscribed to a belief in the divinity of kings – became Emperor of Germany, taking the name Kaiser Wilhelm II.

Within four years of his Uncle Edward's death the Kaiser would make clear that the new century had not ushered in a better time. It had simply provided the last poignant pleasures of a world dying from its naiveté.

The dog days of summer.

Turkey Trots and Tangos

One of the conditions of even the noblest war is willful blindness: nations hurl themselves into battle proclaiming the need to safeguard what they already have. War, of course, will irrevocably change whatever they are defending.

In 1914 Canadians believed that the fight looming in Europe was necessary to protect the British Empire and its institutions. When the war ended fifty-one months later, the scope of change it had set in motion in Canada was not understood – in fact, it was barely perceived.

It was no less than this: the rural, mainly agricultural country that had gone into battle emerged from the war as an industrialized society, firmly centred in Ontario's cities. In the process of fighting a war to protect its Mother Country, a colony had begun to be a nation, alive, however ambivalently, to its own possibilities and to the future. By 1918 other shifts were visible: what in 1914 had been an unassailable patriarchy was about to open a major portal of power – the ballot box – to women. Social structures and attitudes – marriage, the family, the educational system, moral values, and material expectations – all were being altered. Even more unsettling than the content of change was the fact that what had once occurred subtly, over decades or generations, was now taking place in months or seasons. The very essence of change was itself changing.

A sense of uneasiness with this process was evident even before the war began: in the spring of 1914 an article in *The Canadian Magazine* complained that

> New gods interfere with our religion, divorce courts laugh at marriage, festivity disturbs our homes, slit skirts and transparent waists violate the sanctity of the body, the tango shocks Terpsichore, cubism shatters art, sex stories distort literature, problem plays defile the stage. Our music has become mechanical, our charity an advertisement, our worship a form . . . turkey trots, tangos and theatres . . . bunny hugs . . . cooling off joyrides . . . that is not unusual even in Toronto the good . . . and with it all life is a continuous Coney Island, a parent is but a bank, home a sleeping-place.

Before long, "turkey trots and tangos" would seem like minuets and waltzes compared to the change actually going on. In the lee of shifting social winds after World War I, women would gain the right to run for office in the Parliament of Canada (and to be appointed to graze in the lush political fields of the Senate). Their biological lives would alter even more dramatically than their political opportunities: steadily declining infant mortality rates meant that the desired family size could be achieved without unlimited conceptions; as a result, women began to reject pregnancy as a more or less permanent condition of marriage. Moreover, urban families did not need the muscle of numerous sons and the drudgery of numerous daughters in order to thrive: the city, in fact, made the large family a burden. Having moved away from their helpful maiden aunts and widowed grannies, even those who could afford domestic help found that poorer young girls, now working in factories, could no longer be persuaded to overlook the long hours, low pay, and lower status of housework.

Once the decision had been made for what they saw as valid reasons, couples not constrained by religious considerations created an increased demand for birth control. This demand, in turn, was met by technological improvements in available methods and by increased information on the subject. Although both the sale of devices and the dissemination of contraception information remained illegal in Canada until 1969, the widespread flouting of the law can be measured by fertility statistics: in the middle of the nineteenth century, Canadian women who were still married by age fifty had, on average, borne eight children; by the turn of the century that number had dropped to six. (In 1961, even before the widespread use of the Pill, it had declined even further, to three.)

The translation of technology into consumer goods – especially, in the '20s, automobiles, radios, and refrigerators – would make new demands on disposable income and was another factor in the trend toward smaller families. That trend would accelerate even more after 1929, when just eleven years – almost to the day – after the end of World War I, a Depression levelled much of society. At a time when even one more child could push them from bare subsistence to poverty, some Canadians saw limitation as the only hope for the future of the families they already had.

The Depression was not as sudden as the term "the Great Crash" implies. In fact, the prosperity of the war and the period immediately afterward would prove to be a pause in a long series of economically lean years; 1914 was certainly one of high unemployment and was further troubled by the seeming inevitability of war – a time, in retrospect, that would mark the beginning of so much change. Clearly, England was going to be involved in the conflict – and its involvement presented a call on Canadian participation: no one was prepared to argue seriously with Sir Wilfrid Laurier's words, two years earlier, that "when England is at war, Canada is at war."

Nonetheless, days in that late summer of 1914 held their usual pleasures: eager children looked forward to the "Ex" (still mainly an agricultural fair), even though it presaged the beginning of the school year; there was horse racing in Hamilton, a regatta near St. Catharines; the Maple Leafs baseball team was at its lakeside stadium; there were Highland Games at Exhibition Park and thirty soccer games elsewhere in Toronto.

Lawn bowling was popular in Berlin, the small southwestern Ontario city that marked the terminus of the old Black Walnut Trail. Within two years the city would surrender to attacks on the loyalty of its large population of German descent and change the community's name to honour British Field Marshal Horatio Herbert Kitchener. This same misspent fervour would eventually banish Goethe from classrooms, Beethoven from symphony halls, and sauerkraut from patriotic kitchens – where it was replaced by "Victory Cabbage."

A report of a wartime dog show at the Canadian National Exhibition, in which a dachshund had been entered, is a measure of the lengths to which such patriotism went:

> This lone elongated native of sausage land . . . looked around it with a woebegone expression and actually whined and shed tears when a charitable onlooker stroked it. If it had been a real Hun it would have bit the hand that fondled it, but the dogs of Hunland are more humane than some of their masters.

On the last weekend of July, 1914, Germany declared war on Russia and invaded France. Sunday sermons reviled the Kaiser and his allies: "Instead of being appalled and panic-stricken, we Canadians should thank God that we are allowed to bear our part of the burden to resist and, God willing, to forever put down this military mad group of dreamers," one Methodist clergyman told his congregation that day.

The next morning *The Globe* described

> . . . remarkable scenes last night . . . The people . . . vibrating with unrestrained enthusiasm and a display of what might be termed "Britishism" . . . Hats shot aloft,

Signing up became a proof of manhood.

Butter being churned, as it always had been, on a farm near Cayuga.

> then a thousand throats boomed out a concentrated roar – a warning to the enemy, an inspiration to every soul in the British Empire, Canadians still belong to the breed . . . hundreds of men, waving the Union Jack and Canada's flag, with drums beating and rousing British airs stirring the atmosphere, marched along, an undeniable testimony of Canada's unswerving loyalty.

By August 4 England and her Empire were at war with Germany, Turkey, and the Austro-Hungarian Empire. The next day Canadians learned that their overseas contingent would comprise volunteers, a sensible plan considering the number of unemployed who would welcome the soldier's daily pay of $1.10. In the fizz of excitement (and the widely held assumption that the war would be short – four to six months at most), it took almost no time to raise the First Canadian Expeditionary Force.

That winter, despite some unease at the delay in beating the enemy, the true nature of the war – the first in history to encompass whole countries and whole peoples – was still hidden from the population at large. The stores, after all, were filled with Christmas goodies, including the toys that merchants had prudently imported from Europe before hostilities were declared.

The battle seemed comfortably distant: there were no immediate food shortages, no serious price hikes, no diminished attendance at football games, at the Ex, at the Santa Claus parade; in fact, there was plenty of evidence of continued enthusiasm for what was termed "the British cause." (Even the sillier suggestions were being treated seriously, including an order

Farmerettes substituted for men gone to war.

from one commanding officer forbidding infantrymen to shave their upper lips because it was a scientific "fact" that shaving weakened the nerves affecting the eyes and could, therefore, impede a man's shooting ability.)

By the spring of 1915, however, reality had begun to impinge as newspapers carried lists of Canadians dead and missing. On Friday, May 7, a single incident brought the war irrevocably home. The Germans torpedoed the British liner *Lusitania*, killing 1,198 men, women, and children – more than a hundred of its helpless victims from Ontario. Ironically, the event that caused so much outrage amongst Canadians came at a time when employment in the war effort was on the increase and, as a result, the number of enlistees was dropping.

By the summer of 1915 sermons turned from the glories of battle to signing up as a proof of manhood – which also became a favourite topic of speeches by politicians and other prominent citizens. Every possible forum was used in the drive to persuade men to enlist; for a few pennies you could buy the sheet music for such ditties as "When Jack Comes Back," "We're From Canada," "Johnnie Canuck's the Boy," "For King and Country," and the decidedly edgy "Why Aren't You in Khaki?" The CNE attractions that year included a *Gott Straffe England* brooch as well as "relics of baby-killing raids on English coastal towns," bloodstained clothing that had been worn by "soldiers in the trenches who have given their lives in the service of their country," a review of the British fleet, a march of the Allies, a "grand collection of war trophies taken from the Huns on the battlefield," and a spectacle based on the Battle of the Dardanelles.

For a people still untouched by mass presentations of popular music, radio, television and film, an important emotional outlet for the emotions of war was found in the poetry of the day. *The Globe* and *The Star*, for example, frequently published the works of local poets, including members of their staffs. While only "In Flanders Fields" is remembered by most Canadians today, there were many other poems, covering a considerable spectrum of both subject and artistry, that were widely circulated and read. There was praise for England, for Venice, Shakespeare, French Canadians (" . . . The gayest hearts in battle, the stoutest hearts at sea/ Followed the Leopards of England, or fought for the Fleur de Lis . . ."). The Belgians were a favourite subject, as in Thomas O'Hagan's "I Take Off My Hat to Albert," and, of course, in poems about Flanders. William Pike Osborne echoes McCrae: "On Flanders Plain in summer-time the blood-red poppy waves:/ More brightly now its torch is blown above Canadian graves . . ." J. Lewis Milligan's work promised that ". . . 'Christ is born' shall ring through Flanders/ When the Prince of Peace appears . . ."

There were unlikely poets: Lucy Maud Montgomery wrote of "Our Women" ("Bride of a day, your eye is bright/ And the flower of your cheek is red/ 'He died with a smile on a field of France –/ I smile for his sake,' she said" . . .). In 1916 Stephen Leacock (Class of '91) wrote "*Laus Varsitatis*, A Song in Praise of the University of Toronto" (". . . For those were days of Peace. We heeded not./ Men talked of Empire and we called it rot;/ Indeed the Empire had no further reach/ Than to round out an after-dinner speech,/ Or make material from which John A./ Addressed us on our Convocation Day . . ."). Wilson MacDonald of Port Dover praised "The Girl Behind the Man Behind the Gun," while securities executive John Garvin offered a "National Anthem Amended for Canadians" ("God save our Canada/ Silver-crowned Canada, God Save the King").

If much of the poetry was banal ("Here's to the day, Kaiser, when you shall die . . . Beside the lepers of the world you stand outcast . . ."), there are other images with power undiminished after seventy years. From Duncan Campbell Scott came a wry acknowledgement of the new technology, "To a Canadian Aviator (Who Died for His Country in France)":

> . . . But Death, who has learned to fly,
> Still matchless when his work is to be done,
> Met thee between the armies and the sun;
> Thy speck of shadow faltered in the sky . . .

Second Lieutenant Bernard Freeman Trotter was twenty-seven years old and had been dead for twenty-four hours when his manuscript, *Ici Repose*, reached his parents from the front in France.

> . . . "*Ici repose* –"
>
> Add what name you will,
> And multiply by thousands; in the fields,
> Along the roads, beneath the trees – one here,
> A dozen there, to each its simple tale
> Of one more jewel threaded star-like on
> The sacrificial rosary of France . . .

By 1916 Canadian troops had been bloodied in the horrors of Ypres and the Somme and the war had taken on the persuasive reality of a nightmare. The need for recruits was becoming desperate. One newspaper scheme, dubbed "Give Us His Name," encouraged readers to send in the names of possible recruits; tacitly acknowledging that nominees might not appreciate the honour, the papers said that readers could "sign this coupon or not, as you wish." Pranksters had a field day and, when the campaign ended, it was revealed that, of the 11,608 names submitted, 598 had promised to visit the recruiting depot for enlistment in a regiment with a strength that never exceeded 321 men. (In the fall of 1917 the government enacted conscription legislation in order to raise the needed number of troops; by the time of the Armistice, 616,557 men and women had served in the Canadian forces, all but 10 percent voluntarily.)

There were now several kinds of shortages: business premises turned off their furnaces to observe "heatless Monday," and there was "honour" rationing of sugar and butter. Inflation was beginning to take a bite out of everyone's income; the average weekly budget was $7.96 in 1914; by 1918 it had risen to $12 a week – more than 10 percent of that increase in the last year of the war alone.

There was another problem as well: a labour shortage so severe that, as fighting continued, industry could no longer ignore the women who made up a pool of willing workers. At first they had been consigned to harvesting. ("The report that University girls [at Winona] had hulled strawberries cleaner than any other help . . . caused the Toronto office to be swamped with orders.")

Later, light factory jobs had to be filled by women and, in the final months of the war, Massey-Harris employed a hundred females whom it described as "engaged in drilling plates, bending metal sheets, sharpening mower blades and collecting goods for shipment." In the end, more than 30,000 Canadian women worked in munitions factories, in addition to the thousands who had undertaken other kinds of war work. Their presence, the undeniable quality of their labour and its contribution to victory became keys to opening the ballot box to all women.

Of course women had always worked and, for that matter, the old provinces of Upper and Lower Canada had never passed laws expressly discriminating against them in the matter of suffrage. According to an 1820 account, one Montrealer, asked which candidate she favoured, identified herself as the mother of Louis-Joseph Papineau; she said that she would cast her ballot *"pour mon fils, M. Joseph Papineau, car je crois que c'est un bon et fidèle sujet."*

Unlike Mme. Papineau, women in Upper Canada did not cast ballots, but this was the result of practice, not of the law; it was only in 1849, after the formation of Canada East and Canada West, that legislation actually barred females from voting. The following year women were permitted to vote for school trustees, but it was not until 1884 (the year that the laws relating to the property of married women were consolidated) that single or widowed females with property qualifications were allowed to exercise the municipal franchise. Four years later property qualifications for males, which had been in force since the early days of Upper and Lower Canada, were abandoned; any British male could vote provided that he was at least twenty-one, met residency and citizenship requirements, and was not a prisoner, a patient in "a lunatic asylum," an Indian living on a reservation, a judge, or a holder of any of a list of proscribed public offices.

In those final years of the nineteenth century, women had begun to form and join a list of organizations that eventually included the National Council of Jewish Women, the Imperial Order of Daughters of the Empire, the Catholic Women's League, the Victorian Order of Nurses, and dozens of others. Whatever their original aims, many expanded their focus to include social issues and they fought hard for the right to vote. Whether specifically designed to promote political activism, they had another key function: to provide a training ground in public speaking, research, organization, and recruitment. Moreover, women members ran these clubs – structures within which they attained rank and status, became aware of their own capabilities, and, for the first time, tasted power beyond the confines of the family kitchen.

With the 1888 extension of male suffrage, women's organizations inundated provincial and Dominion politicians with flurries of petitions in favour of female suffrage – all without success; they did not attain even minimal political power until 1916, when the first Canadian females, those living west of Ontario, won the right to vote. The West's less entrenched opposition to female suffrage reflected both its independence of Old Country shibboleths and the visible equality of women in the backbreaking tasks of pioneering.

The old arguments against female suffrage had centred on the frailty of the "gentler sex," the need to protect womenfolk from the ugly realities of politics and (shudder) the polling booth. That picture of "the weaker sex," embroidered with ersatz gallantry, had always been a lie; the fact that women were in factories doing urgently needed war work, freeing men for front-line duty, simply made the hypocrisy more evident. In reality, of course, the same men who spoke so touchingly of the need to protect the "little woman" never faltered in savagery when she dared to insist that she had a right to vote.

Although there was no suffrage-inspired violence in this country, Canadians were the beneficiaries of the hundreds of women, especially in England, who were harassed, imprisoned, and tortured for disobeying laws they had no role in passing. The women who fought on the lines, in front of the National Gallery, in the "ladies' galleries" of the British House of Commons (where they were discreetly hidden from view) were routinely hauled off to prison, force-fed until their throats bled, pardoned – provided that they stop fighting for their cause – and, when they contemptuously refused, hauled back under so-called "cat and mouse" laws.

In the opinion of one of them, it is uncertain that war work alone, without the militancy and violence of the English movement, would have secured the vote for women. Nell Hall (later Hall-Humpherson) was a well-bred, steely-

Nell Hall was only 18, but had already been imprisoned.

willed young woman who spent the last fifty years of her life in Canada but who had been born in England to a distinguished family of social activists. The Halls counted among their friends Lord Byron, the utopian William Morris, the Webbs, the Pankhursts, George Bernard Shaw, and the novelist Hilaire Belloc. Grandfather Hall had been a sheriff of Sherwood Forest and Nell's father a founder of Britain's Labour Party.

Nell herself tucked intelligence and an unflinching commitment to justice beneath genteel manners and a charming wit. She and her colleagues baffled authorities, who stereotyped them as traitors to their class, their parents, and their country – and did not flinch from inflicting the most spiteful punishments.

In July, 1913, Nell, in prison after several protests against the authorities, was very ill; she left Birmingham Prison under The Prisoners (Temporary Discharge for Ill-Health) Act. Eleven months later she was back in court. According to Sylvia Pankhurst, member of the famous family of suffragettes:

> Nellie Hall hurled one of her shoes at the Magistrate . . . [she and a co-defendant] struggled and refused to walk, flung themselves to the ground, fought to get out of the dock, and shouted at the top of their voices as continuously as they could. They were refused bail, and were forcibly fed for many weeks before they came to be tried.

Originally charged with being "loose, idle and disorderly" (a clumsy attempt to humiliate her), Nell was eventually prosecuted for being in possession of explosives and for conspiring to commit malicious mischief. It is not difficult to imagine the anxiety and pride with

Training at a Canadian flying school.

Whistler never intended his famous painting to be used as a World War I recruitment poster.

which Leonard Hall read his twenty-one-year-old daughter's letter, written from prison in June, 1914:

> No free spirit has ever been wrecked by a mean spirited oppression yet. And mine won't be either. It is only when the spirit is either unsure or weak that the body can be permanently harmed. I do not care so much now for the appreciation or the indifference of a slave race who do not want to be free, but I do feel happier for knowing that real men and women realise what it all means. I am thankful beyond measure that from my parents I inherit a love of Liberty and the spirit to fight for it. When the call came to you, you answered it. *You* didn't fail. In your heart, dear, you wouldn't like me to.
>
> The public will ever be non-understanding, unimaginative and unsympathetic until by our determination & our enthusiasm we create a new spirit.

Nellie and the others were released just before the beginning of the war, under the terms of a rather plaintive pardon from Buckingham Palace: "The Secretary of State has advised His Majesty to remit the remainder of the sentences of all persons now undergoing terms of imprisonment for crimes committed in connection with the Suffrage agitation." In stiff-lipped capitulation it added:

> This course has been taken without solicitation on their part and without requiring any undertaking from them . . . His Majesty is confident that the prisoners . . . will respond to the feelings of their countrymen and women in this time of emergency and can be trusted not to stain the causes they

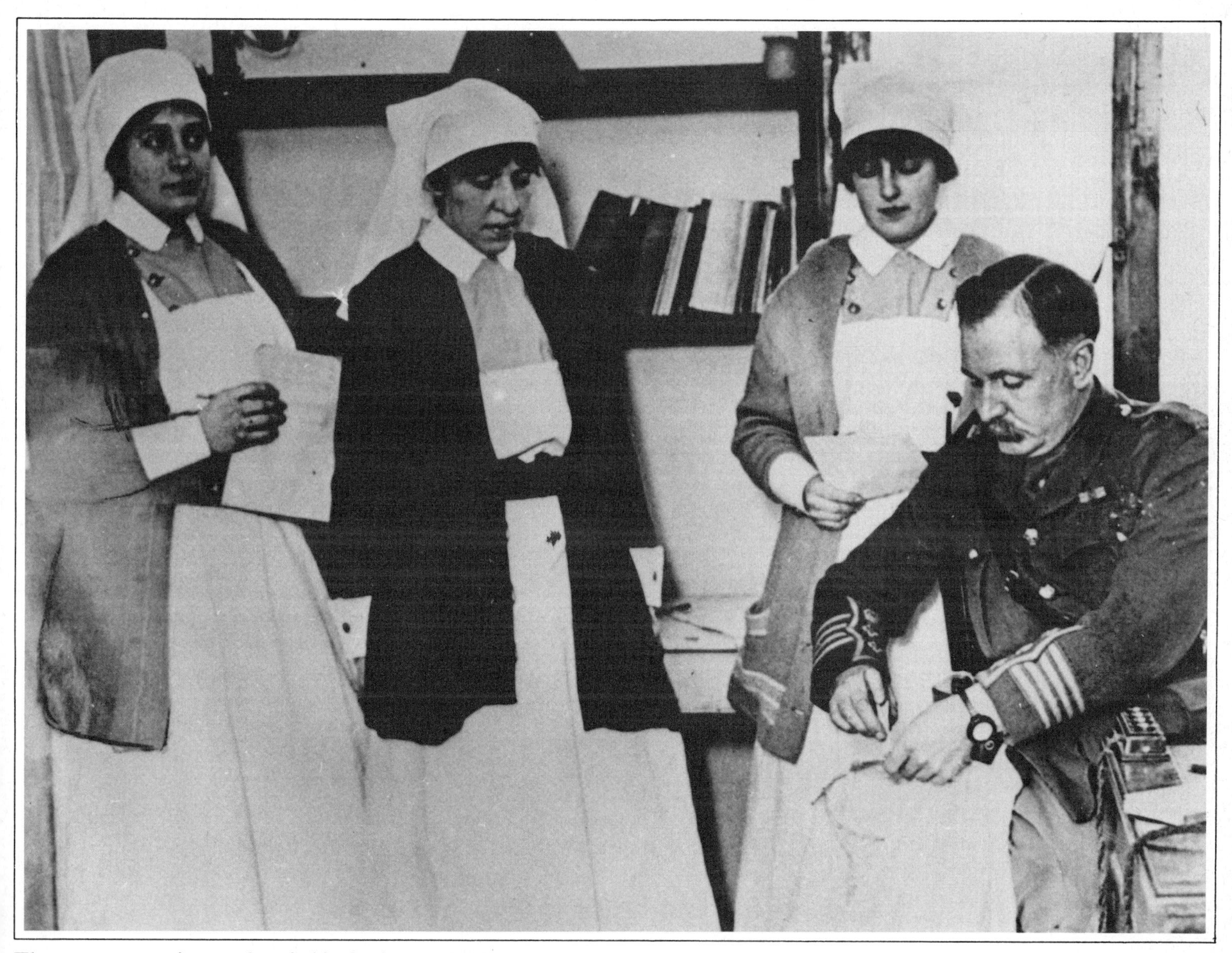

These nurses, serving at a hospital in Orpington, England, in 1917, were among the first women entitled to vote in a Canadian general election.

> have at heart by any further crime or disorder.

Sixty years later, in a short history Nell wrote to the author, she said:

> I often wonder how the liberation of unfranchised women would have evolved without the background of the militant movement before 1914. None will ever know how much the women's war work alone would have influenced the various governments, if at all. . . Violence was the last resort of women who, at that time, had no legal method available to make changes in laws they had no part in making.

Charlotte Whitton, a social worker and long-time mayor of Ottawa who, for two generations, gloried in being a thorn in the side of Canadian politicians of every persuasion, was caustic on the subject of Canadian suffrage:

> . . . the women of this country [she wrote in 1946] . . . are but half-appreciative beneficiaries of rich legacies of freedom, rights and

> privileges, many of which have been bequeathed by greater, earlier crusaders in the two lands to which we are most closely allied – the United Kingdom and the United States . . . Canadian women got the vote as a gift rather than a reward.

Whitton added that there were women who had been "valiant warriors for the vote for over a quarter of a century" and called those in the West "the more vigorous fighters." That fight seemed successful when the Saskatchewan Legislature (followed shortly by those in Manitoba and Alberta) enacted female suffrage bills. On April 12, 1917, the last day of the sitting, the Legislature of Ontario followed suit and passed The Ontario Franchise Act.

It took another two years before the Parliament of Canada passed a similar act. Federally, the final push for the vote began on September 20, 1917, when the House of Commons passed The War-Time Elections Act; it gave the federal franchise to women whose brothers, husbands, or sons had served or were serving overseas. Secretary of State Arthur Meighen hastened to reassure members that the Act was *not* designed to give women rights: it was being passed, he explained, because Canadian soldiers could not vote directly in an election carried on during the war. The bill offered the next best alternative by enfranchising "such of their kin at home who can best be said to be likely to vote in such a way . . . as they themselves would do upon our shores."

There were strenuous objections to legislation that created two classes of Canadians and that ignored the contribution being made by those women who had no relatives in the service. The Minister of Trade and Commerce unctuously acknowledged the injustice of such legislation but insisted that there was a degree of service "still higher . . . which comes from heart strings wrung, which looks out of tear-bedimmed eyes, which comes from sleepless nights and anxious days . . . This is the distinguishing line upon which we base this franchise Bill."

Those living with "sleepless nights and anxious days" quickly included a government that faced continuous uproar in the House of Commons. The Opposition accused Prime Minister Robert Borden of giving the vote only to those women who would support his plan to introduce conscription; they also attacked provisions of the bill that would disenfranchise two other groups of Canadians: conscientious objectors, including Mennonites and Doukhobors who objected to military service on religious grounds, and Canadians naturalized since 1902 but born in what was now enemy country. These groups, the Opposition charged, were actually being stripped of their right to vote because they could be expected to oppose Borden's determination to impose conscription. The bill eventually passed, but only after the government had invoked closure.

The Prime Minister had also been forced to promise that, if returned in the election to be held in October, 1917, he would bring in female suffrage. Having won, he made good on his pledge by personally introducing a bill for that purpose in March of 1918. The ensuing battle inspired members of both the House and the Senate to reach new oratorical heights of anguish, terror, and sheer nonsense. Some expressed concern that suffrage would affect the birthrate and one insisted that

> . . . the Holy Scriptures, theology, ancient philosophy, Christian philosophy, history, anatomy, physiology, political economy, and feminine psychology, all seem to indicate that the place of women in this world is not amid the strife of the political arena, but in her home.

Another quoted French philosopher Auguste Comte to explain what women were meant to do when safely ensconced in their homes: the purpose of progress according to Comte, he said, was "to render the feminine life more and more domestic and to release it more and more from all outside occupation, the better to insure the accomplishment of its end: mating."

The suffragists had defenders as well as opponents; one of the staunchest was the Conservative member for East York, Thomas Foster. A widower whose only child died at the age of ten, he sincerely wanted to help large families by leaving them money in his will; as a result, he is still often confused with an eccentric contemporary of his who sponsored a "stork derby." Seventy-three years old when he was first elected Mayor of Toronto (he held the job for three terms and lived to be ninety-three), Foster in his earlier political career in the Legislature, spoke with rare passion about women's suffrage.

While a member there, he recalled that, during World War I, women

> . . . were prepared to become chauffeurs, to drive automobiles, transportation trucks . . . and to do many other things without which we could not have successfully carried on the war . . . If they have proven their case, as I think they have, that they were in every way equal to the occasion in every

> endeavour, then I think the least we can do in recognition of the noble part they have played in the war is to extend the franchise to the women of this country.

Those were the sentiments that prevailed: although she might not have appreciated the honour, the ninety-ninth anniversary of Queen Victoria's birth, May 24, 1918, became the occasion for Royal Assent to the Canadian Women's Suffrage Act, which was to come into effect on New Year's Day the following year.

Midway through the war, women had also won another major victory: in 1917, the manufacture or importation of alcoholic beverages was made illegal, except for medicinal, scientific, and sacramental purposes. Canada was on the wagon.

(The legislatures of Saskatchewan and Ontario had existing temperance acts, Ontario's having been adopted after a survey showed that 73 percent of those who had voted in the previous provincial election favoured Prohibition. Provincial laws were repealed and replaced by federal legislation.)

Opposition to the drys had been formidable – in part, thanks to their ties to the suffrage movement: "temperance" succeeded because war accented the consequences of alcohol abuse – drunkenness, street violence, rape, child abuse, industrial accidents, absenteeism. Prohibition remained the law for eleven years, but it had consequences of its own and, long before repeal, it became a disappointment to all but its most fervent adherents. Dr. William Victor Johnston, later the father of postgraduate education for Canada's family physicians, was a newly minted general practitioner when, in 1924, he hung up his shingle in Lucknow, Ontario. Near the end of his life he recalled that

> Whatever else this era of Prohibition did, it degraded the physicians [who could prescribe alcoholic beverages for "medicinal" purposes] . . . by making them virtually bartenders and bootleggers. The citizens lost a measure of respect for [them] . . . Many young men learned to drink excessively because it was forbidden and thereby the smart thing to do . . . it allowed the bootlegger with his more dangerous products to flourish and it also prompted the habitual drinker to turn for thirst quenchers to such products as [poisonous] rubbing alcohol.

The fragile suffrage and Prohibition victories of 1916 and '17 were (at least to their supporters) the only patches of sunlight in a period of extended gloom. In Belgium the fields of Flanders were once more awash in water (from the intricate irrigation system the Allies had bombed) and in the blood of soldiers who battled in the resultant mud. On November 4 Canadian troops, after more than three years of costly fighting, gained possession of the muck of Passchendaele.

The losses throughout the war had been appalling: of a total strength of 600,000 Canadians, 68,000 had been killed, wounded, or were missing by November, 1918. For each million Canadians, nearly 8,000 were killed in World War I – more than twice as many per million as would be killed in World War II.

Almost half of all those serving in Canadian forces had come from Ontario – one in every ten citizens of the province had seen service, four-fifths as volunteers. Between the last pre-war and first post-war census, there was a decline of almost four percentage points in the Ontario population of those aged fifteen to thirty-four; war casualties were a major factor in a devastating loss to what was still a labour-intensive, mainly agricultural economy.

There was, of course, one other reason for the loss: in the early fall of 1918, just as victory in Europe seemed assured, there were the first signs of another scourge: a deadly influenza was spreading across Europe. By September it had reached Montreal and, within weeks, had spread to men of the Polish army being trained at Niagara-on-the-Lake. In London 187 civilians, more than two-thirds between the ages of twenty and fifty, died. Between the beginning of October and the end of November there were 2,230 cases and 164 deaths in the Sudbury area; Ottawa suffered almost unbelievably: 10,000 cases and more than 500 deaths. Nearby Renfrew had 1,000 cases and 67 deaths. Throughout the province, classes were suspended, public places, including houses of worship, were closed and business and industry, hit by massive absenteeism, were slowed. By the end of November, when it was over, Ontario alone counted 5,000 dead.

In the midst of the influenza horror, Armistice: "the war to end all wars" was, itself, finally ended. Epidemic or not, the Canadian winter was temporarily made spring by people celebrating the triumph. Ten thousand gathered in Windsor's Ouellette Square and spontaneously began a mammoth religious service of thanksgiving; the Mayor of Kingston declared a holiday and "even street car conductorettes" quit work in such numbers that the cars had to remain in their barns. There were parades in Kitchener, a huge

Amidst the tumult of victory . . .

. . . the aching sense of loss

bonfire in Bowmanville, a procession of troops, Red Cross workers, and female munitions makers through the streets of London. Seaforth's outdoor service featured songs from the united choirs of the town, while the relatives of those who had fallen in France were carried in decorated cars as part of the parade through Thamesville.

In time, of course, it would become clear that only certain kinds of war – not war in general – had ended. There would never be another battle between armies on the field, soldiers fighting each other face-to-face. For the last time, hay for the cavalry would be as vital as ammunition. Nor would carols again float over the trenches in the cold Christmas air, enemy voices joining across no-man's-land to celebrate peace. To this day, however, World War I possesses one horrific distinction: in its name, more Canadians were missing in action, wounded, or killed than in any war before or since.

Although Canadians and Americans had fought on the same side – for the first time – peace chilled relations between the two countries after World War I. Many Canadians recalled with resentment American reluctance to get involved and were particularly galled by accounts of the war flooding Canada from the American media. These often criticized British forces (a term that covered Canadian as well as English, Scottish, Australian, and New Zealand troops) and gave sole credit for victory to U.S. forces.

Stephen Leacock, a provably better satirist than poet, got deadlier the further away the subject was from "Mariposa"; he worried that the American version would give Canadian children a distorted idea of what had actually happened in World War I. Here it was, according to Leacock, as presented in U.S. movies:

> It was occasioned by a quarrel between Woodrow Wilson and a lot of nations living in Europe. Woodrow Wilson, whose only aim was to be good to everybody everywhere, found his efforts thwarted by a crowd of people in Europe. At last he declared war, invoking the blessing of God, of Abraham Lincoln, the Southern Confederacy and the Middle West.
>
> A vast American army invaded Europe. They first occupied France, where the French people supplied a comic element by selling cigarettes, waving flags and talking French, a ridiculous language, forming a joke in itself. Rushing through the woods, trenches, flames and trees, the Americans drove in front of them the Europeans. Exacting nothing in return, they went back to the Middle West, where they were met on the porch by their mother, the spirit of American democracy and the . . . shade of Lincoln.

In 1928 Major George Drew, later Premier of Ontario, included the Leacock description in his stinging denunciation, published in *Maclean's* in 1928, of American claims regarding the war. He was responding to articles that had appeared a year earlier in popular U.S. magazines, especially *Liberty* and *Cosmopolitan* (then more political and less wet-lipped than now). Drew was particularly critical of the Order of the Day that had been issued in August, 1918, to U.S. troops by General John Pershing. "You did more than to give the Allies the support to which, as a nation, our faith was pledged," Pershing said. "You proved that our altruism, our pacific spirit, and our sense of justice have not blunted our virility or our courage." In reply, Drew asked, "Was their altruism or sense of justice greater than that of the brave French and British troops who, for three and a half years before the first American soldier reached the front, had been fighting the same enemy . . .?"

Another galling assertion – that, at the moment of Armistice, the United States had more troops at the front than the British – first appeared in *The Saturday Evening Post* and was repeated in an article in *Liberty* by U.S. Brigadier General Henry J. Reilly. He said:

> There is no better proof of how far the people of a nation really believe in that nation than the readiness and spirit which they display in furnishing men for war. The quick action of our Congress and the slow action of the British Parliament reflected the comparative willingness of the mass of the American and British people to fight for their country.

Drew disputed the point by supplying figures for the entire war, as well as for November, 1918. They show that there were two and a half times as many British as American divisions in battle at the end of September, 1918; that the British mobilized twice as many men, suffered ten times as many casualties and lost nearly eight times as many men as did the United States. There had been 8,654,280 British troops in the war; nearly 3,700,000 had been listed as casualties. More than 20 percent of that number had lost their lives.

The Drew article was more than a childish "who-did-more" exercise; it was one of the first – although hardly the last – worried look at the impact of modern American myth-making on Canadian perceptions. Moreover, the figures supplied by Drew provide a clear perspective for the terms of surrender being imposed on Germany – terms so harsh that they would be cited as a major reason for Hitler's political rise only fifteen years after the war ended.

As Canada turned to peace, the Legislature of Ontario turned to the needs of all of its citizens: from 1914 to 1918, Dominion and provincial legislatures had been concerned almost exclusively with laws that were, however marginally, war-related. The first federal suffrage act, for example, had chosen women to vote as surrogates for their absent relatives; the proponents of Prohibition had convinced others that grains used in the manufacture of spirits were needed in the war effort and that drunkenness hampered that effort.

Now, in the first sweet seasons of peace, there was a new will to rebuild, and change, society. J. W. Dafoe, Winnipeg's legendary newspaperman, described it in the most lyrical, idealistic terms possible:

> Thus the human heart, unconquerable by adversity, resolutely sets about repairing the ravages of time and war. Man rebuilds his reunited home, sets up again the family altars, renews the sweet amenities of life, retills the fields. . . Behind lies the wreckage, the pain, the terrors of those impossible, those unimaginable years of war . . .

In Ontario the first step in the process was rejection of the political past: on October 14, 1919, the government of Sir William Hearst was defeated. (Amongst the disaffected voters: those opposed to Prohibition, those opposed to suffrage, and those first-time women voters who remembered his initial, bluntly worded opposition to them and cast their ballots accordingly.) As the United Farmers of Ontario, under Barrie farmer E. C. Drury, took office, the Superintendent of Neglected and Deserted Children, John Joseph Kelso, was once again going to play a major role in writing legislation. If, as Dafoe had said, it was time to "set up again the family altars," what better way than through the law?

In the previous five years there had been only minor amendments to existing family legislation: the Seduction Act of 1914 permitted parents to sue for compensation for "distress and anxiety of mind, for dishonour received," rather than only for the actual monetary losses suffered when a daughter was seduced. In 1916 the Children's Protection Act had been amended to stipulate that, while a child born within a marriage was deemed to have the father's religion, a child born outside marriage had the religion of its mother.

In the lively Fifteenth Legislature, which sat from March, 1920, to May, 1923, bills affecting every major aspect of family life were presented; there was, after all, a substantial new group of voters – women – and their needs and interests would be ignored at every legislator's political peril. It was all simply backhanded confirmation that Hall-Humpherson and her colleagues had been right when they acted on the assumption that laws passed by a strictly male electorate were different from those passed when there was universal suffrage of both genders. The flurry of activity that took place, especially in family law, in the four years of the Drury regime would not be surpassed or even equalled until the findings of Ontario's Family Law Reform Commission were translated into legislation fifty-eight years later.

Some laws were the result of steps that had been initiated by Sir William Hearst's government and reflected the high degree of concern immediately after the war for the children it had left fatherless. In 1921, for example, Ontario counted more than 90,000 school-aged children whose mothers were widowed – many of them in the recent war. Hearst, in 1918, had appointed the Deputy Minister of Labour, Dr. W. A. Riddell, to explore the advisability of providing public funds for needy women with dependent children.

In 1920 the Deserted Wives Maintenance Act, which required husbands to support wives and families they had abandoned, was amended to increase the maximum amount of weekly support from $10 to $20. (In 1922, in yet another break from past social and legal attitudes, the Act would provide for payments to a mother and her children if they had left their husband/father because of his cruelty or refusal to support them. However, the support order, still for a maximum of $20 weekly, would be rescinded if there was proof of the mother's adultery.)

The same legislative session acted on the results of Dr. Riddell's enquiry and passed the Mothers Allowance Act; in a province that had once refused to enact Poor Laws because it could not justify burdening taxpayers with responsibility for the impoverished, this, indeed, was a break from the past.

Although hardly generous by today's standards, Mothers Allowance legislation did remove the need for some wives to chase their husbands, and it acknowledged that the state would have to provide for families who might otherwise starve. (Like several other pieces of federal and provincial legislation, it discriminated against men by taking for granted that they were always the sinners, never the sinned-against. Until recently, for example, the Criminal Code assumed that only women could be the victims of sexually motivated assaults; on the provincial level, some regulations governing welfare programs have had to be reworked to remove sections that discriminated against single fathers.)

Under the Mothers Allowance Act, a woman was eligible for assistance if she had been widowed; was the wife of a man who was permanently disabled or, for some other reason, would never be able to support his family; or was a deserted wife and had not heard from her husband for at least four years. There were stringent limitations, however: the applicant had to have two or more children under the age of fourteen who lived with her; she had to have been a resident of Canada for at least three years and of Ontario for at least two; and she had to be a "fit and proper person to have care and custody of children." (Six years later, eligibility was expanded to include women caring for disabled husbands or handicapped children of any age, provided that a legitimate child under sixteen was also being looked after in the home.)

The need for such legislation was evident in hundreds of stories of hardship, like the one that appeared in *The Globe* in the summer of 1921. After reporting that the York County Children's Aid Society had taken five children into care, it said:

> For the past 13 days . . . two women have been living in a dilapidated cowshed on Silverthorne Avenue. About two weeks ago [they] came to the . . . district, where they purchased a lot on the instalment plan, paying $2 down and the rest in monthly payments. Questioned . . . if they realized the seriousness of the undertaking . . . they said, with tears, that it was the only way they could contrive to have a place where all could live together. Their average combined earnings amounted to about $12 weekly.

In addition to help for deserted and poor women, the Legislature sought relief for another group of needy people through the Parents Maintenance Act; it spelled out, for the first time, the obligation of financially able children to support their impoverished parents to a maximum of $20 weekly. (Whether because of parental pride or a lack of knowledge of the law's existence – despite the fact that the Parents Maintenance Act has been updated several times – only two cases under the law have been reported in the decades since its first enactment.)

Now, attention was turning to bastards and orphans – war's inevitable offspring. While it is often assumed that changes to the law resulted from thousands of illegitimate children born to Canadian soldiers, records show that, in Canada at least, very few fathered out-of-wedlock infants. In the last year of the war, for example, 214 illegitimate youngsters were taken into care by Ontario's children's aid societies; nearly half were the children of domestics or married women and in only forty-nine cases was the father listed as a serviceman.

Fortunately the law's attitude toward these children, irrespective of their parentage, was going to be both more humane and more realistic than it had ever been before. In the province's early history, legislation had been designed to ensure that children born out of wedlock did not become public charges; now the time had come to change laws that cruelly substantiated the Biblical warning about the sins of the fathers being visited on the children.

The energetic Legislature passed three major bills that focussed on the needs of the young and especially disadvantaged: one established a simple method of adoption; the second rejected the old English common law's dictum that "once a bastard, always a bastard"; the third provided new kinds of protection for those youngsters on whom the law could not confer legitimacy.

Adoption had been referred to in the nineteenth-century laws as an alternative to apprenticeship, but there was no readily available form of it in the laws of Ontario. The concept was hardly unknown: it had existed in Massachusetts as early as 1851, in New Brunswick in 1873, in New Zealand in 1895, and in Nova Scotia from 1896.

Looking back on the decision to enact an adoption law, E. C. Drury recalled that

... in every real sense [it] was my own. Its need was suggested to me on a September night in 1917 when Donald Ross and I were driving together from a Liberal Committee meeting in Collingwood. [Both Ross, a Barrie lawyer and teacher, and Drury were members of the party prior to the founding of the United Farmers of Ontario.] It was bright moonlight, and as we passed a farm Ross told me something of its history which he knew intimately since he had had the settling of the estate. It had belonged to a couple who, when they were past middle age, had taken an orphaned boy whom they had regarded as their son. The woman died first, and not long after, the man, both [without wills]. Distant relatives claimed the estate, and the boy, who had every moral right to inherit, got nothing.

Adoptions could then be made only by a private bill passed by the Legislature – a cumbersome and somewhat costly procedure. Ross pointed out the need of some cheap, simple, and widely available process of adoption. The incident stuck in my mind, and so, when I unexpectedly found myself in the business of making Law, I had an Act prepared by which adoptions could be made by application to a County Judge, at a cost of no more than $3.50. The Children's Aid Society was made responsible for the fitness both of the adopting parents and the adopted child. The fee has gradually been raised to eight dollars. The results have been wholly good.

(Sixty-four years after the event, children's aid societies still have final responsibility for all adoptions in Ontario, although babies may be adopted from private sources. While the latter can entail considerable expense, there has been no fee, since 1978, for an adoption made through an Ontario CAS.)

Another push for adoption legislation came from J. J. Kelso, who had been complaining that it was hard to place foster children in families in which they could never hope to have the same status as natural offspring. The problem had grown more acute with the increased number of children in need of new families, either because they had been orphaned or because the war had left them fatherless.

The Adoption Act of 1921 permitted anyone of "full age" (twenty-one years) to adopt a younger person, provided that the adoptee was not a spouse, brother, sister, uncle, or aunt. Once the adoption had taken place, biological parents lost all rights and were free of legal obligations to the child, who could now inherit from his new mother and father as if he had been born naturally to them. According to a contemporary report in *The Laws of Ontario*, "If we believe at all in the power of that human love, which is a reflection of the Divine, we may hope for great things from The Adoption Act, and the other statutes of which it is a necessary complement."

One of the statutes of which it was a "necessary complement" was the Legitimation Act, also passed in 1921; having rejected a basic tenet of the common law, it legitimated a child whose parents married, even after his or her birth. There were, however, limits to the new law: a previously illegitimate child could inherit only *after* the legitimate children of either his mother or father.

The Act protected his or her right to property only if a parent had willed it without imposing any conditions that might not be fulfilled. For example, the law protected an inheritance that would become effective on the first day of spring of some future year; but it would not apply if the bequest were dependent on the beneficiary reaching a particular birthday. (There will definitely be a first day of spring, but a child may die before reaching any given age.)

A further complement to both the Adoption and the Legitimation acts was the Children of Unmarried Parents Act; it offered some protection to those children whose parents would never marry each other – forever bastards in a world that considered them the cause of shame and the proof of shamelessness. The law was based on suggestions from the Social Service councils of Canada and of Ontario; its purpose, as described in the annual summary of provincial legislation, was that "care and protection of children should result in a higher standard of citizenship, in that it will prevent them from developing into subnormals and criminals, as so many of them have done in the past, owing to neglected childhood."

In the early days few had survived infancy: left with pitiless matrons of private doss houses for needy "girls in trouble," the babies starved to death or were abandoned or smothered when nothing remained of the meagre amounts their mothers had provided for their care.

The English Poor Law Act of 1576 had been the first to recognize the illegitimate child, in order to make his parents responsible for his upkeep and protect the community from any likelihood that he would become a public charge. Upper Canada had, of course,

Mackenzie King had several photos of himself with Sir Wilfrid Laurier doctored in order to emphasize his close relationship with Canada's first French Canadian Prime Minister.

chosen not to adopt either the Poor Law or the next piece of relevant legislation, the Bastardy Act of 1809, which made the father responsible for maintenance.

In 1837, however, the province had passed An Act to Make the Remedy in Cases of Seduction More Effectual, and to Render the Fathers of Illegitimate Children Liable for Their Support. This cumbersome title is an accurate description of the law, which decreed that "any person who shall furnish food, clothing, lodging, or other necessaries, to any child who shall be born after the passing of [the] Act not in lawful wedlock, shall be entitled to [sue] the father of an illegitimate child." The attitude toward such a child is clear in an Act passed by the Legislature in 1859: it punished a person who "leads away, decoys or entices away any child under the age of ten with the intent being to deprive the parent of possession of the child," but exempted a man "who claims to be the father of an illegitimate child." The law seemed to assume that no man would falsely admit to siring a bastard.

Neither this nor any other law had made provision for actually establishing paternity – one of the issues dealt with in the 1921 legislation. Under it, a court could make an order naming a man as a child's father and require him to pay maintenance – on pain of a jail term of up to six months if he defaulted. He could also be ordered to pay the mother's medical expenses as well as those for the burial of either mother or child. There were other provisions that signalled a further difference in attitude toward this group of children: first, of course, the title of the Act described the status of adults rather than simply sticking a label on the child.

For the first time the law provided for a provincial officer who would "act in the best interest of the child" and to whom the mother could apply for advice and protection. If an illegitimate child was neglected, he was now entitled to be cared for, like other youngsters, under the provisions of the Children's Protection Act.

Over the years a variety of laws and court decisions expanded on these more humane concepts: first, the subsequent wife and the child born of a bigamous marriage were given a lien on the estate of the father; in 1924 a court held that there was a presumption of legitimacy when a child was born to a married couple, even if he had been conceived outside the marriage. In 1927 the province permitted an unwed mother to make special application for Mothers Allowance, and, in 1957, specifically made her eligible for benefits under the Act.

One of the last bills in this four-year surge of reforming fervor was the 1923 amendment to the Infants Custody Act, and it is filled with evidence of just how much we had changed in so short a time: it was solidly based on the principle that mothers and fathers were equally entitled to the custody, control, and education of their children, unless the court ordered otherwise. Parents who lived apart might wish to enter into written agreements altering that principle, but neither was assumed to have a greater right than the other. Gone finally, as dead as the "divine right of kings," was the presumption that one family member was the chattel of another.

In the early '20s the sunny determination to improve the world, the fully human desire to give meaning to war's terrible cost, was as much alive in Ottawa as in the provinces. The federal electorate of 1921 was vastly different from that of 1917 – for the first time it included a million and a quarter women

Agnes Campbell Macphail, first woman elected to the Parliament of Canada and, later, to the Legislature of Ontario.

– and it was about to pass judgement on new parties, new leaders, and new platforms. Robert Borden's cobbled-together Union coalition was gone and there was now a National Liberal and Conservative Party, Arthur Meighen at its head. Sir Wilfrid Laurier had been succeeded as Liberal Party chieftain by William Lyon Mackenzie King. Across the aisle sat the Progressive Party; centred in rural Ontario, it won the second-largest number of seats and included amongst its members the first woman ever to sit in the Parliament of Canada.

Agnes Campbell Macphail, a thirty-one-year-old schoolteacher who had been active in the United Farmers of Ontario, won Grey-Bruce for the Progressive Party. A tall, slender woman, ramrod straight in both mien and character, she bore stoically the crass stupidities and spitefulness that greeted her in Ottawa. For example, striving to find the equivalent of the business suits worn by her colleagues, she decided on severe blue serge, a dress that was treated as a national joke by the famed fashion plates of the Ottawa press gallery.

Under the no-nonsense shell, Agnes Macphail was deeply wounded by the treatment meted out to her, much of it by other women:

> The misery of being under observation and being unduly criticized is what I remember most vividly about those first months [she later wrote]. Eating was the worst; it may be they thought I would eat peas with my knife or cool my tea in my saucer, but . . . I was observed . . . so closely that I lost twelve pounds in the first month I was a Member and after that I ate my food downtown for some months.

Nellie McClung.

Emily Murphy.

It would probably not have lessened Macphail's misery had she been able to foresee that the petty humiliations inflicted on her were not personal: several generations of newspaper editors and reporters would treat female members from all parties with the same damaging combination of malice and condescension they expressed toward her.

Macphail sat as a Member of Parliament until her defeat in 1940 and then entered the Ontario Legislature in 1943, once again the first woman member, but lost her seat two years later. She regained it one last time in 1948. A strong pacifist and internationalist, she suffered a small stroke before her 1951 provincial defeat; nearly penniless after a lifetime of public service, she was a popular choice for a seat in the Senate in the spring of 1954. Although Agnes Macphail might have ornamented that chamber, with its few outstanding members and full complement of political hacks, she died in February of that year, before Prime Minister Louis St. Laurent had made up his mind on the appointment.

Across the aisle from Macphail sat another member of unusual, and very different, character: William Lyon Mackenzie King. Today's version of King is a weird little fellow, hidden beneath so many layers of psycho-sexual varnish that it is hard to imagine the presence of an actual human being; but, in his time – before the current hunger for Gossip as History – he was judged to be a brilliant academic, experienced public servant and politician, heir of Laurier's ideas (as well as of his house), confidant of the Rockefellers and Andrew Carnegie. But he was also secretive, cautious, aware that not making a decision was, itself, a form of decision-making, and, in the least generous sense, political; all those traits would prove telling in events that had begun in Edmonton in 1916, that dogged the first King government, and that would not be resolved until years later in Ottawa.

As is so often true in our most significant history, the impetus for this particular change sprang, not from the grandeur of philosophy or the sweep of events, but from the essential character of its major participants, making it necessary to understand them in order to appreciate the issue. They were five women who decided to reshape Canadian law; from different backgrounds, they shared similar strong beliefs. All lived in Alberta – and all had been born elsewhere.

The most famous was probably Nellie Mooney McClung who, as the author of *Sowing Seeds in Danny* (more than 100,000 copies in print in Canada and the United States), was this country's first best-selling novelist. Born to a Scots-Irish family in Chatsworth, Ontario, she was brought up in Manitoba. As a young woman, she married a pharmacist and cared for their family of five children – in addition to being involved in community activities, especially the causes of temperance and suffrage. (Her most inspired and effective ploy was a mock Parliament, with anti-suffragist speeches as delivered by Manitoba's legislators – only references to gender changed: "... Politics unsettles men, and unsettled men mean unsettled bills – broken furniture, broken vows – and divorce ...")

British-born Irene Marryat Parlby had grown up in India and Ireland and met her husband while visiting Canada; they began married life in a sod shack near Alix, Alberta, where she was soon a force in provincial politics.

Like Nellie McClung, Louise McKinney was born in Ontario – in Frankville, not far from Brockville; she taught school in North Dakota, married, and settled in Claresholm, Alberta. Well known for her advocacy of temperance and of public ownership of grain elevators and flour mills, she was elected to the Alberta Legislature in 1917, but was defeated in the following election (in which both McClung and Parlby won seats).

The fourth woman, Henrietta Muir Edwards, was older than the others by at least a generation. Born in Montreal in 1848, she moved to Macleod, Alberta, after marrying and was instrumental in the formation of the YWCA and in efforts by the National Council of Women to promote social programs for women and children.

The four, each having made her individual impact on life in this country, came together to write a common page in our history at the urging of Emily Ferguson Murphy. An author who signed her enormously popular pieces "Janey Canuck," Murphy was the daughter of a distinguished Cookstown, Ontario, family. Her maternal grandfather, Ogle Robert Gowan, sat in the Legislature for twenty-seven years and is credited with founding the Orange Order in Canada (he saw it as a "union between Protestants and Roman Catholics against the gloomy Yankee factions ... called for alike by the dictates of policy, justice and mutual security to keep up British ascendancy over the Yankee or American interest").

The equally distinguished Ferguson side included a Member of Parliament and a Supreme Court Justice; three of Emily's brothers became lawyers and she herself had a lifelong interest in politics and law. A graduate of Bishop Strachan School, she was nineteen when she married Arthur Murphy, a charismatic Anglican clergyman whose assignments led the family to travel throughout Canada and, for two years, to live in England. The couple were flushed with professional and personal success: there was Emily's well-received collection of travel sketches, *Janey Canuck Abroad*, Arthur's work for a British missionary society, and the Murphys' three young daughters.

Then, in quick succession, Arthur contracted typhoid and, just as he was getting on his feet, discovered that the missionary society, low on funds, was not going to continue employing him. Then Emily became ill with typhoid and, in the sharpest blow of all, their youngest child died of diphtheria. Badly shaken, the Murphys moved to Manitoba where Arthur put aside the ministry for a time and developed a timber limit in the Swan River region. Before long, they looked even farther west, to Alberta, and moved to Edmonton. Once settled there, Emily organized three more books of sketches and involved herself in a variety of community activities. In 1916 the Attorney General of the province, responding to pressure for a court to try cases involving women, asked Emily to sit on the bench of such a court. She did – and became the first woman in the British Empire to become a police magistrate.

An incident on her first day in court proved prophetic: the counsel for one defendant objected to Emily's presence on the bench on the grounds that she was not a "person" within the meaning of the British North America Act. That objection was repeated several times over the next couple of months, always noted by the magistrate, who went on calmly to hand down her judgements. In December of 1916 the province appointed another woman to act as police magistrate in Calgary, where counsel appealed a ruling on the same "person" grounds.

Mackenzie King finally pays tribute to the "Famous Five," in the company of (left to right, back row) Senator Iva Campbell Fallis, Senator Cairine Wilson, and (front row) Mrs. Henrietta Muir Edwards, Mrs. J.C. Kenwood, daughter of Emily Murphy, and Mrs. Nellie McClung.

The problem stemmed from ambiguity in interpreting the relationship amongst three sections of the BNA Act: 22, which described the composition of the Senate; 23, which listed qualifications for appointment; 24, which said that "The Governor General shall from Time to Time, in the Queen's Name, by Instrument under the Great Seal, summon qualified Persons to the Senate and . . . every Person so summoned shall become and be a Member of the Senate and a Senator." But sections 22 and 23 used the masculine pronoun *only* ("He shall be of the full age of Thirty Years," etc.). It was argued that, in light of the pronouns in 22 and 23, Section 24 meant "men" when it spoke of "persons."

The 1917 decision of the Supreme Court of Alberta seemed to clear up the matter: it held that "applying the general principle on which the common law rests, namely of reason and good sense . . . there is . . . no legal disqualification for holding public office in the Government of this country arising from any distinction of sex."

Heartened by an eminently sensible judgement, various groups pressed the government of Canada to appoint a woman to the Senate; Emily Murphy, in addition to her court work, was active in many of those organizations. Over a period of time she held, among other offices, that of president of the Canadian Women's Press Club and of the Federated Women's Institutes of Canada, and was a vice-president of the National Council of Women.

By 1921, when the Montreal Women's Club forwarded its resolution to Prime Minister Arthur Meighen, there was increasing consensus that the first woman Senator should be Emily Murphy. Meighen replied that the Department of Justice had advised him that the appointment of a woman was not possible under the terms of the BNA Act. In his election bid later that year, Meighen promised that, should he win, he would seek to have women admitted to the Upper House.

Meighen's party lost, but the question continued to be discussed for the next five years: Prime Minister Mackenzie King wrote Mrs. Murphy in 1922 to promise his support and, two years later, in a speech in Calgary, told the Women's Canadian Club that he would act on the issue. In 1924, '27, and '28 the National Council of Women sent delegations to Ottawa, pleading for the government to act – all to no avail.

Mr. Justice William Ferguson of the Supreme Court of Ontario, Emily's brother, suggested that one sensible answer might be to have her appointed to the Senate and then, if it wished, that body's Privileges Committee could obtain a judgement on the BNA Act issue.

When his solution proved unacceptable to King's government, Mr. Justice Ferguson drew yet another law to Emily's attention: Section 60 of the Supreme Court Act, which directs the Supreme Court of Canada to rule on any constitutional point in the BNA Act if five interested persons petition it to do so. When Emily, thoroughly fed up with King's inaction, decided to take the initiative, the issue was finally joined.

Murphy's political judgement and shrewdness were evident in her choice of the other four persons who, with her, signed the necessary petition in August, 1927. (Always generous, she had the signatures arranged alphabetically, which is why the case is known as *Edwards v. Attorney General of Canada.*)

When it was heard by the High Court, beginning on March 14, 1928, the Solicitor-General of Canada, the Honourable Lucien Cannon, led the arguments on behalf of the government; the "five" were represented by the Honourable Newton Wesley Rowell, a former Opposition leader in the Ontario Legislature and a long-time advocate of female suffrage. The province of Quebec took its stand with the federal government, appointing a special counsel to assist Mr. Cannon, while Alberta reaffirmed the 1921 decision of its Supreme Court by asking Mr. Rowell to act on its behalf as well for the five.

The government argument: the Fathers of Confederation, acting at a time when no women held public office, did not mean women to do so, and it was necessary to interpret the BNA Act in that context.

The "interested persons" argument: in 1867 Lord Brougham's Act, which stipulated that words referring to the masculine gender shall also be taken to refer to the female gender, was in force; moreover, in 1920, when the Dominion Elections Act was passed, the section of the BNA Act dealing with elections law was interpreted to include females.

The judgement of the court, given by Chief Justice Francis Alexander Anglin on April 24, 1928: under the BNA Act, women were not eligible for Senate appointments. On that same day King's Quebec lieutenant, the Honourable Ernest Lapointe, Minister of Justice, announced that the government would begin immediately the lengthy task of amending the British North America Act (a move that, considering opposition from Quebec, as well as from some quarters within the Senate, might be stalled forever or fail completely).

The five women were not prepared to sit around waiting for the future, and, as soon as Parliament rose for the summer (without any action on the promise to

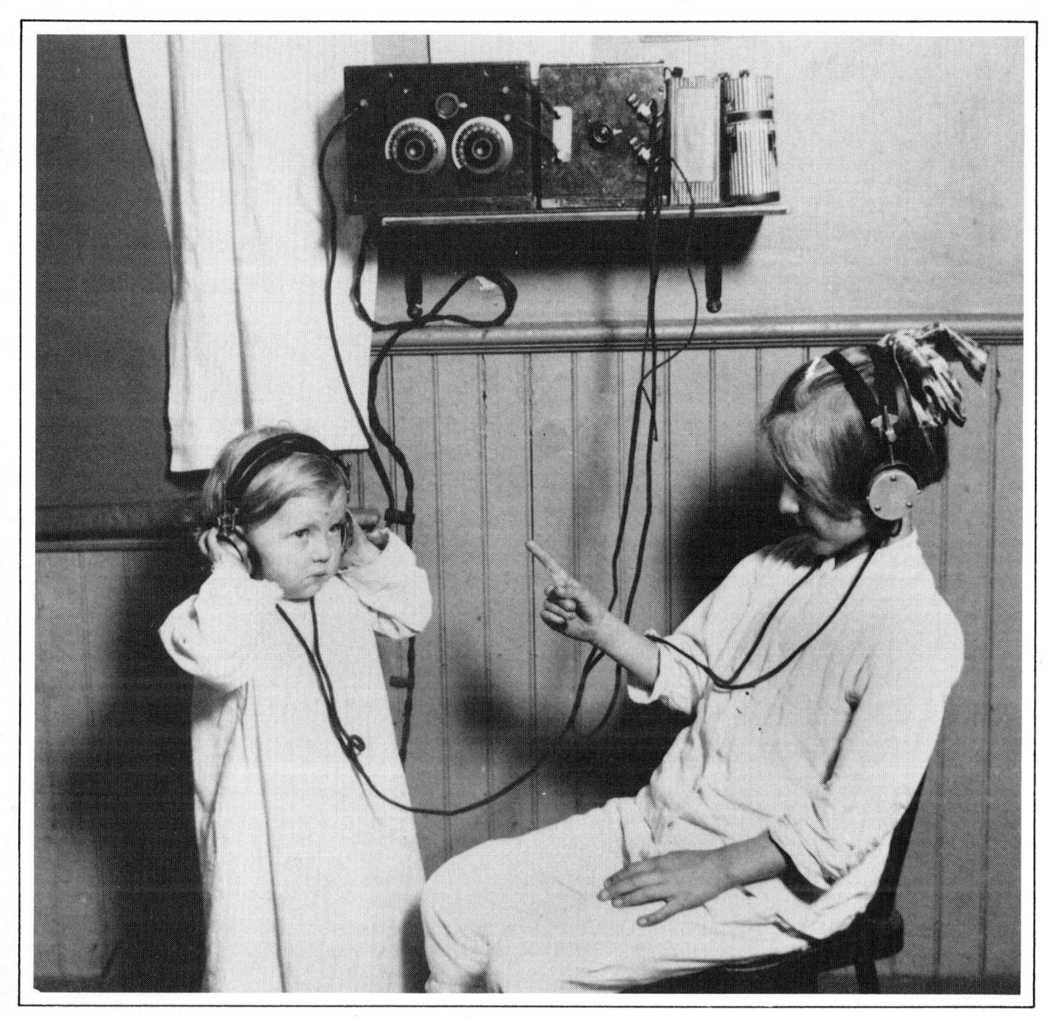

In 1924 family members were happy to wait for their turns at the radio.

amend the BNA Act), they asked leave to appeal to the Privy Council in London. The Justice Department cooperated by agreeing to pay the costs of the action before the Council's Judicial Committee (which, until 1948, had the power to review decisions of the Supreme Court of Canada). Rowell agreed to go to London on behalf of the five, Alberta sent its own Attorney General to assist him, and Quebec cooperated by withdrawing its assistance to the Crown.

For four days, beginning on July 22, 1929, the "Persons Case" was argued; according to a contemporary report:

> In a quiet room at Number One, Downing Street, five great judges, with the Lord Chancellor of England at their head, and a battery of bewigged lawyers from Canada and from England, were wrestling with a question, propounded on behalf of their sex, by five Alberta women . . . Deep and intricate questions of constitutional law are debated back and forth. The exact shade of meaning to be placed on certain words is argued to the finest point . . . and so it goes on, and probably will continue for several days. At the end of all these endless speeches, lessons on Canadian history, and questions by five great judges of England, it will be decided, if one may hazard a guess, that women undoubtedly are Persons. Which one may say, without exaggeration, most of us know already.

The guess turned out to be correct: on October 28, 1929, in a judgement delivered by Lord Chancellor Sankey of the Privy Council, it ruled that "the word persons includes members of the male and female sex, and that therefore the question propounded . . . must be answered in the affirmative; and that women are eligible to be summoned and become members of the Senate of Canada." (In England itself the House of Lords did not permit women to take seats that were theirs by inheritance until twenty-eight years after the five persons judgement.)

Irrespective of political bias, it is clear that Emily Murphy had earned the right to a Senate seat. But perhaps King resented her Conservative politics or perhaps he simply objected to her zeal in pursuing the matter – Ottawa has always preferred public shows of reticence, especially from females. Whatever the reason, he made the first appointment of a woman in 1931, choosing Cairine Wilson, prominent in women's organizations and possessing what is still the prime qualification for a Senate appointment – the "right" political beliefs.

That snub is more a measure of King's character than of the importance of Murphy's battle. If the decision had gone the other way – as it would have if the Canadian Supreme Court had been the final judge of the issue – it is entirely possible that the many laws containing references to "persons" would have been the focus of lengthy, time-consuming legal battles. Even more critically, it would have stamped Canadian society as one in which women were immutably inferior. Finally, the judiciary would not include the women who now sit as judges – most notably, of course, Madam Justice Bertha Wilson of that Supreme Court itself.

Ironically, King's government was defeated in 1931 and the Right Honourable Richard B. Bennett, an old ally of Mrs. Murphy, became Prime Minister. When a Senate vacancy from Alberta occurred in January, 1932, it was widely assumed that she would go to her just political reward; Bennett, however, decided that the seat belonged traditionally to a Roman Catholic, and made the appointment on that basis. Two years later Mrs. Murphy, who had retired from her police magistrate's position, died, aged sixty-five.

Today, a plaque honouring the "five" is mounted on the wall outside the Senate Chamber, a backdrop to a handsome marble bust of Senator Cairine Wilson. It, too, lists the five in alphabetical order but, in a small enough gesture of reparation, it goes on:

> To further the cause of womankind these five outstanding pioneer women caused steps to be taken resulting in the recognition by the Privy Council of women as persons eligible for appointment to the Senate of Canada.
>
> This movement was inaugurated by Magistrate Emily F. Murphy.

How Many Children Does That Bridge Have? Ontario Gets a Divorce Court

Except as otherwise provided by this Act, all Laws in force in Canada, Nova Scotia, or New Brunswick at the Union, and all Courts of Civil and Criminal Jurisdiction . . . existing therein at the Union, shall continue . . . as if the Union had not been made; subject nevertheless . . . to be repealed, abolished, or altered by the Parliament of Canada . . .

The British North America Act, 1867
(renamed the Constitution Act, 1867,
by the Constitution Act, 1982).

Because, for nearly seventy years, Parliament made no move to "repeal, abolish, or alter" the laws "existing therein" (at least, as they related to divorce), there were vast differences in practice in the constituent parts of the new nation.

The three Atlantic provinces, for example, had had a long history of permitting divorce: adultery had been grounds in Nova Scotia since 1758, cruelty since 1761. Prince Edward Island and New Brunswick reached all the way back to the reign of Henry VIII (and the early Church's concept of "sacramental marriage") to establish that "the causes of divorce from the bond of matrimony and of dissolving or annulling the marriage are and shall be frigidity or impotence, adultery and [forbidden degrees of blood relationship]." New Brunswick had had a divorce court since an act of 1791, which superseded an even earlier law; as far back as 1835, Prince Edward Island had a court with the power to consider divorce proceedings (although it was 1945 before the rules and procedures were proclaimed under the Act, making the legislation applicable).

As Canada stretched west of the Manitoba-Ontario border, each jurisdiction (including the Northwest Territories and the Yukon) stipulated as a condition of joining that the English Matrimonial Causes Act of 1857 would become the operative law of divorce in its courts. The residents of Ontario and Quebec continued to present petitions to Parliament where individual bills of divorce were considered and, in the majority of cases, passed. Which, with three major exceptions, was how matters rested from Confederation through World War I and into the mid-'20s.

The first change came in 1925, when the Parliament of Canada finally exercised the power in the divorce field that it had been given under Section 91 of the British North America Act. The subject, once again, was inequality between husbands and wives.

Women in Quebec, Ontario, and Prince Edward Island – provinces without their own matrimonial courts – sometimes found that applying to Parliament for relief had one advantage:

because this legislative body has broad powers to enact laws as it sees fit, wives might be granted a divorce on the same grounds as husbands: adultery. In the rest of the country, however, as in England until 1923, only a husband could obtain a divorce on the sole ground of adultery. A wife, on the other hand, still had to have proof of two marital offenses: adultery plus either desertion, incest, rape, bigamy, sodomy, or bestiality.

Agnes Macphail, for one, was outraged, seeing in the discriminatory grounds a parallel to the economic inequality of Canadian women. In a sometimes tempestuous debate on the subject, she said:

> I believe the preservation of the home as an institution in the future lies almost entirely in the hands of the men. If they are willing to give to women economic freedom within that home; if they are willing to live by the standard that they wish the women to live by, the home will be preserved. If the preservation of the home means the enslavement of women, economically or morally, then we had better break it . . . I would ask men to think of that and think of it seriously. I do believe that the economic freedom of women is one of the things that is causing increasing divorces, because women will not tolerate what they once had to tolerate. You can smile about it if you like, but I know a lot of men who talk very learnedly on a subject like this and who want women to be very pure and chaste when they themselves are not fit to associate with a pure and chaste woman. So, when we have a single standard for men and women, both morally and economically, we shall have a home that is worth preserving, and I think we can be quite sure it will be preserved.

When the debate was over, Parliament passed the Canada Divorce Act of 1925; it gave wives in provinces that had matrimonial courts the right to sue their husbands for divorce on precisely the same terms as their husbands could sue them.

Five years later Parliament took the next step – this time, to ease, however slightly, a jurisdictional rule having to do with domicile in divorce cases. Although the word "domicile" is normally used to mean "home" or "dwelling place," it has a slightly different connotation in law. Used since early times, it is meant to clarify questions that arise because human beings tend to travel and therefore become subject to a variety of legal systems. Under which laws, for example, should a Scot travelling in Wales be tried for injuring an Italian who is a resident of Spain? Even within the same country there are jurisdictional problems: which province should hear the divorce case of a couple who lived in Quebec – she was born in Ontario and he in New Brunswick – until he left and returned to New Brunswick, while she got a job in Manitoba? (He would probably be considered domiciled in New Brunswick.)

Traditionally, since the married woman was not a person apart, her domicile was that of her husband. Divorce laws required that she sue in her husband's *current* domicile; but changing domicile, although somewhat more complex than simply moving house, is not impossible for the man determined to thwart a divorce suit: if he has a summer cottage in New Brunswick, it might be sold and a retirement home purchased in British Columbia – a possible factor in determining his domicile. Or, if he is a businessman, he might sell all his Moncton interests, start a company in Toronto, and insist that that was his domicile – even though he lives, for the time being, in New York.

In 1929 a bill was presented that would have permitted separated women to establish domiciles of their own, but it failed in the Senate (and was strongly opposed by the Solicitor-General for Canada, the Honourable Lucien Cannon of "five persons" fame). The successful version, the Divorce Jurisdiction Act of 1930, represented only a small improvement on existing legislation: it allowed a woman to sue her husband in the place that had been his domicile *at the time of separation*.

In the same year a divorce court was finally established in Ontario – thanks to the campaign waged by a western clergyman of the sternest moral rectitude and patience. He was James Shaver Woodsworth, a Methodist minister (and later founder of the Cooperative Commonwealth Federation), originally from the southwestern reaches of Toronto, in what used to be the village of Islington. Pennsylvania Loyalists, the Woodsworths had once been a prosperous family of businessmen; J.S.'s father, a Methodist preacher of modest circumstances, had

In the midst of economic blight, the Premier of Ontario, Mitch Hepburn, admires a small natural miracle, one of the Dionne quints.

moved his family frequently, finally heading west when the boy was eight years old. As a young man, James returned east to obtain his theology degree from Victoria College; there, he became deeply involved in the ongoing arguments about the place of the "social Gospel" – the here-and-now and its relation to the hereafter. Woodsworth spent a year in England, returned home, married, and took up his duties in a fashionable Winnipeg church. But by the end of World War I he had made drastic changes in his life: a pacifist who eventually left the ministry, he was, at various times, a civil servant, a longshoreman, a unionist, and finally a politician.

In 1921 Woodsworth was elected as the Member for Winnipeg Centre (a seat he held until his death in 1942), another of those historically important and enduring people who first came to Ottawa in the Fourteenth post-Confederation Parliament. A man with a strong moral sense and high personal standards (travelling by train, he took cheap sleeping berths and brown-bagged it across the country), he had no fundamental interest in divorce as such, but he was appalled by the use of Parliament as a matrimonial court.

In the six years between Woodsworth's entry into the House and the beginning of his protest, there had been more than 1,000 divorce bills before Parliament (and another 1,300 Canadians had obtained American divorces). This number contrasted strikingly with the total of 604 cases presented in the sixty-four years between Confederation and 1921. The increase was a reflection of the upward surge of divorce throughout the country; after a long period of stability in which there were 6.4 divorces for each 100,000 Canadians, the rate had climbed every year but one. By 1935 it was 13.2 divorces for every 100,000 people. (The most recent figure, for 1978, was 243.4 divorces per 100,000; Macphail's honest admission that economic freedom is a factor in the higher incidence of divorce has been amply borne out.)

In 1921 W. G. Nickle, the member for Kingston, introduced a bill into the House of Commons designed to make the Exchequer Court of Canada (predecessor of today's Federal Court) a national divorce court to administer the law as it existed in England in 1870; his bill did not succeed and, although the idea was a sound one, it was never revived.

The 1928 crop of divorce bills – 95 percent from Ontario – was so large that Prime Minister Mackenzie King proposed passing seventy-five of them as a group, rather than having them scrutinized individually. Woodsworth was heartily sick of the amount of work that each bill entailed – three separate readings in the Commons and another three in the Senate – but there were other problems that he kept bringing before the House:

> I object to the present procedure because poor people cannot come to Ottawa to avail themselves of the divorce court here. It remains a privilege of the better-to-do . . . Further, the poor man who is charged with being guilty of a crime that calls for divorce has no opportunity of defending himself . . . in that case, and in all these cases, we are making no provision whatever for alimony . . . More serious still, there is no provision whatever in these cases . . . for the maintenance of the children.

Therefore, on April 20, 1928, Woodsworth firmly set out to force the issue by insisting that each bill of divorce be passed separately, "not in batches." The next day's *Toronto Telegram* headlined its story, "Woodsworth Objects to Sacred Tie Being Broken in Chunks," and went on to describe how

> . . . the little Winnipeg preacher got up on his hind legs and howled. He declared that this divorce legislation was being treated altogether too lightly by the Commons. Some day he was going to demand that the House go into details on one of these bills. Then it might be necessary to ask the lady member to leave, to clear the galleries, and to ask Hansard [the verbatim report of proceedings] to cease to function.

When several attempts to pass Senate bills establishing an Ontario divorce court failed, Woodsworth, true to his plan, discussed the nastier details of two cases before the House and made it clear that he would continue the public laundering of marital woe until an acceptable solution had been reached. Well aware of both Woodsworth's steadfastness and of the nature of divorce cases (a suit was generally undertaken only when the couple had already dipped into the more squalid possibilities of human behaviour), members knew they were facing endless, grim sittings.

Woodsworth questioned each bill carefully: Were there children? What was being done to ensure that they were going to receive support? Would the Member moving the bill, and the one seconding it, please explain these points? Could the bill's sponsor give the House an outline of the case? (In her memoir of him, Woodsworth's daughter says that his habit of asking questions had become so firmly ingrained that, when a bill dealing with a bridge was presented amongst a batch of divorce actions, her father stood up in the House and asked, "Are there any children?")

The stakes were clear: Woodsworth, polite and implacable, would ask questions until Ontario got a divorce court or until hell froze over – whichever came first. By the time either occurred, Parliament's business would wobble to a halt. Mackenzie King, therefore, finally appeared to capitulate: in the 1929 session he promised that some action would be taken to solve the problem in the following year. In 1930, King having failed to come through – not for the first time – Woodsworth reintroduced his Ontario divorce court bill and forced a rapid second reading of it. Various delaying tactics – substituting an educational campaign to cut down on divorce rather than establishing a court, setting the bill aside so that "it can be thoroughly digested by the people of Ontario" – did not get needed support. On May 6, 1930, by a vote of 100 to 85, An Act to Provide in the Province of Ontario for the Dissolution and Annulment of Marriage was passed by Parliament. Less than a page long, it decreed that "the law of England . . . as that law existed on the fifteenth day of July, 1870, . . . shall be in force in the province of Ontario." Couples in Ontario could now sue each other for divorce in the courts of Ontario.

Perhaps the most astonishing aspect of Woodsworth's fight for an Ontario divorce bill was that, seven months after the recognized beginning of the Depression, he had been able to capture Parliament's attention at all. Thirty-five years would pass – years of economic disaster, global war, upheavals in every aspect of social outlook and behaviour – before enough attention would focus on family law to make it the subject of a provincial study. And it would take four years beyond that before Parliament passed the next legislation relating to family law.

The Depression was the most overwhelming concern of 1930: the forces that caused it and the reasons it finally ended have inspired as many theories as there are schools of economic or sociological thought. What is beyond dispute, however, is that it remains to this day the worst economic catastrophe that ever struck Canada.

In the West the news was worst of all as nature's now-malevolent hand turned off the rain, drying lush farmland into sand beaches on which generations of work and hope were marooned. In the 1928-29 season Saskatchewan's farmers were Canada's most prosperous; by 1932 they were Canada's poorest – their income had dropped by 72 percent in those four years. The people of the Atlantic provinces suffered a less precipitate rate of decline – but only because the supposedly "Roaring Twenties" had already left large numbers of Maritimers on the edge of bare subsistence. Nonetheless, in the years between 1929 and 1933, the value of fishing, Maritime Canada's chief industry, declined nearly another 50 percent.

Proportionally, Ontario's burgeoning manufacturing and retail industries were in as bad shape: women making garments for the T. Eaton Company in 1929 were paid $3.74 for sewing a dozen voile dresses; two years later they received less than half that for the same work. At the peak of the 1929 stock market the fifty leading Canadian stocks on the Toronto and Montreal exchanges had a total value of more than six billion dollars; by the 1932 lows those same stocks were worth less than nine hundred million, a loss of nearly five and a half billion dollars – 85.9 percent of their value. In 1933, 400,000 people in Ontario were on direct relief, receiving an average of $4.22 per family per week; the number of building permits in twenty-five Ontario cities had fallen to an eighth of what they had been just three years earlier.

Although only the most destitute families were eligible for public assistance, more than 15 percent of Canada's total population was on relief by 1933. In May of that year almost a third of all Canadian wage earners were unemployed. Building was 11 percent of what it had been in 1929 and the dollar value of exports had declined by more than half. Families, companies, whole jurisdictions, went into debt. Newfoundland, proud possessor of a unique and uniquely preserved culture, had been a self-governing Dominion of the British Empire for several decades; now, even though relief payments were low ($1.80 a month for adults), government costs were rising while income dropped. The Dominion's credit collapsed and it lost the right to self-government, becoming the responsibility of a British government committee. (Nonetheless, hardy Newfoundlanders worked out a plan for funding visiting health nurses for the remote outport settlements: the island's women, legendary knitters, sold handmade garments to some of North America's poshest stores and used the $12 they received *annually* to subsidize the visiting nurses.)

A few Canadians escaped the bleak realities of the Depression and some even prospered, building the foundations of future empires. The country's banking system, which had always been more sternly controlled than its American counterpart, was solvent and its retail branches remained open – in contrast to the frighteningly common newspaper pictures of American depositors who arrived to discover bank doors locked and their life savings gone.

In Toronto, Conn Smythe opened his successful ice hockey barn on College Street; in North Bay, Roy (later Baron) Thomson bought a radio station, the first outpost of a media empire that would eventually include the mighty *Times* of London. For those who wished to dwell in marble halls, John David Eaton opened his home-furnishings store, two blocks west of Smythe's arena, and promised that it would become the most successful such outlet in Canada. Quickly characterized as a white elephant, Eaton's College Street was always pleasantly (but unprofitably) uncrowded and was eventually sold. (Today a part of the elegant old building is used for provincial courts.)

Speaking to a *Maclean's* writer long after the Depression was over, J. D. Eaton remembered it with astonishing obtuseness, recalling that

> Nobody thought about money . . . because they never saw any. You could take your girl to a supper

R.B. Bennett could not translate his personal kindness into effective public action.

> dance at a hotel for $10, and that included the bottle and a room for you and your friends to drink it in. I'm glad I grew up then. It was a good time for everybody. People learned what it means to work.

A 1931 letter, written by Richard Bedford Bennett, shows that Canada's Depression-era Prime Minister was similarly out of touch with the realities being faced by millions of less well-heeled Canadians. A millionaire himself, thanks to friends who had left him a controlling interest in the E. B. Eddy paper companies, Bennett complained that

> The people are not bearing their share of the load . . . I do not know what the result . . . may be, but unless it induces men and women to think in terms of honest toil rather than in terms of bewilderment because of conditions which they helped to create, the end of organized society is not far distant.

Before he left office four years later, Bennett had become much less lofty about the lives of fellow Canadians. Proud or angry, humble or shell-shocked by their experiences, they wrote to their country's leader, certain that *he* had solutions to the hopelessness and helplessness that baffled them. From Chadwick, Ontario, Mrs. Stewart Nolan wrote:

> No dought you will be surprised to receive this letter I have been advised by a friend of your's to write you in so doing I am asking you to Please not let this be Known in Public as my husband doesn't like me to ask for help from any one we have had so much sickness in our family . . . my heart has gone bad my two girls 10. and 12

> yrs old have both be sick since Feb. under medical treatment I have not the money to give them or myself the medicine we should and we are all in need of clothes if you have any suits or clothing for men you have given up I wish you would send some . . . if you knoew how hard we have tried . . .

D. Woodstock of Kincardine started by assuring the Prime Minister of her family's loyalties:

> My husband . . . presided at your meeting here (in our rink) and we afterwards had a cup of tea with you at Miss Linton's. . . If you could be so extraordinary kind to find a job for our boy or our daughter, you would win a harassed mother's undying gratitude.

Seven-year-old George Bancroft of Ruthven, Ontario, was prepared to point out the advantages, both sacred and profane, of replying to his request, and started by presenting his credentials:

> I am just 7 yrs old probably you won't take time to read my wee letter. But however I have had a terrible experience in my short lifetime I am eight yrs old on 14 day October which is election day and I was wondering if you could give me some help to be able to attend school & walk once more. By supplying me with an artificial leg. My leg was shot off last November with a shot gun at close range with a boy who picked it up at another house. I wasn't expected to live atall. But I am here today . . . I am active & well every other way so when I play I often get hurt, if I just had a leg I could go back to school . . . if you don't believe my history just ask Dr. Shellington of Windsor he took off my leg along with Dr. Metcalfe of Kingsville he is my Doctor. If you will say you will help me a little, I will send you my phota. We live on a farm a rough one havn't been able to pay our interest for 2 years now & principal the same., so you understand our circumstances. Probably you will be able to get me an artificial limb for my birthday the 14th day of October so as my people will feel like going out to vote that day. The price of my leg would probly mean alot for a fellow when the judgement day comes I know there are many other little crippled boys & girls too But I feel if I had my leg I would be able to help some poor Robin back in his nest again. Now Would you like me to send you my picture I will do so. Hoping you will be so kind to give me the price of an artificial leg or pay for it when I get it, as we can't afford it & it maybe joy in the skies for you.

On a more bitter note, Leo Gadali of Toronto enclosed a newspaper clipping about the death of a twenty-two-year-old unemployed bookkeeper who jumped 1,500 feet from the wing of a plane, "bidding a smiling farewell to his instructor . . . I would say," Gadali wrote, "the Dominion Government was the murderer of this young Canadian . . ."

Bennett sometimes answered letters himself, passed on the names of job applicants to various government boards and agencies, or filled requests for clothing (even ordering long underwear for a destitute western farmer). One of his three secretaries reported "great difficulty in restraining him from sending money to everyone who asks for assistance," and finally a special fund was established, the gifts usually doled out on the basis of judgements made by Bennett's staff. The amounts were small – almost never more than $5. Although the generosity was not always disinterested – the number of $5 donations increased sharply as the 1935 election neared – it was sincere. It has been estimated that the Prime Minister spent some $25,000 annually on donations, in addition to sending silver mugs to children whose parents had christened them Richard Bedford, giving gifts of flowers and candies at Christmas, and, it is said, paying for the education of as many as eighteen people at one time.

(Although Bennett authored his own Canadian "New Deal" in 1935, the courts eventually ruled much of it outside federal jurisdiction, and he is most vividly – if not always fairly – remembered as unable to cope with the events of his time in office.)

Technically, the worst of the Depression had subsided by 1933, although the economy remained slack until half-way through World War II. In the words of one Canadian historian of the period, war

> . . . was far more than a project of outdoor relief for the masses. But in this country it was also that. Many young Canadian men, a group unusually hard-hit by the

> Depression and the resulting unemployment, must have preferred being trained to kill – and perhaps eventually killing or being killed – to living off their parents, riding freights across the country, marking time in relief camps, working for small wages under the constant threat of unemployment, or losing self-respect when only relief vouchers, grudgingly supplied, kept them from starvation.

The Canada of those pre-war days was so unlike the nation of today that it might as well have existed only in the imagination. Eleven million people lived in that long-ago country, a third of the breadwinners without work – and, a decade before unemployment insurance, with no way of stopping the slide into poverty. (By contrast, the unemployment rate in 1982, the worst year of the most recent recession, reached a high of 12.8 percent.)

In 1931 a labourer worked, on average, only thirty-two and a half weeks a year and he received $14.74 a week. (The effect of the Depression on wages lasted for a very long time: by 1941 labourers worked for an additional month and a half or two months annually but earned, on average, 44 cents less a week. Even managerial and professional earners, least affected by the lack of work during the Depression, made $9 less each week in 1941 than they had received ten years earlier.)

Despite the Depression, home ownership was still the dream of most couples: more than 12 percent of all Canadians (13 percent in Ontario) owned their own houses, while a mere 4 percent lived in apartments. Only one in ten Canadians had a phone, one in five a mechanical refrigerator, one in four an electric vacuum cleaner, one in three a car – although the people of Ontario were more likely than other Canadians to have these luxuries – but three out of four owned radios. (Radios were handsome pieces of furniture – the smallest the size of a mantel clock – with large speakers, glowing eyes, and, in the more expensive models, short-wave bands. All were subject to taxation through an annual federal licensing scheme.)

Married women were not eligible for jobs in the federal civil service unless they could show personal need or capabilities necessary for the public good. Those females who joined the service while single had to resign when they married; since no one willingly gives up a job in economic hard times, many couples married secretly – and even maintained separate residences so that they would not be cashiered for immoral behaviour. Some bank tellers were obliged to seek company permission before marrying: at salaries of less than $2,000 a year, it was thought that the responsibilities of marriage might tempt employees to dip into the till.

Ontario's major city, Toronto, had several buildings tall enough to require elevator service and each car, of course, had a gloved and uniformed elevator operator. Personal service of all kinds was taken for granted, whether it was the twice-a-day, six-day-a-week mail delivery or the free calf's liver the butcher tucked into the order because he knew how much everyone appreciated the little treat for the family cat.

The large Eaton's and Simpson's department stores had circulating libraries where eager customers paid three cents a day to borrow popular fiction. (Of course, books were in hard cover: the first paperbacks, from England's Penguin Books, did not appear in Canada until just before the war – and were only moderately successful.) The credit card was neither known nor needed; Hall's Dairy, Canada Bread, grocery stores, all delivered and some even ran tabs for their best customers. Deliveries, of course, were sometimes delayed in winter, when horses slipped on the city streets. In summer, there was the problem of manure disposal. In the streets, vendors carried heavy blocks of ice into homes where sturdy oak iceboxes were still used to keep food cold; outside, kids climbed onto the trucks to steal the chipped-off slivers.

Even in the big city, restaurant menus centred on roast beef, gravy, peas, and mashed potatoes. Eaton's was noted for its chicken salad; at Simpson's the best dish was chicken pot pie, which was served in both the Arcadian Court and the Men's Grill (the latter open to women only when in the company of men). Across the street, at Bowles Cafeteria, there was a Depression tomato soup, popular with the clients but not with the management: hot water was a nickel, add ketchup and stir. In winter, it at least was warming.

Thrift was an important virtue in Ontario and had less to do with the Depression than with Old World concepts of goodness and godliness. Like all key social values of the day, it was inculcated at home – by precept as well as by necessity – reinforced by the church, and strongly supported by the school. In Toronto, for example, the Board of Education ran a Penny Savings Bank: each Monday morning children brought their precious hoards of pennies – some were the large, handsome

The radio was an imposing piece of furniture and the family gathering place.

"coppers" still in circulation – to class. The bank paid a very generous 3 percent interest on deposits.

The department stores had a scheme under which customers *lent them* money on which they paid interest rather than, as with credit cards, the other way around. A client made a deposit in "her" account (it was, of course, actually in her husband's name, since even this type of "credit" was never extended to married women in their own right); as she shopped, the cost of purchases was deducted from her deposit, which she then replenished. (These so-called "deposit accounts" still exist, although neither Eaton's nor Simpson's has opened one in more than a decade.)

Banks had evolved their own architectural style – Early Intimidation – and cheques were made out in the Spencerian script taught relentlessly at school; in order to clear, the face of each cheque had to bear a three-cent postage stamp, a form of federal taxation.

Sometimes crabbed and quaint, especially when seen from the distance of fifty years, Canadian society was also more than the sum of its parts: a well-behaved populace lived with a degree of stability that would ease the adjustments that war soon demanded. In the mid-'30s that catastrophe loomed ahead, unseen.

In 1934 a new Ontario government was elected under the leadership of St. Thomas farmer Mitchell Hepburn, a member of the federal Parliament who until then had never been elected provincially. The Legislature had shrunk from 112 to 90 seats – one of thousands of cost-saving moves the provincial government had had to make. As he took office, the worst of the Depression had passed, but Hepburn still faced staggering economic problems. The immediate crisis, however, was more homespun: on May 28, precisely two weeks before the election, a poor housewife in the northern mining town of Callander gave birth to quintuplets – a genuine rarity of nature in the days before fertility drugs. With unstinting help from Toronto's Hospital for Sick Children (which became a world leader in multiple-birth genetics), the babies survived. Within a short time the Ontario government had to decide whether to leave them with their parents, who seemed to be vulnerable to the blandishments of promoters wanting them for exhibition in American freak shows, or to step in and take the girls from their natural parents, who were guilty only of breaching the laws of probability.

The government managed to combine the worst of all possible solutions: the Dionne quints were made wards of the province, kept physically and emotionally isolated from their parents, brothers, and sisters. They were exhibited to an adoring public – a rare, bright moment in the midst of so much despair – and made a mint for the province, for their parents, and ultimately for themselves. In exchange, they traded the warmth, grubbiness, and uncertainty of family life for beguiling cuteness and emotional antisepsis amongst a staff of paid keepers.

(Even if anyone had recognized that these five were genuinely "needy and dependent children," there was no John Joseph Kelso to help. He had retired in the year of their birth and died a year later, leaving accounts of his remarkable career that are blurred only by the standard pieties of his time. His interest in poor children may have come, as he claimed, as a Christian response to conditions he had seen as a newspaper reporter. But he must also have been moved by his own painful childhood experiences, gathering bits of wood for his impoverished family, depending on another man's generosity for some of his education and on his own gritty determination for the rest.)

In the third week of 1936, that exemplar of royal and familial duty, George V, succumbed to old age. Raise the glasses high: The King is dead, long live the King. But wait – on December 8, 1936, the uncrowned King in the second part of the equation declined to take the throne. He could not reign, he told the world, "without the help and support of the woman I love" – a twice-divorced American named Wallis Warfield Spencer Simpson. Even those who fancied themselves "liberal" in such matters were shaken by a man who turned his back on duty – however symbolic – to regularize an affair that had been a secret only from the people of Britain. The strong-jawed Duchess and the weak-willed Duke had done nothing to give divorce a good name. (There was a royal dust-up in Ottawa when the Prime Minister and his Cabinet gave assent to the British Act of Succession by which the throne passed to "Bertie," now King George VI, rather than recalling Parliament from its winter recess.)

There was one last moment of pleasure before war began: in the shimmering spring of 1939, the new King and his Queen Elizabeth visited North America. Gentle, courteous, and, in his own life, a brave man, the King and his sweet-faced wife inspired unparalleled affection amongst the crowds who cheered them every inch of their way. This loyalty, too, would have its uses in the time ahead.

Today, those who remain are past middle age: the boss, the retiree, somebody's father or grandfather, relics of the last war sanctioned by society. In September, 1939, however, they were young enough to feel invulnerable – naïve and eager for the battle. By war's end, 1,086,771 Canadians – including 49,251 women – had served in the armed forces and 41,992 of them had been killed.

They were, of course, much more than statistics, although, more than forty years later, it may be impossible for anyone who did not know them to appreciate their idealism and sweetness. Here is the story of just such a man, born in the midst of one war, killed near the end of another.

Irving Reider was born in Toronto on May 7, 1916, the anniversary of the sinking of the *Lusitania*, at a time when it seemed sickeningly possible that the Germans might still be victorious. His father, originally from Rochester, New York, died when Irv was only seven. His mother, a Polish immigrant, was determined that her only son would be well educated, and in 1933, after graduating from Harbord Collegiate, Irv enrolled in chemical engineering at the University of Toronto. His marks in the sixteen subjects he carried each of the two years he attended ranged from middling to excellent – 52 in calculus, 96 in hydrostatics – and he might have been expected to make a career in some branch of applied science.

There were other factors, however.

In 1941 Veronica Foster was the popular "Bren Gun Girl" at work and, off-duty, a talented jitterbugger.

Members of the Canadian Women's Army Corps arrive for training in Newmarket, 1941. They are no longer farmerettes, but not soldiers either.

First, of course, money: the $300 tuition was reasonable but an intolerable burden at home, even though he was working part-time. There was also a sense of uselessness: it was no secret that Jews – and Irv was Jewish – could not expect to find work in engineering. Another member of Irv's class remembers that, just before graduation, the dean called the four or five Jewish students into his office to tell them, regretfully, that they should not plan on staying in the field since their chances of obtaining work were almost nil.

(Anti-Semitism, in fact, was an accepted part of life in Canada before, during, and after the war: signs in many of the best Muskoka resorts warned "No Jews or Dogs Allowed," and the Premier of Quebec won an election by charging that his opponents were in league with the "International Zionist Brotherhood," an organization that existed only in his feverish mind.)

Bright, attractive, and eager to test himself in the real world, Irv found work "on the avenue," selling dresses for a manufacturers' agent, Ben Rosenberg. He had the use of Ben's old Durant and then of a second-hand Chevy he bought for $700, travelling from Oshawa to Windsor selling "better" specialty-sized (i.e., large-size) dresses that wholesaled for up to $12 each and retailed for about twice that. A champion swimmer, he practised in the Harrison Baths, played cards with old school buddies, took the occasional flyer on the slowly recovering stock market – although he turned over most of his pay to his mother – and went to baseball games with his brother-in-law. His friends described him as good-natured, "a devil with the ladies," and "a guy who knew the name of every piece of classical music ever written and could tell the name of the composer too." He read fiction (*The Grapes of Wrath* and *Of Mice and Men* were favourites) and hated to get up in the morning.

As soon as the war started, he began to talk about joining the services. His father had lost a son in 1920 as a result of gas poisoning suffered in the trenches in 1917, and Irv decided that he would reach out to the half-brother he had never known – and to his dead father – by enlisting in the American forces.

In 1941 he was accepted as an officer trainee in the U.S. Navy Air Force but, after a dumb prank kept him from pilot's school, he transferred to the Army Air Force. Commissioned a lieutenant in 1944, he returned home on leave, talked of being engaged to a beautiful young woman from the Peterborough area, and went off, his friends remember, happy and excited, to the war.

Irving B. Reider, born May 7, 1916, Toronto; died October 4, 1944, Bari, Italy.

On October 4, 1944, after a bombing run on the Rumanian oil fields at Ploesti, his seventeenth mission, Irv's Liberator bomber failed to return and was listed as missing. His mother, now twice widowed, was told that he had been captured – a lie that her family hoped would eventually be proven true. On January 4, 1945, the International Red Cross sent word from Geneva that the plane had been discovered near Bari, Italy, all ten crew members dead.

Both of Irv's sisters, one niece, a family friend, and a rabbi were present to tell his mother that he had been killed. Instantly, and in keeping with Jewish mourning custom, she removed her shoes; for hours, until a doctor arrived to sedate her, she paced up and down the first-floor hallway, crying brokenly for the young man – "my prince" – who had died.

That fall, by which time the war in Europe had ended, a postcard arrived from Italy. It showed a mountain near Bari, with a pinhole marking on one of the topmost slopes. "Your son lies high on this mountain," the stranger had written, "close to the God he served so well."

Because of the condition of the Liberator and its crew, burial was in a common plot in Jefferson Barracks, Missouri, the war cemetery most central to the families of the ten men. Irv's mother and his elder sister attended the final interment service; they returned to Toronto with a light wool flag, one of ten that had decorated the common coffin. His mother moved the pictures of King George and Queen Elizabeth that had decorated her "front room" since the Royal Visit of 1939, and placed a small standard with a gold star in the middle of the largest bay window.

The following year she learned that all the members of her family, perhaps 200 of them, had perished in the ovens. (She herself died in 1959, long before two young history professors in Toronto revealed that, before and throughout World War II, it was the established policy of the Canadian government to keep this country safe from Jewish refugees, including the thousands of dazed orphans who had sought sanctuary in the last days of the war. Some of the country's most senior civil servants, including the Honourable Ernest Lapointe, King's Quebec lieutenant, and Vincent Massey, later appointed Canada's first native-born Governor General, used their considerable influence on King to keep Jews out.

(Numbers tell precisely how successful they were: between 1933 and 1945, the United States accepted more than 200,000 Jewish refugees; Britain, battling just to survive, allowed 70,000. The impoverished countries of South America were proportionally at least as generous: Argentina took 50,000; Brazil, 27,000; Bolivia and Chile, 14,000 each. In that same twelve-year period, Canada managed to welcome 4,000.)

On May 7, 1945 – ironically, it would have been Irv's twenty-ninth birthday – the war ended. The *Toronto Telegram* reported that, "before ten o'clock this morning, people were streaming out of offices on Bay Street, hatless and coatless, to celebrate the unconditional surrender of Germany in a blizzard of paper, streamers and confetti." King having already promised that no Canadian would be obliged to fight in the Pacific Theatre of Operations, the country was aching to begin the time of peace.

The emotional post-war air was resolutely clear and sunny, but the giddy pleasures of peace turned out to be transitory: six and a half months after the Japanese surrender of August, 1945, Winston Churchill spoke of "an iron curtain" that had settled over Eastern Europe. Yesterday's invincible ally had become today's shifty nemesis and soldiers who had fought a war billed as the prelude to everlasting peace could be forgiven their cynicism.

Inevitably, World War II would force on us a reconsideration of the very meaning of being human – and a new understanding that we are a darker, more complex species than we had previously acknowledged. In time, this reality would be expressed in Hannah Arendt's words as "the banality of evil" and, just as memorably, in the observation of a comic-strip opossum named Pogo ("We have met the enemy and they is us"). The recently vanquished were not a monstrous "they" but people who, like us, came in varied moral and cultural shapes: some practised Beethoven by night and genocide by day; others wrote limpid poetry, or studied flower arranging or ancient dance, in order to renew themselves for the tiring work of organizing death marches. "They" were different from "us" – not by kind but by degree. Given the "right" circumstances, we, too, might have betrayed our friends, requisitioned Zyklon B gas, pried gold from the molars of the dead. Having mistaken victory for righteousness, we learned just how fragile human decency is.

Those who survived the battle's terrible lottery came home to a world that was, as Jeanette MacDonald warbled, "waiting for the sunrise." They faced a reality that was less rosy. The stagnant Depression years had left a housing shortage and there was a dire need for 320,000 new homes, some for the 40,000 Canadian men who had married overseas. But at last there was prosperity: servicemen received $7.50 for each month of domestic service and $15 for each month overseas; long-term vets received up to almost $2,000, more than a year's wages.

The federal Department of Veterans' Affairs made it possible for thousands of vets to go to universities, colleges, and trade schools; others, however, returned heartily sick of anything that even resembled regimentation and went job hunting. In government and in private industry, war widows and returnees had priority in obtaining employment (often at pre-war wages). A Veterans' Land Act helped those who wanted to farm or fish and there were credits toward the down payment for household furnishings, or for establishing a small business.

There were problems as well: the kids who left had come back as men. They were now face to face with families who could not possibly live up to the images they had carried with them onto the field; children who had not seen their fathers for years, if ever, were struggling to "make room for Daddy." No one had heard the theories about emotional damage when parents and children are not physically close at birth or about the natural estrangement that results from long periods of separation.

If those who had gone away had changed, so had those who remained behind. There were thousands of second honeymoons as people reached across the span of different experiences – and, sometimes, of many months or years – to renew their knowledge of each other. But time and the unshared past could not be repealed. The women who had faced problems, made decisions, accepted consequences alone, were not likely to meekly hand over autonomy – or the chequebook – or to pretend that everything could remain the same.

Only family law, unaltered since 1930, could go on as if the world had remained the same in all those years. The first acknowledgement that this was not true did not come until 1964, when the province passed the Ontario Law Reform Commission Act.

In the following spring, the commission began a project

> . . . to analyse the existing law affecting all areas of family relations within the legislative competence of the Provincial Legislature, to evaluate the adequacy of those laws in view of changed economic and social conditions pertaining to the family, to state the basic principles required for a modern code of family law in Ontario and to suggest remedial legislation to establish such a code.

It had taken more than twenty years for the shift in values to begin permeating the law, especially the law of the family. But, when the changes finally came, they would be the most substantive in the eight centuries since the church, and then the state, had moved to regulate the formation and behaviour of families.

Victory.

Farewell, *Filius Nullius*

Ultimately, there is no way those who grew up within the circle of that 1940s world can describe it to those who did not. The larger differences, of course, are the easiest to grasp – there were no computers, television sets, birth control pills, jets, cocktail bars, bank cards, frozen foods, detergents, plastics, multinationals, hi-fis, stereos, no 33⅓rds, videos, cassettes, video cassettes, no Highway 401, no Sunday movies, no Sunday sports – no Sunday anything.

Boys were still being given names like Shirley, Beverly, and Marion. The first "miracle drug," penicillin, had been used at the battlefronts but was not yet available to the general public; doctors routinely x-rayed patients or handled radium and lost their fingers – or their lives – to cancer. Aids were defined as "helps or supports," but infantile paralysis – or polio, as it was sometimes called – stalked innocent victims each autumn, leaving them crippled or dead. (In really bad years children revelled in the delayed opening of school, oblivious of terrified parents hovering over them.)

The telling differences, however, were more subtle: a decent woman did not smoke on the streets and she wore a hat and gloves while out and about; people did not appear in white clothing, white shoes, or straw hats before the May 24 weekend or after Labour Day. Those were the "rules" – a rule being anything that "they said" or that "everyone knew." Despite the upheaval of a world war, the Ontario of 1945 was closer in its customs and attitudes to the province of 1845 than it was to the one that exists today.

Certainly, there was no interest in post-war years in changing the laws affecting Canadian families. In the House of Commons, the Cooperative Commonwealth Federation was carrying on in the tradition established by J.S. Woodsworth: from time to time it attempted to clog House business by examining individual divorce bills being presented on behalf of Quebec residents and, after Newfoundland joined Confederation in 1949, on behalf of its citizens as well.

Which is where matters stood in May, 1960, when CBC television producer Ross McLean and his staff aired the first of two programs on the subject of divorce. Seen from the distance of more than twenty-five years, both shows look like reports from the Lost Planet of Smug: in the first, a woman claims that she acts as a paid co-respondent in divorce actions. In the second, broadcast two months later (while the CBC dithered about the sensation it had innocently created), thirteen men and three women talk about divorce. A psychiatrist describes it as a "form of mental illness"; hollow-voiced with horror, the on-camera host warns that 6,000 Canadian couples will be divorced that year.

Today, no one remembers who first suggested that *Close-up,* the CBC's national magazine program, undertake an in-depth look at divorce, although the law was ripe for just such an examination: there were endless stories of wives unable to find deserting husbands so that they could sue for their freedom; men tied to women they loathed; children growing up in an atmosphere poisoned by mutual hatred and despair; divorces obtained by deceit or outright perjury.

Initially, the intention within the *Close-up* team was simply to interview representatives of the various groups touched by divorce and separation: some clergymen, politicians, a lawyer, a psychiatrist, a social worker, a divorced woman, and one who was separated but unable to get a divorce. (As a pointed reminder of social attitudes of the period, the last two were shown in shadow, a style television now reserves for Mafia defectors and undercover narcotics agents.)

The idea of including a "professional co-respondent" was hardly earthshaking: almost everyone, particularly in Ontario's larger cities, knew someone, or knew someone who knew someone, who had used the services of one. They were women who, for a fee, purportedly concocted evidence of adultery – in the eight provinces where that was one of the few grounds for divorce. (In Canada, a divorce action is instituted by a "petitioner," who files a "petition" against a "respondent" or "respondents." The person accused of having committed the marital offense with the spouse being sued is, therefore, the "co-respondent," a term that comes from the English law and" practice.")

In the usual scenario, the hotel room was rented by the "guilty" party – almost always the man, since only the most desperate woman, willing to risk the loss of friends, community standing, and even the custody of her children, would subject herself to the shame of being branded an adulteress. The co-respondent arrived, followed shortly by a detective who, having discovered that the room had been rented in the name of Mr. and Mrs., "burst in" on the couple, noted their deshabille (nightclothes or partial clothing, one obviously used bed; et cetera). The tableau had the precision of Kabuki dancing.

Often, after suitable expressions of shock and outrage, the interloper (usually a detective but sometimes a lawyer, relative, or friend) and the "adulterers" would sit down, have a quick celebratory drink; then everyone could go home, wait for the service of papers, describe to the court what had happened (omitting only the friendly toast), and live more or less happily ever after. Although we did not lack for genuinely adulterous relationships, only those people young enough to believe in the tooth fairy or too old to care were assumed to be ignorant of the existence of professional co-respondents.

Initially meant to be simply one of seventeen segments, the interview with *Close-up*'s purported co-respondent proved to be, with very little editing, interesting enough to warrant a separate program, which senior staff decided to air first. All hell broke loose.

One Toronto newspaper dubbed the woman "The Shady Lady" and promptly proclaimed its painful public duty to find out who she was. The program touched off other, even more bizarre, events: the Attorney General of the day assigned his newest Crown attorney to find out whether The Shady Lady had been telling the truth. The young Crown attorney was unable to find evidence that the CBC's interviewee (eventually revealed as a young Toronto mother in the midst of her own divorce) had ever been a co-respondent in a single case, let alone on the 120 occasions she had claimed. His searches through old divorce files, however, did turn up one lawyer who was using pictures of an innocent client in order to concoct evidence of adultery in other cases and who was eventually disbarred and jailed.

The newspaper continued to attack the integrity of several people involved in *Close-up*, and watched circulation soar with each pious condemnation. Then the next sensation came along and the lady was pushed into the shade for good.

But the program and its aftermath had focussed attention on the hypocrisy of divorce law, and the subject moved centre stage in a way that had never occurred before. Canadians considered themselves amongst the world's most law-abiding citizens; we were delighted during the war, for example, when the New York *Daily News* ran a series describing how our honesty and national spirit of cooperation kept wartime inflation under control and limited black market activities. We prided ourselves on being cautious, responsible, decent – and modest about it all in the bargain.

By 1960, however, the fictitiousness of that description was becoming obvious, a portrait of Dorian Gray in which society appeared unblemished while it ignored the rot eating away beneath the surface. Arnold Peters, one of the CCF members leading the divorce filibuster, pointed out on the second *Close-up* show that "when a thousand people are caught in hotels or motels in Montreal in a year . . . there's something going on." He criticized parliamentary divorces for people in Quebec and Newfoundland as a system for the wealthy and spoke of less fortunate couples who had saved up for ten or twenty years in order to present their cases in Ottawa. Whatever the financial disadvantages of this system, Peters pointed out that couples who appealed to Parliament were able to sway members with the kind of evidence that divorce courts would not even permit lawyers to introduce. "Parliament does dissolve marriages for cruelty and neglect, though the records show adultery. In the [divorce courts of the] provinces, the judges have to stick to adultery."

Senator Arthur Roebuck, a former Attorney General of Ontario, Chairman of the Senate-Parliament Divorce Committee, a courtly octogenarian who was one of the House's most respected members, talked about the distance between the existing law and the real reasons people yearned for marital freedom: desertion, cruelty, insanity, life imprisonment. Arthur Maloney, then federal Member for a Toronto riding and later Ontario's first Ombudsman, explained that, as a devout Roman Catholic, he did not vote on bills of divorce because he found them "distasteful"; "I would like to see Parliament relieved of the obligation if you could work out something acceptable to Quebec and Newfoundland," he added.

That, of course, was a crucial constitutional issue; Quebec had joined Confederation with the assurance that it would not be forced to abandon its traditional refusal to set up divorce courts; it had permitted Ontario to set up a divorce court in 1930 and, perhaps, by 1960, it would not have obstructed modernization of the federal Divorce Act for other provinces. In any event, in another seven years a federal Justice Minister, who came from Quebec, would move to change the law of divorce.

Certainly, there were – and are – jurisdictional tangles in the laws concerning marriage and divorce. Under section 91 of the Constitution Act of 1982 (successor to the British North America Act of 1867), the federal government governs grounds for divorce and makes the rules defining the capacity to marry (i.e., those regulations, originating in the ancient Ecclesiastical

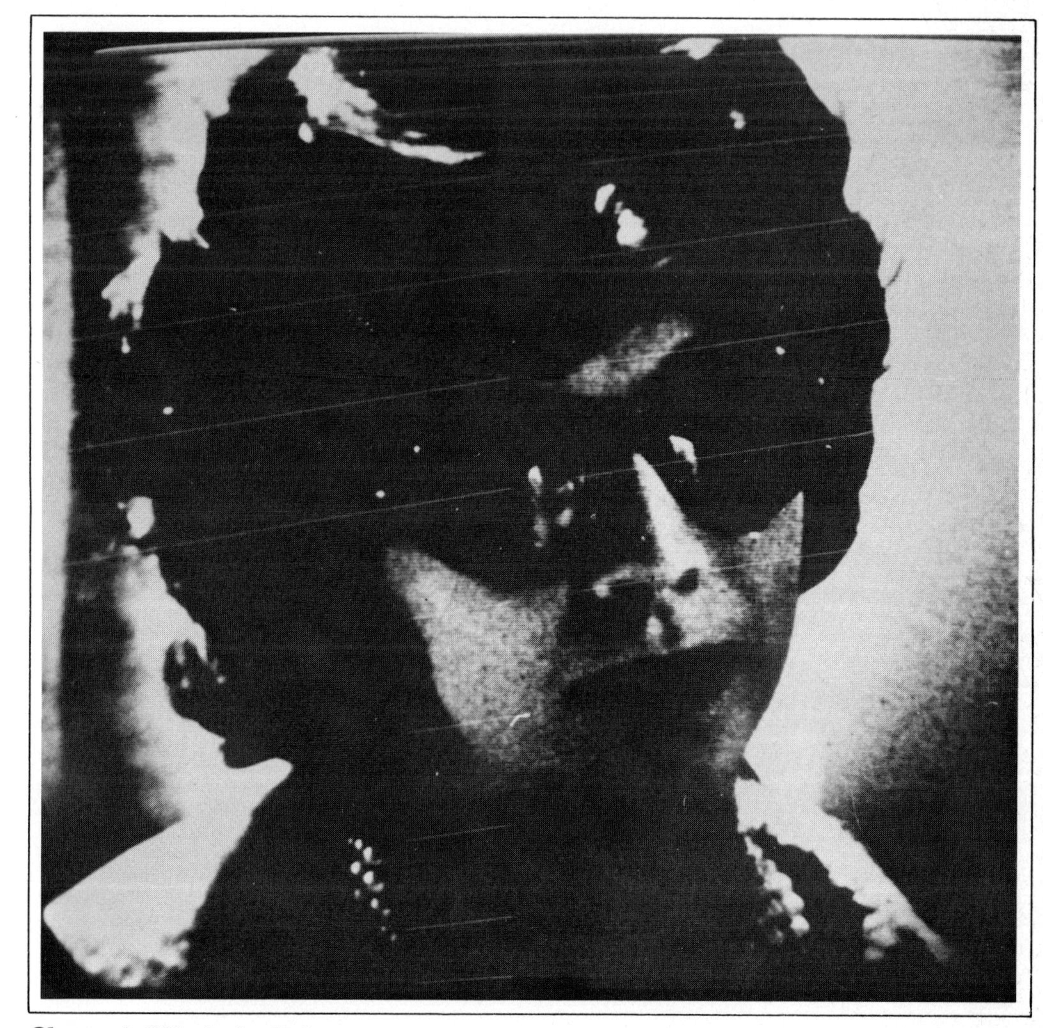

***Close-up's* "Shady Lady."**

The courtly and beloved Senator Arthur Roebuck.

Courts, that cover degrees of blood relationship, ability to consent, and so forth). The provinces have the right to decide who may solemnize a marriage, the precise subject of the Cartwright-Simcoe fight of early Upper Canada. It has been said that the federal government gets to decide on the beginning and the end of marriage and the provinces on everything in between.

Unfortunately, it is not quite that simple. Under section 96 of the Constitution Act, the federal government has the right to appoint judges to the senior courts (in Ontario, the District and Supreme courts). Only those judges are authorized to grant divorces; in addition to the dissolution of marriage, the federal Divorce Act covers support and custody, *if those are issues in the divorce suit.* Otherwise, support and custody decisions can be made by judges of several courts, including the Provincial Court (Family Division). And to further confuse matters, criteria for support are different under federal and provincial laws. In all, a person seeking a divorce, custody, and support might be heard by judges in one or possibly two from amongst three different courts.

But there is even more overlap: although a judge of the District or Supreme Court may make an order for support or custody, normally a judge of the Provincial Court (Family Division) enforces those orders. He or she cannot vary them, however. Furthermore, although provinces make laws regarding support and legislate the division of property when marriages end, a case involving a person's property rights must be heard by a section 96 judge. (Not surprisingly, some lawyers and judges admit to uncertainty about the effects of the most recent decisions in this complex area.)

If the reasons for the jurisdictional stew are difficult to comprehend, the results are not. They are: uncertainty, inconsistency, and, in earlier times, a reluctance by politicians to get caught up in the mess. Not a single act concerning the rules of marriage, custody, support, or divorce was passed, federally or provincially, between 1930 and 1968.

Finally, in 1967, the then-federal Minister of Justice, Pierre Trudeau, announced plans for an overhaul of the Divorce Act; the legislation, passed into law the following year, was based on some of the recommendations of a joint Senate-House Committee chaired by Senator Roebuck; it had heard submissions from various interested public bodies, many urging that any new rules end the adversarial process with its tradition of labelling one party "innocent" and the other "guilty."

Under the Act, however, the category of fault grounds was *expanded* to include disappearance or imprisonment for more than three years; non-consummation for at least a year; "gross addiction to alcohol or a narcotic"; participating in a bigamous form of marriage; "physical or mental cruelty of such a kind as to render intolerable the continued cohabitation of the spouses"; sodomy; bestiality; rape; or homosexuality.

A non-fault ground, marital breakdown leading to separation for at least three years, was added, but even it had an element of fault: the deserting spouse had to wait for five years before seeking a divorce, while the deserted spouse had to wait only three. Couples

In 1949 Canada's first public housing project was taking shape in the downtown Toronto slums. The Bluett family posed happily in their old and new homes – a telling contrast.

who separated by mutual consent could begin divorce proceedings after three years.

The traditional matrimonial offense of adultery was retained (and, along with it, another relic of the Ecclesiastical Courts of England, which treated adultery as a quasi-criminal activity. To this day, there is only one question in a Canadian court of law that a witness cannot be compelled to answer: "Did you commit adultery?").

The 1968 Act contained another important change: for the first time a divorce action could be instituted in the domicile of either partner, rather than just in the husband's place of domicile; gone were the days when a woman could be chained forever to a long-gone husband simply because she did not know where he lived or claimed domicile.

At last, thirty-eight years after Ontario's first divorce court and after 101 years of parliamentary divorce, there was a new Act. Characterizing its effects with absolute certainty is an exercise in futility, since they are so pervasive that they can be used to buttress almost any argument.

One result is unarguable: the Act unleashed a torrent of divorce cases. In contrast to the 6,000 Canadian couples who had so exercised *Close-up*'s host, five times that number sought divorces in 1970, two years after the new Act became law, and, in 1982, the figure was more than 70,000. Even in absolute terms, the increase was staggering: the divorce rate per 100,000 Canadians rose nearly 100 percent between 1972 and 1982.

(According to the 1981 census, in June of that year there was one couple cohabiting outside marriage for every sixteen who were married. If even more recent figures from the Alberta Institute of Law Research and Reform are true across Canada, the trend is gathering momentum: in the adult population of that province, one in every eight persons has been divorced; one in six is a former cohabitant outside marriage; and one in twelve currently lives in an unmarried relationship.)

The costs, however calculated, have been astronomical: 500,000 children have been affected by divorce proceedings since 1969; in fact, they are involved in half of all divorces. In the last ten years alone, Canadians extricating themselves from marriages have spent an estimated half-billion dollars just in legal fees.

Moreover, people divorce at an earlier age and earlier in the marriage: between 1969 and 1982 the average length of marriages ending in divorce declined from sixteen to twelve years. The numbers, however, do not necessarily establish a cause-and-effect relationship between marriage failure and liberalized divorce legislation. (It was just five years earlier, in 1963, that Betty Friedan's seminal treatise, *The Feminine Mystique,* was published, an event that neatly marks the beginning of the modern "feminist movement" in North America – and the beginning of all the emotional, economic, and cultural changes implied in that term.)

As it has turned out, 1968 is remembered more as the year of international political turmoil, the assassinations of Robert Kennedy and Martin Luther King, and the year in which the scope and horror of Vietnam were widely recognized for the first time. (A generation born only after the end of World War II now had its own reasons for

The Vietnam demonstrations continued throughout the '60s.

asking questions about the right of the state to enforce personal morality; many young Americans paid heavily for that right, choosing exile rather than obedience to their government's policy in Vietnam. Perhaps as many as 100,000 Americans, draft dodgers and their mates, came to Canada – the majority to Ontario. This was a new generation of Loyalists, committed not to any political system but to their own standards of ethical political behaviour.)

Ultimately, of course, the 1968 Divorce Act was not about making divorce easier, about discouraging or encouraging marriage, or even about changing its quality; it was not about feminism or any other cause, however just. It was an overdue recognition that the law, which has long protected the right of people to enter the state of marriage voluntarily, could not keep them there under legal duress, however disguised.

Despite the lack of legislative movement in family law after World War II, the field had not been entirely ignored. In 1948, for example, Walter Williston, a leading member of the Ontario bar, left one of Toronto's most exalted law firms to join Osgoode Hall as full-time faculty member under Dean C.W. Wright. The following year, Wright resigned to reopen the Faculty of Law at the University of Toronto (originally set up in the mid-1850s, but almost entirely dormant ever since).

In 1949, Williston began teaching family law in a separate course, the first in Canada; until then, it had been incorporated into other subjects. According to H. Allan Leal, later dean of Osgoode:

> . . . there simply was no perceived need to treat it separately until after World War II. Then there was a realization that – not just in family law, but elsewhere as well – the rules and principles, as set out, were out of whack with changing economic and social conditions, with the entire social reality; clearly, it was time to take another look. That conviction led to the establishment, for the first time, of a permanently based, adequately funded commission directed to bring law into the twentieth century in Ontario.

In 1964 Ontario passed the Law Reform Commission Act "for the purpose of promoting the reform of the law and legal institutions"; Leal became chairman of the commission, the first such body anywhere in the Commonwealth. (This move, like so many other pioneer steps in Ontario's legal system, would eventually affect other parts of Canada as well. For example, Quebec's Office of the Revision of the Civil Code began to make proposals for the reform of the matrimonial property system in that province; Alberta, Manitoba, and Sas-

katchewan set up reform commissions of their own; an English commission was formed in 1965; and in 1969 Ottawa established a Law Reform Commission that included the Honourable James McRuer, an original member of the Ontario body.)

The Law Reform Commission's first order of business was the establishment of the Family Law Reform project, a mammoth task that resulted in a six-volume report, issued between 1969 and 1975, recommending change to every aspect of the law as it affects the family, from the ancient concept of bastardy to the responsibility that family members bear each other in automobile accidents.

Because its job was so complex, the commission decided to start with relatively straightforward issues and move on to more difficult topics. It chose as its first the law of torts: those non-criminal wrongs people commit that injure others or damage property.

It was an appropriate beginning: many cases, especially those involving car accidents, showed that the traditional legal view of a couple's responsibility toward each other and between parents and children, as it was affected by torts, was badly outdated. Because the common law viewed husband and wife as one legal person, neither could sue the other for a tort – although the various married women's property acts had altered the concept enough to permit wives to sue in tort when husbands damaged or misused their property. Until the reforms passed in 1978, however, the legal liability of children and parents for damages against each other had always been unclear.

Members of a family, however, could sue nonmembers who were responsible for a death that resulted in lost family income; in the case of a wife's death, a husband could also take action for the "loss of consortium": guidance, care, replacing them, and an amount for loss of a wife's sexual services. The commission recommended that the law be extended to cover nonfatal as well as fatal accidents; that it will apply equally to husbands and wives (instead of to husbands only); and that parents, children, grandparents, grandchildren, and brothers and sisters be allowed to sue for the loss of guidance, care, and companionship.

It suggested, however, that a husband should no longer be able to sue for criminal conversation – the humiliating procedure establishing the sexual ownership of wife by husband that had so outraged Caroline Norton. It also urged that fathers should no longer be allowed to sue for "loss of services," a device for obtaining money when a daughter had been seduced.

Although it would take almost nine years before the recommendations regarding torts would be passed into law, all of the commission's suggestions, as published in 1969, were eventually adopted.

The second report, released in 1970, did not fare as well, perhaps because, in recommending that the age of marriage without consent should be different for men than for women, it was less in step with prevailing attitudes. The commission suggested that the minimum age (which had been fourteen and, for pregnant females, twelve), be raised to eighteen for men and sixteen for women. It viewed as "being extremely significant . . . the fact of the earlier attainment of physical and social maturity in women than in men" and gave, amongst its other reasons: "Because males, statistically, tend to marry persons younger than themselves; because it is essential that a young man shall have achieved a degree of emotional and financial independence and self-sufficiency . . ."

When the time came to frame the legislation, however, the Ministry rejected the idea that men needed a pool of younger women from amongst whom they could choose mates, or that they had needed more time to establish themselves financially. With very minor qualification, the law, as later presented and passed, set sixteen as the age for both sexes.

The second volume of the commission's study also recommended that, in addition to clergy and judges, the law permit court officials, court clerks, sheriffs, and municipal clerks to perform marriages; it saw this as one way to meet the needs of couples who did not want a religious ceremony but had difficulty finding judges with enough time to officiate at weddings. However, the law, when it was passed, extended only to justices of the peace (a group of minor judicial officials, usually not lawyers, whose responsibilities include issuing summonses and presiding over limited kinds of trials, including those related to parking and traffic offenses.)

There was another, very sweet, recommendation that did become part of the law: a man and wife could now repeat their wedding vows without going through all the legal formalities again. Previously, they had been trapped between the law's requirement that a license be issued before each wedding service and its refusal to grant marriage licenses to already married people.

In 1973 the Law Reform Commission published the third part of its report and it, more than anything else, represented a major departure from the old common law. Its most important recommendation is found in the opening section: "For all purposes of the law of Ontario, a person is the child of his or her natural parents, and his or her status as their child is independent of whether the child is born within or outside marriage."

And in those few dry phrases, enacted in 1977 and in force since 1978, the Province of Ontario, by the stroke of the legislative pen, abolished bastardy. The mean-spirited concept of *filius nullius,* the hoary lie that had cloaked penny-pinching in a mantle of virtue, disappeared. The law now acknowledged what common sense should always have known: "illegitimacy" is a description of a grown-up relationship used to brand a child. Canadians living outside Ontario must be ashamed that, to this day, no other province has adopted similar legislation.

Paternity, however, is an issue separate from legitimacy, since it is necessary to establish the identity of the child's father in order to seek child support from him. Under the law that existed until the reforms were adopted, a mother would apply for an affiliation order that named the father and required him to support the child (but not the mother). They were difficult orders to obtain: the mother had to apply within two years of her baby's birth and she needed corroborating evidence of paternity. Generally, witnesses would swear that the couple had spent time together under circumstances that implied they had "opportunity and inclination" to have sexual relations. The cases were unpleasant and research suggests that the evidence of all parties before the court was unreliable.

Today, as the result of changes recommended by the commission, either the mother sues on the child's behalf or the child sues in his or her own right. In trying to establish paternity, a court may now order the mother, father, and the child to have blood tests; any of the parties can refuse, since the legislation does not make tests mandatory. Judges, however, do have the right to draw a negative inference from such a refusal or by the same token may give little weight to blood test results.

Volume three also tackled the difficult problems of custody and access to children: since 1855, when women were given their first, grudging custody and access rights, the law had stopped viewing children as their father's chattels and had begun to understand that they were separate human beings with discrete needs and interests, and to base decisions on what were deemed to be "in the child's best interests." Theoretically admirable, the principle was deeply flawed in practice because of a tendency by judges to apply their own rules of thumb: "children of tender years" (i.e., seven or less) were better off in the custody of their mothers, but older boys should live with their fathers, and so on.

The use of the "best interests of the child" doctrine as a judicial guide had been strengthened by a 1951 Privy Council decision in the case of an American couple named McKee. In 1946, Mr. McKee had brought his six-year-old son to Kitchener, Ontario, after losing his final legal appeal against a California court decision giving custody of the boy to his mother. Once Mrs. McKee located them, she began a fight for the youngster's return which ended five years later in London, England; there, on March 15, 1951, the Privy Council overturned the Supreme Court verdict and gave Mr. McKee custody.

The Councillors held that the decision hinged on the need to act "in the best interests of the child," which, according to the majority, lay with the father. By then, they pointed out, the boy had lived most of his life with his father and barely knew his mother. However unintended, the somewhat less lofty subtext of the decision, of course, is that kidnapping, if successful long enough, overturns court custody rulings.

The McKee case did, however, establish clearly that the child had interests that might not coincide with that of a parent. The Law Reform Commission went even further and said that judges "should ascertain the wishes of the child if the child is capable of having and expressing wishes and should take account of them to the extent to which the court thinks fit, having regard to the age and maturity of the child." That became part of child welfare law in 1978 (and was later incorporated into the Children's Law Reform Act, 1982, as a specific requirement in custody decisions).

By the time the Law Reform Commission's next volume appeared, the process of reform had begun to sharpen and, to some degree, alter public perceptions of family law. And it was in 1974, while public consultations on the commission's recommendations were under way, that Canadians learned just how much women suffered economically in Canada when their marriages ended: the Murdoch case.

The undisputed facts: Irene and Jim Murdoch, who lived in Turner Valley, Alberta, had been married for twenty-five years when they separated in 1968; both were hard-working ranchers. Mrs. Murdoch did the usual farm chores; in addition, she hayed, raked, mowed; she branded, vaccinated, and drove cattle; she worked alongside her husband to a degree that freed him from the necessity of hiring a hand and, during Mr. Murdoch's frequent illnesses, carried on even without his help.

When she sued for half-interest in their property, cattle, and other assets, both the lower and the higher courts of Alberta found against Irene Murdoch; she then appealed to the Supreme Court of Canada. The verdict of the majority came down to this: Mrs. Murdoch was not entitled to a cent of the value of the property; they agreed with the judge who first heard the case that she had not made "a direct financial contribution" to the ranch and that "what [she] had done, while living with [her husband], was the work done by any ranch wife." (Of the five Supreme Court judges who heard Murdoch v. Murdoch, only one, the late Chief Justice Bora Laskin, disagreed, and he suggested past cases that could be construed as supporting the wife's side.)

Irene Murdoch.

Mr. Justice Bora Laskin.

There was a particularly infuriating irony in the outcome: if the Murdochs had *not* been married – if she had been, legally, a "stranger" – Mrs. Murdoch would have almost certainly wound up with her portion. The state, which traditionally supports marriage as a stable form of social organization, was now defining it as a term of slavery: as a wife, Mrs. Murdoch was expected to hoe, mow, dehorn, brand (and cook, clean, and bear and raise children), with no hope of a share of the property when the marriage ended.

It was the kind of injustice that mobilized public opinion about family law in a way that had never occurred before in Canada and that probably has its only precedent in the mid-Victorian furor that surrounded the Nortons. In their outrage, people wrote an avalanche of letters to press and government. As Craig Perkins, Ontario's senior policy adviser on family law, recalls:

> It was on everyone's mind as few court cases in Canada – other than sensational murder trials – have ever been.
>
> It seemed to come at just the "right" moment: everybody's attention was focussed on issues of justice to women, thanks to the work of the Royal Commission on the Status of Women. The federal divorce reform legislation had passed only six years earlier and divorce rates were beginning to rise sharply; suddenly, a lot of people worried that they might be affected someday. That was very different from the attitude just a few years earlier, when almost nobody knew someone who was divorced; now most people did and they also knew of the bitterness, the unfairness, the economic hardship under which women lived. Put that together with consciousness-raising and you had a furious response.

The ongoing consultations on law reform in Ontario made it clear that the province would have to enact its own legislation if it wanted to thwart future "Murdochs." In anticipation of the completed reform process, the Attorney General of the day, John Clement, asked members of his staff to draw up a minimal legislative proposal that would provide safeguards, at least until and if the Legislature later decided on more extensive reform.

The result was the Family Law Reform Act, 1975. First, it abolished the common-law doctrine that a husband and wife were to be regarded as one person, the theoretical underpinning of Murdoch. Second, while it militated against the interests of some women, the new Act also abolished presumption of inequality, a law that permitted husbands to make gifts of property to their wives, either jointly or as sole owner, but, at the same time, insisted that the properties wives put in their husbands' names, either jointly or solely, were intended not as gifts but only as trusts to be held and managed prudently.

The underpinning of the old law was society's view that women are flighty and unable to make binding decisions; the new one accepted, instead, the equal ability of husband and wife to make their intentions clear when making a gift. There was another significant change: if a property was held in both names, the law assumed that each person was owner of a half. Until then, a spouse (usually the husband) could avoid paying creditors by purporting that a piece of property held in both names was not his and, at the same time, avoid paying his wife by insisting that it was.

Third, the Act specifically drove a narrow, negatively worded stake through the heart of future Murdochs by stating that one spouse who contributed work, money, or money's worth to the property of the other was not disentitled to an interest in property simply because he or she was the spouse of that property's owner. ("Money's worth" is the provision of goods or services other than work: for example, trading in the wife's old car and using the proceeds toward buying a tractor.) In other words, in case there still was any doubt, the law of Ontario no longer held that married couples shared a single legal identity. The 1975 Family Law Reform Act was so far-reaching that the Attorney General was convinced that no further reform would ever be needed. Events would shortly prove him wrong.

In the meantime, however, attention focussed on the next volume of the Law Reform Commission's Report, which was published in 1974, in the aftermath of Murdoch; coincidentally, it recommended a total rethinking of the division of property at the end of marriage, a topic that would prove the most contentious of all and that, unlike the other recommendations, would require *two* major rewrites of the law.

The commission wanted fundamental change: anything acquired before marriage would continue to belong solely to

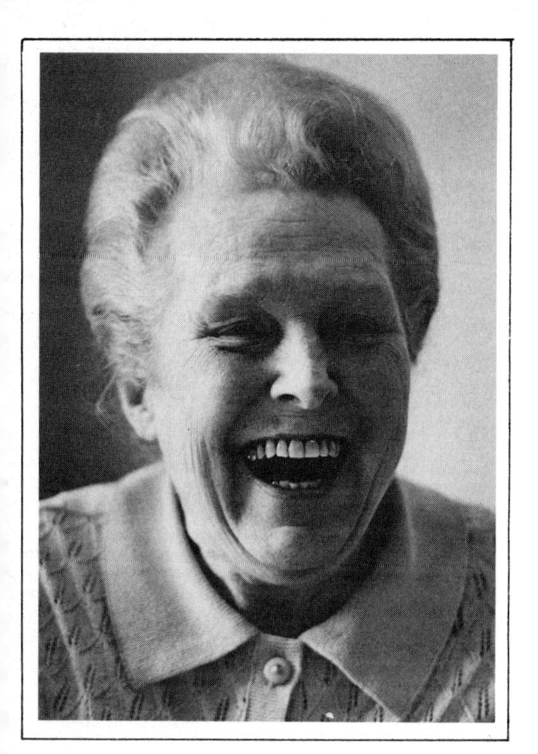

Margaret Campbell.

its owner and a married couple would still be entitled to acquire and dispose of assets separately; however, once a marriage ended (whether by separation, divorce, or death), the value of all the assets they had amassed – pensions, stocks, farms, the family home, furniture, cars, businesses, professional practices, vacation properties – would be divided equally; in fact, the courts would have virtually no discretion in matters of equal sharing. (This concept is known variously as "deferred community in property," "deferred sharing," or, in Quebec, "partnership of acquests.")

The only exceptions would be gifts, inheritances, or settlements for personal injury (but not for property damage). The other exception would be the matrimonial home, which could be held in the name of either party or in both their names, but, when marriage ended, would be considered to belong to both, irrespective of when it had been bought and by whom.

The commission also proposed that couples should share in any *gain in the value or the income of assets* acquired before marriage – not the asset itself, but the increase in value or income since the marriage. Here is how that kind of property division would affect the hypothetical Mr. Smith, who is a partner in an accounting firm, and his wife, who is a lawyer. If they separate, all their assets belong equally to them both and each is required to obtain an evaluation of their professional practices.

Smith is older, has been in business longer, and, since the marriage, his firm has *increased in value* by $200,000. Mrs. Smith's legal partnership has also become more valuable, although only $100,000 *more* than it was before she married. Each is entitled to one-half the *increased value* of the other's firm – Smith to $50,000 and Mrs. Smith to $100,000 – leaving him owing Mrs. Smith $50,000. (Apparently, there is an unending need to emphasize the difference between dividing an asset and dividing its increased value; ten years after the commission's report, newspapers were still having trouble grasping the concept. In December, 1985, one headline warned: "New Ontario laws forcing divorcing couples to split almost everything they own . . ." and an editorial shrilled that ". . . a spouse who runs off with a lover is still entitled to an equal share of the partner's business, pension, savings plan or farm.")

In reality, the commission recommended that, to prevent forced sales of assets to pay off debts, payments between spouses should be made in instalments over a period of time.

The commission also recognized that couples might misrepresent their finances to each other; to prevent financial loss resulting from a spouse's negligence or misstatements (failing, for example, to reveal the existence of business debts), it provided that one spouse would sue the other to protect property.

During public consultations that took place between the publication of the recommendations and the writing of new family law legislation, it became clear that there was strong opposition to deferred sharing: a few women and several vociferous men's groups objected, and, in order to ensure passage of the long-overdue reforms, the idea was shelved. Moreover, many of those involved were sure that it would become law in the not too distant future – an optimistic belief that eventually proved to be out by more than a decade.

The property provisions of the 1978 Family Law Reform Act, therefore, were limited to the treatment of family assets (the matrimonial home, furnishings, the cottage, or anything else both partners used), which were presumed to be owned equally when a marriage was ended by separation or divorce, but not by death.

Three provinces found other ways of tackling the division-of-property problem: Manitoba and Saskatchewan took action to protect farm women – which was not surprising since they, like Mrs.

Murdoch's native Alberta, have many farm communities and both were directly affected by her plight and by the public reaction to it. However, the new laws themselves caused a great deal of controversy: in Manitoba, there were demonstrations on the steps of the Manitoba Legislature, first by men when NDP Premier Ed Schreyer passed an Act that divided all types of property when a marriage ended, and then by women when the Conservative government of Stirling Lyon repealed it even before it could come into force.

Eventually, a compromise bill became law in Manitoba; unlike the original, it gives courts a great deal of discretion in deciding whether to divide assets equally (in cases, for example, where marriage lasts only a short time). Recently, Saskatchewan's Law Reform Commission has been urging that the province's property act, which is much like Manitoba's, be weakened to exempt any farm brought into a marriage or the increased value of such a farm – a move that would open up holes large enough to swallow the Murdoch decision whole.

In Quebec, the civil code has always been a North American anomaly because it is based, not on the old common law of England, but on the Napoleonic Code that came into force after the French Revolution. Intended to reflect revolutionary ideals of equality, it included community of property, which turned out in practice to stress the *fraternité* and forget the *égalité*. In order to protect themselves from their husbands, therefore, wives living under the Napoleonic Code have traditionally obtained marriage contracts.

In 1970, Quebec brought in "partnership of acquests," which permits a wife to keep and manage property she has bought herself; when marriage ends, however, any marital assets not covered by a marriage contract are evenly divided.

While the public was still arguing over its property recommendations, the Law Reform Commission released the fifth part of its report, on the family courts themselves. The courts volume, while it may have seemed of interest only within the legal community, actually contained far-reaching recommendations that could affect the way family courts are set up, judges are appointed, and families are treated. It urged that a single court, which would include both section 96 and provincially appointed judges, be given jurisdiction for all family law in Ontario. That recommendation, combined with recommendations of the federal Law Reform Commission, led to the Hamilton Unified Family Court, which was established in 1977 and still functions as a possible model for the future. (Prince Edward Island's Supreme Court has jurisdiction in all areas of family law; British Columbia has made a partial attempt to initiate one unified court; and there are projects in Newfoundland, Manitoba, and Saskatchewan.)

The Hamilton court is, in many ways, a great success; it makes the system simpler by offering all family law-related services in one building: the courts, conciliators, intake workers, and legal-aid duty counsel for child welfare and domestic assault cases. The court also maintains links to community-based services such as therapy, marital counselling, battered women's shelters, and other social agencies.

The federal and provincial governments consult on choosing judges for Hamilton, but, in order to ensure that they have the widest possible authority to hear cases, actual appointments are made by the federal government under section 96.

After nearly a decade, there is no indication that the unified family court will become standard. There are still many problems – economic and jurisdictional – to be solved. One stumbling block, of course, is political: governments do not easily give up their right to make appointments, especially appointments to the bench.

Whatever the eventual outcome of the Hamilton experiment, the immutable reality is that no court is better than its judges and that few judges are better than the system by which they are chosen. In Canada today, although bar committees are consulted about appointments, they complain of being asked the wrong question: is this person (or political supporter or personal pal) qualified?, rather than: is *this* the best person for the job?

Furthermore, if politicians treat the bench as a reward, they are tempted to assume that appointees to lower courts are not "owed" the opportunities for advancement that judges, like other professionals, need if they are going to stay involved in their careers. (And, without such opportunities, the best-qualified people will be reluctant to serve.)

In 1975, six years after the publication of its first volume, the Law Reform Commission released its sixth and final report, on support and maintenance; its recommendations were adopted almost in their entirety when the Family Law Reform Act of 1978 was passed.

The commission recommended and the Act said that, unless behaviour causes financial harm (i.e., a wrench is thrown into a threshing machine), courts, as a rule, should treat it separately from support, since needs are more relevant in determining support than such marital misconduct as adultery or cruelty.

The Act also permitted men, for the first time, to sue their wives for support – as the federal Divorce Act has since 1968. In order to further rationalize some of the jurisdictional tangle that had overgrown family law, the commission urged the federal government to repeal the maintenance and custody sections that had been written into the 1968 Divorce Act in response to then-outmoded provincial statutes. (At that time, Ottawa maintained that there was a need for uniform support standards that only the federal law could provide; by limiting itself to custody and maintenance matters only as they form part of a successful divorce petition, the federal government acts within its constitutional jurisdiction. Now, the commission said, it was time to leave those areas to the provinces, which have jurisdiction over all other aspects of family law. The new Divorce Act, however, retains and expands the custody and maintenance provisions of the 1968 statute.)

In the last volume of its report, the Ontario Law Reform Commission reiterated its stand on abolishing bastardy by recommending that support for children should be equally available in or out of marriage. It also urged that the law drop the offensive *dum casta* clause, which stipulated that a woman was entitled to support only as long as she remained chaste after the marriage ended. From the Latin *dum casta et sola vixerit* – as long as she shall live, chaste and alone – the clause meant that a man could control his wife's body even *after* they were no longer married. Although the courts no longer used it in their decisions, it was still a feature of some separation agreements.

With the completion, at least for the time being, of its monumental task of rethinking family law, the Law Reform Commission turned its attention elsewhere; within the Ministry of the Attorney General, the question of writing recommendations into law was now well under way.

It was almost exactly at that moment, on October 9, 1975, that Roy McMurtry, a forty-three-year-old lawyer, former guard and linebacker for the University of Toronto's football squad, was sworn in as the twenty-sixth Attorney General to serve in Ontario since Confederation.

A practiced civil litigation lawyer, McMurtry had had clients with family problems, including many women who had suffered under the existing law, and he was determined to use his new role to push for family law reform. Rather than moving cautiously, McMurtry decided to grab what might be his only chance ("There could be another election before long and I had no idea whether I would be back," he remembers) and he began a campaign that lasted for the rest of his Legislative career. Fortunately, the issue seemed certain to gain all-party support in the minority House; most New Democrats favoured new legislation and many Liberals were enthusiastic, most significantly that party's justice critic, Margaret Campbell.

The husky-voiced, outspoken Campbell is an experienced lawyer as well as a successful mystery writer and part of the first generation of influential female politicians in Toronto's history. A veteran of City Council's powerful Board of Control, Campbell was the first woman ever to make a serious bid to become Toronto's mayor – the only election she ever lost. A family court judge after she left City Hall and before entering provincial politics, Campbell would play a small but crucial role in what became the very lengthy process of enacting new family law legislation.

It quickly became clear to the new Attorney General that, although his colleagues would support a reform solution, they believed that the property division recommended by the Law Reform Commission was politically dangerous. The first job, then, was to find a formula that *would* get through the Legislature.

Members of the Ministry's policy development staff laid out two possible options: either maintain the status quo (the English system of making decisions without any defined guidelines) or distinguish between family and business assets and divide family assets only. The first alternative was unsatisfactory: aside from the enormous number of cases that had to be litigated, it hardly qualified as "reform." The second, suggested by Karen Weiler (who had run the public consultation program and is now a District Court judge), was less than what McMurtry favoured personally but, he says, he recognized that

> . . . it was important to have a reasonable level of support in the community generally; otherwise, courts find ways of frustrating the intention of legislation. In the long run, the most important issue was to diminish the adversarial content of marriage breakdown, to bring a greater degree of certainty to the process, and to encourage early settlements.

The new legislation did follow the commission's recommendation for protecting the matrimonial home (usually the family's largest single asset); although either spouse could own it, the home could be sold or mortgaged only with the consent of both partners.

That requirement replaces the dower right, another of those concepts that reach back into history, this one more than a thousand years, before the Norman Conquest. The English adopted dower from the Saxons and we in turn got it in 1792 as part of the received law of England; over time, it was codified in a statute known as the Dower Act.

Perhaps its very antiquity explains why a mythology, based mainly on misinformation about its meaning, now covers dower like a soft moss; certainly, some people were alarmed when they discovered that it had been abolished by the Family Law Reform Act. In reality, dower was simply the right of a widow to receive a life interest in *one-third* of the land to which her husband held legal title at any time during his life or to which he held equitable title at the time of his death.

In lay terms, this meant that a woman had the right to remain on a part of her husband's property as long as she lived – but she could not leave it to anyone, nor could she mortgage it beyond her own lifetime – an essentially useless form of ownership since no one would mortgage or buy a piece of property from a person whose right to it died with her.

In modern times, dower continued to permit a widow to live on her husband's property or, in addition, to obtain a sum of money for giving up her right to do so – which sounds pretty good: a townhouse in a large city, after all, worth, let us say, $150,000, meant that her third interest was $50,000. Right? Wrong. She was entitled to only *a third of a life interest*; the courts held that, actuarily, chances were fifty-fifty that a woman would die within eighteen years of her husband, even if she were very young, and it computed her life interest at no more than eighteen years.

That being the case, judges estimated the value of a lease of the property, multiplied by no more than eighteen, and awarded most of the result to the wife. First, however, they subtracted from that amount the interest that the money would have earned if it had been invested for that many years. By the time the dust and arithmetic had settled, there was not much left for a widow, especially one with a young family.

There was another dower-related myth as well: that somehow a woman's dower interest prevented her husband from buying, selling, or mortgaging property. In fact, however, he could get around her refusal to "bar her dower" by having the purchaser pay a portion of the sale money into court to represent the wife's dower interest. She could certainly get that money – when her husband died.

A husband could also frustrate the supposed protection of the dower right by buying property as a nominal trustee for a third person named by him. The property was then considered a trust not subject to his wife's dower rights. Or he could put a mortgage on the property before taking the transfer of the ownership (simply by registering the mortgage immediately before registering the deed); that made the mortgage company, not the husband, the legal title holder (even if the mortgage was for only one dollar) and, again, meant that the wife was unable to collect her dower interest.

(Although the concept of dower has been abolished, the 1986 Family Law Act did resurrect one of the dower rights, adapted to modern circumstances: on the death of either spouse, the survivor has a right to remain in the matrimonial home, without charge, for sixty days.)

The Family Law Reform Act's prohibition against one spouse selling or mortgaging the matrimonial home without the permission of the other (except by court order) makes up in economic equality whatever it lacks in romance. Recently, an Ontario appeal court ruled that a mortgage company had access to sufficient knowledge of a man's circumstances and, therefore, should have known that it needed a proper signature from his wife before giving him a mortgage. As a result, the court said that the company could not collect from the wife and had to make a personal claim against its client, who had forged his wife's signature to the mortgage papers, collected the proceeds, and left the country.

Aside from complex property matters, there were other aspects of the commission's report that had to be turned into legislation. The Minister and his staff decided to bring the proposals to the Legislature in three packages: the first to deal with children, the second with wills and estates (which had been a related but separate Law Reform Commission project), and the third with matrimonial property and support. Passage of all of them seemed a foregone conclusion; the only likely criticism was that the third did not go far enough.

In the spring of 1976 the first proposals for a new Family Law Reform Act were presented to the Ontario Cabinet's Justice Policy Committee, which gave them its fullest support. However, because the proposed laws would affect the status of children outside marriage and the ability of women to collect support (both of which would affect welfare recipients), the Social Development Committee was invited to review the bills.

At that point, opposition began to mount from both politicians and civil servants worried that it would be costly to bring child and family welfare benefits into line with the new laws (if, for example, either parent – rather than the mother only – could obtain support for a child, whether or not born in marriage).

There was a five-month delay while the Social Development Committee studied implications of the proposals; in the meantime, religious leaders were meeting with both the Premier and the Attorney General to discuss support obligations between persons living together outside of marriage (so-called "common-law unions" – a misnomer, since the common law has never recognized those relationships). The bill imposed responsibility for support on couples who live together continuously "in a conjugal relationship" for five years or who have had a child in a union that had some degree of permanence.

In July, 1976, a white paper was prepared for presentation to the Cabinet; in August, McMurtry invited Cabinet colleagues to discuss the issues directly with his officials, and was pleasantly surprised afterward when he was asked to draw up legislation as soon as possible.

Although members of the clergy were satisfied that the law was not encouraging nonmarital relationships, the possible public and political reaction to even limited recognition of cohabiting made careful management of the bills vital; a timetable was worked out to present the legislation in October. For the next eight weeks Ministry officials worked frenetically, not just to write the actual acts, but to write a book that would explain what was being proposed. McMurtry was determined that the bill would be preceded by a preamble (relatively rare these days) because he wanted to clarify the philosophy behind the legislation: the family is still the basic social unit, but marriage is an economic partnership. McMurtry held out against those who worried that a preamble would only provide more grounds for legal wrangling. As finally written, it said:

> Whereas, it is desirable to encourage and strengthen the role of the family in society;
>
> And Whereas for that purpose it is necessary to recognize the equal position of spouses as individuals within marriage and to recognize marriage as a form of partnership;
>
> And Whereas in support of such recognition it is necessary to provide in law for the orderly and equitable settlement of the affairs of the spouses upon the breakdown of the partnership; and to provide for other mutual obligations in family relationships, including the equitable sharing by parents of responsibility for their children . . .

And the various provisions of the Act followed.

On October 26, 1976, the Honourable Roy McMurtry rose in the House and introduced the children's law reform, succession reform, and family law reform bills.

No one could have known, on that heady day, that it would take nearly two years to bring family law into the twentieth century and that those years would be filled with mornings of elation and nights of despair.

In November the three bills were read a second time and referred to the Legislature's Standing Committee on the Administration of Justice, under the chairmanship of NDP Member Ed Phillip. Although public hearings were held quickly, it became apparent that there was insufficient time to complete consideration of the legislation before the House rose for the Christmas holidays.

A new session was scheduled for the spring of 1977 and, in its earliest days, bills 6, 7, and 8, as they were now numbered, were reintroduced in a single day by the Attorney General. This time they died on the order paper when the Legislature was dissolved and an election called.

After the election (of a second Conservative minority) the House resumed sitting in June, the bills were reintroduced, and two, the Children's Law Reform Act and the Succession Law Reform Act, were passed.

The Succession Law Reform Act made several basic changes to the law of wills and estates, some affecting families: first, it expanded the definition of what assets in an estate the courts could include when giving financial relief to dependent survivors and, second, it permitted surviving cohabitors and children of unmarried parents to sue as dependents.

The Children's Law Reform Act (which appeared in two parts, the second of which passed in 1982) was packed with ideas that family law had never before contained. For example, it encouraged mediation, a concept of negotiating custody and support settlements, using "helping" professionals, before going to court. It also urged the use of modern assessment techniques as a way of evaluating children's needs and helping judges make decisions that are genuinely "in the best interest of the child." (Mediation and assessment, which are costly, are now used most frequently by middle-class families who know about such services and can afford them.)

The Act, for the first time in Canada, set out factors that clarify "the best interests of the child": continuity of care, stability, the desire of each parent to take responsibility for the child, his or her emotional and financial ability to do so.

Gone are the rules of thumb ("tender years," "a boy needs a father") that, at best, are only general; instead, judges were given guidelines to be applied on a case-by-case basis, placing parents on an equal footing before the law. (Although there have been complaints that custody decisions still overwhelmingly favour mothers, there is no clear-cut evidence that this is actually so; in an admittedly small sample, an American survey showed that, when parents fight for custody, fathers win more frequently than mothers.)

The biggest impact of the Children's Law Reform Act, however, has been that it enforces custody orders and reduces childnapping by the non-custodial parent. Now, courts in one province respect orders made in another; moreover, as only one of four countries that have signed and ratified the Hague Convention on international kidnapping (France, Portugal, and Switzerland are the others), Canada has served notice that it will enforce custody decisions made elsewhere in the world.

Within Ontario itself, judges have tough new powers to ensure that a custody decision in favour of one parent is not willfully annulled by the other. A judge may order police to recover a child and can force a parent suspected of planning to abduct a child to deposit a passport and/or substantial sums of money with the court.

By the same token, the parent who has custody is expected to obey access orders: a judge of the Provincial Court (Family Division), sitting in Toronto, recently sentenced a mother to several weeks in jail when she repeatedly refused to allow the children's father to exercise rights to access that the court had granted him.

Encouraged by the fact that two of the three bills in the reform package were now law, the Attorney General reintroduced the Family Law Reform Act in the fall of 1977; it was referred once more to the Standing Committee, and, as another Christmas and the end of another session approached, failure again began to seem likely.

McMurtry, however, was determined not to let the issue, and the legislation, die. With the cooperation of members from both opposition parties, the House unanimously passed an unprecedented special resolution that kept the Family Law Reform Act alive; the resolution also authorized the Standing Committee to hold meetings in order to consider the bill after the end of the session. And, in the same generous spirit, it speeded up the process by stating that, on the first day of the new session (which opened in March, 1978) the bill would be deemed to have been reintroduced, given second reading, and referred to the Standing Committee of Justice.

(A special resolution is hardly the stuff of headlines but, it was, in fact, a rare courtesy in a group that jealously guards parliamentary rules and its own prerogatives; moreover, the spirit of cooperation was a noticeable contrast to the tense partisanship that had characterised the successive minorities.)

The Justice Committee met and heard more briefs in February, 1978, and began clause-by-clause study of the legislation, completed in early March. It then reported to the House, normally the last step prior to third reading of a bill. But, on this occasion, uncertainty about the implications of the legislation resulted in a decision to send it for further detailed study to the House sitting as a Committee of the Whole.

Some members believed that the delay doomed the Family Law Reform Act and it certainly gave people time for second thoughts; New Democrats were beginning to get signals from members of the public that the property provisions did not go far enough and that women's organizations, especially, were displeased. Twenty months had passed since the introduction of the legislation and the need to get it through was increasingly urgent, before members got bored or irritated with considering the same problems again and again. McMurtry decided to talk again with Margaret Campbell, the single strongest woman member of the Legislature, who still had reservations about the bill.

The two agreed that Campbell and her legal adviser (who had been a member of both the Ontario and the federal law reform commissions) would meet with McMurtry's staff and with Arthur Stone, senior counsel of the Legislature, in order to fine-tune some of the wording of the Family Law Reform Act.

The result, contained in sections 4(5) and 4(6), are known historically as "the Campbell amendments." The first emphasized the principle of dividing property, recognizing the contributions of the spouses as equal, even though those contributions might take different forms. The second gave effect to the first by permitting the division of non-family assets when a spouse made an indirect contribution to their acquisition. In essence, "the Campbell amendments" clarified the legislation by

Municipally operated day care, which became common in the '60s and '70s, began modestly in Toronto's Bellevue Day Nursery, whose first class, in 1943, included this serious young *artiste*.

providing a blunter instrument to ensure that sharing resulted from its various provisions.

On Thursday, March 16, the debate was beginning to wind down; the NDP had moved a series of amendments (most related to deferred sharing) that had already been rejected by the other parties in the Standing Committee on Justice. Before adjourning on Friday, March 17, 1978, the Legislature of Ontario passed the Family Law Reform Act, to come into effect precisely two weeks later.

Jubilant members of the Attorney General's staff convened in a restaurant at the Sutton Place Hotel, a block from the Legislature, and celebrated the beginning of a new era of family law in Ontario.

For the next four years Ontario was considered a North American leader in the field of family law, and it appeared that even the compromise on division of assets would not pose a serious problem. In fact, some judges were interpreting the law quite liberally and their decisions might, in time, have led to the more equitable sharing of nonfamily assets favoured by the Attorney General, the Law Reform Commission, and some politicians and women's groups.

And then, just before Christmas, 1982, the Supreme Court of Canada released its first judgement under the Family Law Reform Act: the Leatherdale case.

Mr. and Mrs. Leatherdale, a Toronto couple who had been married for nearly twenty years, separated in 1979 and were subsequently divorced. By the time they appeared in court, they had reached agreement on the custody of their only child and on all other issues except the ownership of two assets held in Mr. Leatherdale's name: Bell Canada stock and a registered retirement savings plan that had been purchased from the proceeds of a sale of some Bell stock; Mr. Leatherdale was a Bell employee and the company had deducted payments at source from his wages.

But, except for ten years she spent keeping house and rearing their child, Mrs. Leatherdale had always worked outside the home. She felt, and the trial judge agreed, that she was entitled to an amount equivalent to half the value of those two assets. Mr. Leatherdale appealed to the Ontario Court of Appeal, which held that Mrs. Leatherdale was not entitled to a cent of the value of either the Bell stock or the RRSP.

She appealed to the Supreme Court of Canada, which gave her a quarter of the value of the disputed property. In the decision, written by the Chief Justice (usually a signal that the matter is considered particularly important), Bora Laskin said that, since Mrs. Leatherdale had worked outside the home for half the life of the marriage, she was entitled to only half of a half of the value of the nonfamily assets.

That reasoning was actually consistent with the 1978 Family Law Reform Act, under which nonfamily assets were to be shared only if "the court is of the opinion that a division of the family assets in equal shares would be inequitable, having regard to . . ." (It then listed various factors, including the length of time the couple lived together, the length of time they have been apart, how the property was acquired, and so on.) The Supreme Court found no evidence that the Leatherdales' division of their family assets resulted in an inequity that would necessitate a division of the RRSP and pension, which were nonfamily assets. The decision was a stark reminder that labelling some assets divisible and some not was still distorting the actual value of the homemaker's contribution to the family's finances.

(While it failed to acknowledge that a wife's housework increased the family's ability to acquire assets, Leatherdale did recognize that a wife's earnings, used for the family, contributed to them. That, at least, was a step in the right direction – until Leatherdale, the courts had held that the contribution had to be directly to the given asset, i.e., with *that* cheque she bought *that* chair and had a clear right to *it*.)

The Leatherdale decision aroused a storm of criticism, much smaller than the one that had followed Murdoch, but a storm nonetheless. Suddenly the limitations of the Family Law Reform Act were obvious. The Ontario Status of Women Council, in a brief to a Ministry group reviewing family law reform, supported the Law Reform Commission's original recommendations. The Canadian Bar Association, Family Law Section, however, was less certain: its eighteen-person committee was divided almost exactly down the middle and it set the issue aside.

Other cases continued to focus attention on weaknesses in both the federal and the provincial legislation, especially as they relate to support and property issues. Furthermore, as time passed, the pattern of court decisions was, if anything, narrowing the intent of the

Family Law Reform Act. The trend was pinpointed by Frances Gregory, a legal author, in a paper arguing that the goal of maintenance (which still most often takes the form of money from a husband to a wife) should be to provide financial security for a former spouse, not to rehabilitate her.

Gregory's paper says that "rehabilitation" (usually through time-limited support orders) is not realistic in today's society and gives several major reasons for that conclusion: first, Gregory argues, marriage is an equal partnership in which the unpaid labour of one should be viewed, not as making her dependent on the other, but as having created interdependency that benefits all members of the family.

Moreover, as a housewife, a woman creates assets for the husband that will outlast the marriage (his career, for example) while she is creating liabilities for herself that will also outlast the marriage (especially, Gregory says, in a world where women who are "expected to become self-sufficient after marriage breakdown face the same discrimination as all women, plus the disadvantages of lost seniority, accumulated experiences, pension rights and technological fluency."). Furthermore, the true costs to the custodial parent (usually the mother) are never calculated accurately to include her labour, even if expenses are shared. Finally, Gregory says, maintenance decisions are made on the basis of a genuine economic equality between the sexes that does not exist in reality.

The Family Law Reform Act actually set out sixteen factors that courts were to consider when making maintenance awards. The major ones: each spouse's capacity to support him- or herself; the effect of their various responsibilities on their earning abilities; child care or other domestic services "in the same way as if the spouse were devoting the time spent . . . in remunerative employment and . . . contributing earnings . . . to the support of the family." The law, however, does not rank the guidelines or suggest how judges should weigh them against each other when making decisions.

The resultant uncertainty is reflected in a hodgepodge of court decisions; in some, the fact that the spouse (usually the wife) can support herself means that she is not entitled to maintenance, irrespective of her contribution to the family (despite the fact that, if she had worked outside the home, she would probably have been eligible for some form of pension). In others, her right to educate herself is seen, in Gregory's words, as "a last resort" – for example, in an Ontario Unified Family Court judgement that refused a bookkeeper's request for support so that she could be retrained as an interior decorator but, ironically, awarded maintenance because of her "faithful performance of her duties as a wife . . ."

Several decisions suggest that there really is one law for the rich: the wives of wealthy men are not expected to go into the labour market to begin supporting themselves, while those married to wage earners are expected to do so, often without regard to their age, health, education, skills, or ability. Or, in the ineffable words of a 1981 Ontario decision, "The only hope of financially resolving the dilemma of inadequate income is generally that the dependent spouse will in time find other means of support by remarriage or employment or both."

The court was blithely unaware of the sheer effrontery of suggesting that a woman find herself a man in order to keep herself in food and shelter, but it was hardly alone. According to a study on second families and the law of support, by Judge Norris Weisman of the Provincial Court (Family Division), "a . . . wife and children will usually be restricted to the standard of living offered by the second relationship. Conversely the trend seems in favour of giving the husband's second family every opportunity to succeed, even at the risk of casting the first family onto the public purse." The strong inference is that a wife had better find herself another dependency relationship as soon as possible, but, even if she does, she could well wind up on welfare. (And judges make it more likely by using the kinds of decisions quoted by Judge Weisman as the reason for making minimal support payments to first families, arguing speciously that there is no point in rendering a judgement that will not be obeyed.)

On February 1, 1985, while the arguments about support and maintenance were heating up again, the Honourable Roy McMurtry, having unsuccessfully contested the leadership of his party – and having used the campaign to continue his fight for further improvements to family law – resigned both from Cabinet and from his seat in the Legislature. On May 1, McMurtry took up duties as Canada's High Commissioner in London.

The following day, Ontario went to the polls and, as it had in two of the three previous elections, the majority voted against the Progressive Conservatives who had governed the province since 1943; this time, however, the split amongst the three parties was so close that, for six weeks, it was uncertain which of them would be able to form a government. On June 26, the Liberals, who had supported further family law reform, took office.

Roy McMurtry.

Whereas . . . Marriage is a Form of Partnership

The past, to be sure, is prologue. But prologue to what? The process of change is relentless and key court decisions still confirm and confound the past equally. Ontario has a brand-new law, the Family Law Act, 1986, and a new Divorce Act has been implemented by the federal government. Is it possible, then, to put family law on the back burner, secure in the knowledge that reform of it is finally completed?

Probably not. The "law" (as distinct from "laws") is an always imperfect attempt at justice and fairness. Especially when it is intended to regulate the intimate behaviour of human beings, no law can take into account the variety of their beliefs, experiences, needs, and activities or the complexity of their feelings and relationships with each other. Quite aside from the question of whether its division of property was adequate, the Family Law Reform Act, 1978, could not have worked perfectly or for an indefinite period of time. The enduring importance of that Act, in any event, is not its individual sections but its historical place as Ontario's first attempt at even-handed family law, incorporating more social change than any piece of legislation passed in this country. That alone makes it significant to the people of Ontario, even if they never know how it came to be or why.

With the passage of time, the way the courts interpreted the Act, once it moved from legal theory into the real lives of real people, emphasized the need to change it. Dissatisfaction with property division was still a sore point, but there were other issues that had to be considered, some involving new technology and others a Constitution that had not even existed when the Family Law Reform Act was written.

On a wet Ottawa Saturday afternoon in April, 1982, the Queen and the Prime Minister signed the Constitution Act, 1982, which gave Canada sole powers over Canada's Constitution. Certain of its provisions have had a direct impact on family law, which was further affected three years later when section 15 of the Constitution's Charter of Rights and Freedoms came into effect. The section says that:

> Every individual is equal before and under the law and has the right to the equal protection and equal benefit of the law without discrimination and, in particular, without discrimination based on race, national or ethnic origin, colour, religion, sex, age or mental or physical disability.

The prohibition against sex discrimination was a remarkable victory that has not even been achieved by American women, despite attempts since 1923 to obtain a similar guarantee in their

Doris Anderson at the Conference on the Constitution, 1982.

Constitution; it was included after a dazzling display of hard work, persistence, and political savvy by individuals and women's organizations across Canada (and because of Doris Anderson's skill in focussing public attention on the issue).

Among the implications of the new Charter provisions:

- Changes to child welfare laws as they affect unmarried parents. The traditional tendency in such laws is to give more power to the mother (whose relationship to the child is evident) than to fathers (whose relationship may be harder to prove). It is only fair that mothers (who usually have to support and care for children by themselves) have the power to relinquish their youngsters if they wish, but it is harder to defend cases in which, unless a father is readily available, he is not informed that his child is up for adoption. Almost certainly, this procedure will be challenged.
- Changes to welfare laws as they affect the support of single mothers. Welfare agencies that have "man-in-the-house" rules that punish women living with males, even if the men are not supporting them, face court challenges. The move will be welcome if it ends decisions like that of a Hamilton-area judge who sentenced the single mother of eight children to a one-year jail term for obtaining welfare while living with a man – although there was no evidence that she had ever received a cent from him for herself or her children, some of whom had to be placed in foster homes while she served her sentence.
- Changes to the law as it affects sharing of property. Some legal authorities suggest that attempts may be made to use the Charter as an avenue to gaining deferred equity in those provinces where it does not already exist.
- Changes to property law as it affects unmarried cohabitants. When the 1978 Family Law Reform Act was written, the status of unmarried couples was politically and socially delicate; the statute, therefore, acknowledged a support obligation only in cases where couples had lived together for five years or, if a child had been born, sooner. Contrary to a widespread misreading of the 1978 law, however, cohabitants did not enjoy the property rights of married couples: there was no right to deferred sharing of family property, and, although a dependent survivor could sue under the Succession Law Reform Act, there was no automatic right to a portion of the estate of a partner who died without a will.

Although Ontario's new legislation makes it possible to claim support after only three years of cohabiting, a further possibility, with major social obligations, is that the Charter's provisions may be construed to mean that the property of married and unmarried couples must be treated identically under the equality section. Is it discriminatory to make property rules that are applicable only to married people? Or can it be argued that, if it exists, such discrimination (to use the language of the Charter) is "demonstrably justified": some people choose to live outside marriage *specifically* because they wish to avoid its consequences, including the requirement that property be shared.

In addition to the uncertainty arising from section 15, there is section 7 of the Charter, which comprises only twenty-seven words: "Everyone has the right to life, liberty and security of person and the right not to be deprived thereof except in accordance with principles of fundamental justice." Despite its brevity, section 7 will produce major challenges over the next few years, the extent depending on the Supreme Court of Canada's view of both the intention of section 7 and the court's role in interpreting its meaning. Among the potential issues:

- Protection of family privacy and the freedom of individuals within the family. In the United States, the Supreme Court has given particular emphasis to the freedom provisions, especially as they involve the family. For example, it has ruled that health care facilities cannot always require parental consent before performing a medical procedure; i.e., requiring parental consent for a girl who decides to seek an abortion can be deemed to violate the liberty interest of a "mature minor." (The Children's Aid Society of Toronto recently lost a case in which it applied for wardship of a twelve-year-old dying girl who refused blood transfusions as being contrary to her religious beliefs; the judge held that the patient had been discriminated against on the basis of her religion, contrary to section 15, and that her security of person, guaranteed in section 7, had been infringed.) Canadian courts may well rule, as American courts have, that laws forbidding access to contraceptives interfere with the family, as do prohibitions on specific types of sexual activity between consenting adults.

A state duty for the Queen, the culmination of a dream for the Prime Minister: the signing of the Constitution Act, 1982.

• Limits to state interference in the family. The liberty section has been used in the United States (and undoubtedly will be tested here) to clarify the sometimes vague guidelines under which children's aid societies define a child as "neglected" and apply for protection orders or Crown wardship.

If the Charter has drastically altered the rights of Canadians, reproductive technology has overturned old limits to the way they conceive, bear, and raise children; the law still has to grapple with the legal implications of what has happened in the laboratories. It is now possible to take an ovum from one woman and fertilize it with the sperm of a male (whom she may or may not know), and implant it in the womb of another woman, with the resultant infant being raised by one, by some, or by none of the above.

Surrogate motherhood, sperm and/or ova banks, and *in vitro* fertilization raise a host of issues that government has never had to consider before. Among them: as the biological father, should the sperm donor be responsible for any future support of the child? Should he have any parental rights? Does paying a woman to act as a surrogate mother actually legalize the selling of children? Is it prostitution? Is it adultery? Is it just a business arrangement? How should the courts respond when, as happened in the United States, the surrogate mother delivers a physically handicapped child and the people who purchased the woman's services refuse to take delivery of the infant? In general, what control should the law impose on medical use of human material?

In June, 1985, the Ontario Law Reform Commission recommended that the courts supervise all aspects of contracts that deal with surrogate pregnancy: payment, the emotional and physical suitability of the various parties, testing, consent, termination of the pregnancy, responsibility for defective children, and failure by the natural mother to fulfill the terms of the contract (for example, by refusing to give up the child). The report recommends that the law prevent sperm and ova donors from claiming any parental rights to children that result from their donations and that it free them from legal or financial responsibility for such children. (Lawmakers may be disconcerted to learn that, in the United States, a group has been organized for the children of sperm donors seeking to find their biological fathers.)

Under the commission's recommendations, the records kept by sperm and ova banks would have to ensure the anonymity of all parties (although there would be "linkage" for medical purposes). The banks would also be required to discard unused human material (sperm, ova, *in vitro* fertilizations) – which, in theory, can be kept indefinitely – within ten years.

Geneticists are particularly concerned that, in our highly mobile society, it is all too possible that adoptive or sperm-bank children may unknowingly meet and mate with their siblings or half-siblings. That is one reason that confidentiality laws are an increasingly contentious issue as they affect adopted children. In recent years, in our admirable zeal to give the adopted child the same rights as one born naturally to its parents, we have been caught up in a lie, which is that the youngster's biological parents never existed. Now there is more and more pressure to permit adopted children to find their natural parents, for medical or emotional reasons.

Dimpled and pleased with the world, Louise Brown is oblivious of her role as history's first *in vitro* conception.

By the time the Law Reform Commission reported on reproductive technology, it was too late to include its recommendations in the Family Law Act, which had almost been completed. In fact, it will be many years before those moral, ethical, legal, and medical issues are considered adequately by society and absorbed into the law.

In late 1984, the attention amongst family law specialists was beginning to shift to Ottawa, where the federal government was about to begin public consultations on new divorce legislation; the proposed Act shortens, from three or five years to just one year, the time needed to obtain a "no-fault" divorce and maintains the right to an immediate divorce in fault cases (adultery and either physical or mental cruelty).

Some groups, especially those representing fathers, had pleaded with the federal Department of Justice to make joint custody or shared parenting mandatory; although the Act, which came into force on June 1, 1986, makes reference to the concept, it sensibly does not impose it. (Joint custody, which gives both the custodial and noncustodial parents equal say in major child-rearing issues, is an admirable idea that works well when both parties are able to set aside their own differences and cooperate in caring for their children. But that is harder to do in a society where women, who are most often the custodial parents, still get inadequate financial and social support.)

The new federal legislation takes a firm position on mediation, imposing a duty on family lawyers to discuss the concept and to inform clients about resources in their community. Like shared parenting, mediation is excellent in principle: studies indicate that, when it is successful, it decreases the amount of time needed for people to begin building new lives for themselves, minimizes the amount of disruption and bitterness associated with the end of marriage, and therefore lessens the emotional and financial toll involved.

Nonetheless, it has to be approached realistically: any kind of mediation is most successful when both sides have roughly equal power. Women are beginning to argue that, as long as men earn and have more than they do, marital mediation involves economically mismatched opponents: a husband with enough money to fight, little to lose (he can always turn down the mediator's recommendations and hope for better terms at trial), and a clear-cut advantage over the frazzled woman whose more limited economic and emotional resources are needed by her children. As a result, some lawyers are urging women to submit only non-economic issues to mediation and to settle money matters in court.

The new federal Act sets four objectives for judges ordering spousal support: to recognize and redress the economic advantage or disadvantage either partner suffered as a result of the marriage or its breakdown; to relieve economic hardship that results from the breakdown of the relationship; "in so far as practicable," to promote economic self-sufficiency on the part of each spouse within a reasonable amount of time; and to apportion the financial consequences arising from the care of any child of the marriage.

In addition to setting out those objectives, the law lists specific factors that judges should consider when making support awards. Amongst them: the conditions, means, needs, and other circumstances of each spouse and of their children, including the length of time the couple cohabited and the functions of each performed during the relationship. The inclusion of "functions" in the guidelines is meant to reward the person (usually the woman) who has been the homemaker by recognizing that she is at a disadvantage in preparing for the job market; in order to prevent traditional attempts to tie material behaviour to support, misconduct is barred as a factor. Objectives and guidelines will be of only limited use, however, because they are just listed in the Act, without any indication of which, if any, are paramount.

The Trudeau government had drafted a new divorce bill with many similar measures in the fall of 1983 and then-Justice Minister Mark MacGuigan spent part of early 1984 travelling across the country seeking professional and public reaction to it; with the Liberal defeat in September, 1984, however, it was widely assumed that reform of the Divorce Act would be delayed or forgotten completely. The fact that, quite the contrary, the new government was as committed to reform as the old one seemed to promise fresh opportunities and a greater need to press for change to family law in Ontario.

However, delays once again dogged the Ministry's timetable: the premier's resignation, followed in quick succession by the leadership fight to succeed him; McMurtry's resignation; the election of a minority government and the uncertainty that followed it; and, six weeks later, the formation of a new government, the first led by the Liberals in forty-two years.

Throughout that entire period, officials within the Ministry of the Attorney General continued with their preparations for a new Family Law Act, heartened by assurances that successive ministers were committed to the changes McMurtry had begun. Robert Welch, who took over from McMurtry, was enthusiastic, although powerless: shortly after he was sworn in, he had announced that he would not run in the election then expected at any moment.

Reform turned out to be a durable campaign issue: both the Liberals and NDP supported new legislation; the newly elected leader of the Progressive Conservatives, Frank Miller, would only say, however, that his party was committed to "improving family law."

In the six weeks after the May 2 election, while he sought a formula that would allow his government to cling to power, Miller moved closer to the other parties on most issues, including family law. The importance of the reform bill was underlined by the fact that the new Attorney General, Alan Pope, presented it on June 4 as Bill 1; in addition, on June 13, Pope moved first reading of Bill 14, the Support and Custody Orders Enforcement Bill. Family law reform might have a brand-new priority, but almost every member present doubted that Pope would be in a position to bring up either act for further study. The government lasted only eight sitting days in the Legislature before being defeated on June 18.

Eight days later, on the steps of the mellow old Legislature, flags flying and thousands of citizens watching from the broad sweep of the front lawn, Ian Scott, Ontario's twenty-ninth Attorney General, was sworn in. He was a popular choice: according to a professional peer, the fifty-year-old litigation lawyer "already had an excellent reputation as a brilliant, hard-working straight-shooter, respected even by his opponents." Superficially, he is unlike his old friend and predecessor in more than just politics: while Roy McMurtry is a cigar smoker, a genial bear of a man who responds instinctively to issues, Ian Scott is a cigarette smoker, more cerebral and naturally eloquent. As it quickly became clear, however, the new Attorney General was every bit as determined to reform family law as the old one had been.

Scott underlined that commitment by quickly allowing Bill 1 to be brought forward without change and, for a while, it seemed likely to become law in the hectic eight-day July sitting with which the new government began its career. The deadline was pushed back, however, when the New Democratic Party announced that it needed more time to study proposed changes.

The House reconvened on October 15 and, exactly one week later, Scott presented the Family Law Act for second reading, the stage at which legislation gets its most thorough consideration. This time, the bill had all-party support: after Scott urged members to pass the legislation quickly, Evelyn Gigantes spoke on behalf of the NDP; in addition to the Conservative justice critic, Terry O'Connor, Norman Sterling, who had been McMurtry's parliamentary assistant throughout the events leading to the 1978 Act, represented the Official Opposition.

In November, the Support and Custody Orders Enforcement Act was given third reading . (It will come into effect by the spring of 1987.) At about the same time, Bill 1 was sent to the Standing Committee on the Administration of Justice for public discussion and clause-by-clause consideration.

Groups supported or condemned the Family Law Act or, in some cases, talked about other topics entirely. Although custody and support are not dealt with in the legislation, committee members listened gravely as grandparents pleaded for access rights and groups of fathers and second spouses argued that support orders should be limited to two years (an argument that one observer characterized as "treating a former partner like a car: you got rid of it, so why bother buying gas?").

Representatives of three Jewish organizations asked for amendments to Bill 1 that they felt were needed by Jewish women: in addition to a civil divorce, Orthodox couples who wish to remarry must obtain a religious divorce (a *get*); males, who must agree to a *get*, may remarry, in a religious ceremony, without one, although their ex-wives may not. Some husbands have been using the *get* to bargain for favourable support or custody terms.

While the Attorney General and even some Jewish feminists oppose the legislation (it seeks civil remedies for religious wrongs, which is potentially dangerous and possibly contravenes the Charter) a free vote was taken in the Committee and two provisions, designed to prevent such situations, were passed. One forbids a person who fails to remove "all barriers that are within his or her control and that would prevent the other spouse's remarriage within that spouse's faith" from presenting a case under the Act or, if that person is a defendant, from presenting evidence. The second permits a court to set aside any agreement or settlement if "removal of barriers that would prevent the other spouse's remarriage within that spouse's faith was a consideration . . .".

The most contentious issue the committee considered, however, was in a key section of the bill, under which a court could award less or more than half the net difference in assets if it was of the opinion that an equal division "would be unconscionable . . ." The last of those words was the subject of lengthy heated debate, some members

"Whereas marriage is a partnership": Premier David Peterson and Attorney General Ian Scott look on as Lieutenant-Governor Lincoln Alexander signs the Family Law Act, 1986.

and family lawyers arguing that it set so high a standard that judges would *never* be allowed to vary from equal division; they preferred the word "inequitable" ("unfair, unjust") that had been used in the Family Law Reform Act. The Attorney General, however, had been so impressed with arguments about economic injustice in divorce, made by American sociologist Lenore Weitzman, that he had copies of her book, *The Divorce Revolution,* distributed to all members of the standing committee. Weitzman's studies show that divorced women suffer a 73 percent decline in their living standard, while divorced men experience a 42 percent increase; moreover, equal sharing of property forces the sale of the family home – usually the only real property the couple owns – and does not divide intangible property (education, professional licenses) that is owned by one partner but is usually the result of the work of both. Scott brought the committee around to his view and "unconscionable" ("outrageous, inordinate") remains the criterion of the Act.

By mid-December, the committee had completed clause-by-clause study of the bill and members expected that it would pass third reading on December 20, the last day the House sat before recessing for Christmas. Three Conservatives, however, decided that they had reservations about the bill and, once again, time ran out before it could be passed. House Leader Robert Nixon planned to schedule it for January 10, the first Friday after the Legislature resumed sitting, but a small technical flaw, discovered at the last minute, sent the bill back to the committee for amendment. Finally, on January 17, 1986, the Family Law Act, 1986, was passed. It took effect on March 1.

The legislation closed a major gap between people who are widowed and those who separate or divorce. The law's traditional reluctance to interfere with any competent person's right to bequeath property meant that, while separated or divorced spouses had rights to family assets, widows and widowers could be left *nothing*, irrespective of how assets were acquired. Their only recourse was to appeal to the courts as surviving dependents, a skimpy and humiliating solution. The 1978 legislation had had the effect, however unintended, of making it financially more advantageous to separate or divorce than to wait to be widowed. The new Act applies equally to a marriage that ends in separation, divorce, or death; a widow or widower can choose either to take the division of properties, as set out in the Family Law Act, or to take a bequest instead. (For example, their comparative value might make it preferable for a survivor to take proceeds of a large life insurance policy, which are exempt from the Act, rather than half the value of assets.)

The new law provides guidelines for awarding exclusive possession of the matrimonial home to either spouse: first, of course, the best interests of the children; but, in addition, any division of property or support orders, the availability and affordability of other suitable accommodations; and the special needs of the spouse seeking exclusive possession. (The overall intention of the law, and the tendency of judges, is to minimize the upheaval that young children suffer by permitting them and their custodial parent to remain in the matrimonial home until they can cope and, after that, to require that it be sold and the proceeds divided.)

The new legislation is also designed to cushion the effects of the rapid changes contemplated in the new Divorce Act; it gives spouses two years after divorce or six years after separation, whichever is the shorter, before they have to apply to the courts to divide property under the Family Law Act. (Because the limitation on separated couples is new, an initial six-month grace period, during which any separated person could apply under the Act, was included.)

But, beyond all its other provisions, the major change in the new Family Law Act is that it makes "deferred sharing" the law of Ontario and, in the words of the 1978 preamble (which it repeats), it regards marriage as truly "an economic partnership." The difference between the 1978 and 1986 acts is basic: the first divided property according to the way it had been used, while the second covers almost everything. Unless it was a gift or an inheritance, if it was acquired during the marriage, or if it increased in value during the marriage, it is divisible.

(Although, on the whole, members of the family bar agree with the intent of the Act, some predict already that parts of it will be heavily litigated: the division of a pension's capital rather than its proceeds, for example; the division of the matrimonial home that represents part of an inheritance; the acceptable margin of error when evaluating practices or businesses retroactively.)

The major concern, however, is about the indirect effect of the Family Law Act: that, at least in the short term, it will lead individual spouses to sign marriage contracts that destroy all the rights that have painstakingly been safeguarded for them in the last two acts. Roy McMurtry used to worry that "marriage contracts could leave women especially in a less advantageous position than before," and he saw it as the only possible negative consequence of deferred sharing.

Even before the Family Law Act was passed, Attorney General Scott warned lawyers that there would be "a lost generation" of men and women unable to understand the personal implications of reform.

Lenore Weitzman's contention, that equal division of property leads to long-term injustice to women and children, is more troubling. If the courts give property on the one hand and, on the other, deprive women of adequate support for themselves and their children, or if they fail to recognize the career sacrifices women make by staying home and they place unrealistic time limits on spousal support, the new law, however well intentioned, will simply perpetuate old injustices in a new form. That would be unfortunate; in treating all property as belonging equally to both partners, the Family Law Act is a long overdue attempt to deal with the way married people actually acquire their assets. In Scott's words, the law

> ". . . encourages *real* stability – not the supposed stability that cloaks economic terrorism and that makes marriage less a vehicle for profound emotional attachments than a state of bondage. People will have to be educated to make their own economic, as well as emotional, bargains when they marry, conscious of all the elements of a relationship. The end object is to develop a community that is aware of what it is doing, able to order its own affairs, a society where men and women enter – and leave – marriage pragmatically. The Act means that people can no longer enter marriage unthinkingly, blind to its consequences.

Taking Scott's view a little further, the Act should give all society, not just its feminist members, an urgent new motive for improving the economic status of women because, until that happens, husbands will be paying out painfully large sums of money – proof, if proof is still needed, of the financial disparity that currently exists between men and women. Until then (a very long time, indeed), it is wise for the partner who is, and will likely remain, economically disadvantaged to avoid signing a contract and to be wary of pressure to do so.

The Support and Custody Orders Enforcement Act, which is companion legislation to the Family Law Act, establishes an Office for the Enforcement of Support and Custody Orders within the Ministry of the Attorney General; the office will relieve spouses from the burdens of collecting money owed to them and will ensure that custody judgements are obeyed.

Ontario's office is being patterned after a similar scheme in Manitoba: unless an individual creditor decides otherwise, each court order for support or maintenance is filed with the office and all payments are made to it. Because all information about each case can be computerized, it is easier to locate an errant spouse and even to identify assets.

The law seems harsh – until it is measured against the number of maintenance orders in Canada that are in default – estimated at 60 to 70 percent – almost every one representing the unmet needs of women and/or minor children. Moreover, disregard for such orders has tended to spiral: as it becomes clear that judgements are not being backed up with action, there is little exterior pressure to obey them, so more and more are ignored.

In the past, there have been sporadic efforts at recovery, always limited to single-support parents already on or forced onto public assistance rolls. Now, provincial muscle backs up court orders, no matter whether they are for the benefit of a millionaire's wife or a millworker's children.

In Manitoba's experience, the results have been just as unambiguous as the message: the compliance rate for support orders has risen from about 30 to more than 75 percent.

The office's mandate to enforce custody orders will back up efforts by a parent seeking a kidnapped child with the considerable clout of Ontario's police and legal systems. A kidnapping parent's knowledge that the police are involved should, by itself, help to reduce the temptation for noncustodial parents to take the law into their own hands; if, however, they do, the odds are certainly shorter that the child will be spirited out of the province or be hidden for years.

Perhaps righting the most troubling wrongs of the past gives us time now to evaluate the consequences, not all of which could have been foreseen, of change. For example, in our desire to free people from the hated chains of unwanted matrimony, have we encouraged a kind of serial polygamy in which discarded mates and children are left without adequate provisions?

Should we take the view that responsibilities must be discharged in the order in which they are incurred, or should we safeguard people's rights to marry and procreate, irrespective of the number of former spouses and children they leave behind? By accepting family breakdown and the right of people to "seek happiness" by making other families, are we relegating increasing numbers of people, women and children especially, to lives of poverty and hopelessness?

This, after all, is a free country and a person should be permitted to form families as he or she sees fit; to suggest otherwise is to return us to the days when people were punished for life for making unwise matrimonial choices. While a more equitable division of property reduces financial problems in a number of families, support is vitally important to the majority. In times like our own, when governments face difficult funding choices every day, should the public purse be used to pick up the tab when support is inadequate, or should we treat family support responsibilities like a form of mortgage: the third does not get paid until after the second and the second does not get paid until after the first?

Considering the complexity of the problem, should society search for methods of automatically guaranteeing support when marriage breaks down? Should we have a type of insurance? Should we harness computer technology to deduct maintenance and support orders, like income taxes, at source?

How can we protect ourselves, as individuals, from the vagaries of support decisions? Or are the inequalities pointed out by Frances Gregory, Judge Weisman, and others inescapable? The broader judicial issue is the enormous discretion permitted by most family law – a reasonable power since a judge must respond differently to different couples and their situations. But judges are as susceptible to inbred biases and stereotypical thinking as the rest of us. According to one study, they make decisions, in part, on the basis of their own social and economic backgrounds; furthermore, those with heavier workloads tend to react more negatively to colleagues and to other professionals; they are also more likely to impose fines and to operate under the old-style rules of thumb. (Which is not to accuse judges of improper behaviour, since they, like the rest of us, are affected by personal experience and belief.)

Many decisions, however, even those apparently dealing only with financial matters, are disguised value judgements: the court that limits support in the case of a mother who wants to stay home and care for her children, thus forcing her to work, is not just making a dollars-and-cents decision: it is also overriding the mother's belief that her children need her at a difficult time in their lives.

In a pluralistic society, value-loaded decisions may eventually lead to increased pressure to find ways of "structuring judicial discretion": permitting differences but encouraging a greater degree of predictability in the courts. The danger is that too many restraints on decision-making could hamstring judges – another sure way to discourage the brightest, most experienced men and women from accepting judicial appointments. The answer is to define more clearly and to list, according to priority, the factors that the courts should use in decision-making and to back up guidelines with professional research.

Today, courts emphasize, instead, "continuity of care": whenever possible, children should be left with the parent who has been caring for them. Access by the noncustodial parent, however, is crucial: studies show that ongoing contact with both parents is absolutely crucial to the child's mental health. Courts, therefore, grant access in all but cases of the most inappropriate or potentially dangerous behaviour by the noncustodial parent (and, in a well-publicized Ontario case, a judge even directed a boy to pay monthly visits, in penitentiary, to his father, who had murdered his mother). Shared parenting, discussed in the new Divorce Act, stresses the importance of maintaining parental relationships. The danger is that it will become another fad, taken up enthusiastically, applied inappropriately, and, when a backlash sets in, just as inappropriately dropped. (It will be viewed suspiciously as long as its proponents insist, as most now do, that it can be applied across the board. The mother struggling to support small children whose father is in arrears or whose visits to them are sporadic, may not take kindly to the suggestion that he should have some say over which church or school they attend, or whether they should see a dentist.)

Not only we, but our various governments, live in economically uncertain times. The limits to public spending that have become the hallmark of the '80s restrict society's ability to respond to complex social issues; they frustrate even our best intentions and most scrupulously decent laws, the work of our most intelligent and devoted judges, lawyers, and lawmakers. Compassion comes easily to the prosperous because it does not test them, but economic anxiety makes us, collectively as well as individually, less generous.

Today, we are building an increasingly complex quasi-legal system around family law. We want couples to attend counselling sessions so that they will marry wisely; therapy sessions so they will separate only with regret; mediation sessions so that they will discharge their obligations to each other decently; joint parenting sessions so that they will be responsible and cooperative parents. But, to use two favourite contemporary words, support networks cannot be wished, and they certainly cannot be legislated, into existence. They are easy to describe in utopian pastels, but they can be willed into reality only in the crisp truths of the financial pages: Who pays? How much? What are the priorities? Those are the tough questions we still have not tackled; until we do, it is hard to imagine what family law will be like even a decade from now.

The history of the Province of Ontario has a clearly defined shape: it starts with a small group of colonials whose devotion to one principle – the Crown of England – was surrounded by a range of individual traditions, beliefs, and even crotchets. In family law, its momentum has been exclusively in one direction: toward a body of rules acknowledging that people have different attitudes and beliefs, that they choose different structures for their lives and relationships. It recognizes, without judging, their human capacity for folly and attempts to protect the weak from the strong, the powerless against the powerful.

The way the law now accepts people's differences would have been hard to predict even at the beginning of the recent push to reform family law; it is only in hindsight that the persistent desire for people to retain their individuality becomes clear.

The post-war period, after all, had been filled with prognostications of a future in which people dressed uniformly, ate nutritious pills in place of food, and lived in cities composed entirely of large buildings; by contrast, recent history shows that we are looking for more, not fewer, choices. While it is true that many of us work for multinational corporations or in enormous office complexes, there is increasing concern, not about uniformity, but about isolation in the "electronic cottage," with its microcomputer. (Since the workplace is organized for social as well as industrial and technical reasons, it seems likely that human beings will always find ways of pooling their labour; otherwise, a large number of electronic cottagers will have to meet an equally large number of appealing computer repairers to save the race from biologic extinction.)

Food has become less, not more, standardized; while it is technically feasible to produce a pill that will meet all our nutritional needs, the dining table, like the workplace, serves more than a utilitarian purpose. Instead of gulping down the imagined Break-lunch-sup Pill, we are stubbornly buying more cookbooks, more kitchen utensils, more kinds of more exotic foods, than ever before in the history of the world. Not very long ago, the Canadian hostess was content to serve chips to her company and to put out what used to be known as "the lunch" – cold cuts and sweet pickles – a signal that the evening of bridge or conversation was being brought to a close.

Now, in cities large and small, dinner features pasta made in the cunning gizmo that stands between the espresso/cappuccino maker and the food processor; there is often a dish with a scent of framboise or tarragon vinegar (from the gourmet section of the supermarket) and a divine little dessert composed of four kinds of fruit your grandmother never heard of. Leaving a dinner party or a supper ("the lunch" is now something that occurs before two in the afternoon) without asking for at least one recipe is a virtual declaration of a lack of interest in food or of the host's or hostess's inadequacies. In the kitchen, at least, no one talks about a pill anymore. Ironically, the forecasts of food served pharmaceutically have come true only for Africa's starving millions.

We are as staunchly individual in our buying habits as our budgets permit us to be. With a wide range of available synthetics – from sleazy to luxurious – there has never been a greater demand for cotton, wool, and silk. Contrary to predictions, many neighbourhood grocers are still in business, offering individualized services (delivery, telephone ordering, billing) at a premium that busy men and women are prepared to pay. At the same time, the department store is being noticeably affected by the North American love affair with the boutique – the little store that offers just T-shirts or running gear or waterbeds or stockings or weekend apparel or shirts. Of the many unforeseen consequences of the bank-supplied credit card, one of the most significant has been that it removed the large, impersonal department store's unique ability to offer a variety of goods from one creditor. It made the entire plaza or the whole neighbourhood a "department store."

The school, yesterday's temple of uniformity, bubbles (and sometimes bubbles over) with variety in everything from the clothes worn in the classroom to the textbooks used in it. Organized religion, once reliably composed of "Christian" and "other," now comprises every shade of belief and philosophical underpinning – or none.

Family law today exists on the edge between two delicately balanced realities: on the one hand, it recognizes a considerable degree of latitude in people's beliefs and in the ways they choose to organize their lives. At the same time, the state has a greater say in what goes on within the family circle: there are laws that limit the way a parent may treat a child; that mandate a level of hygiene, medical care, education, and emotional succor that must be offered to him or her; that prohibit – even if they do not stop – family violence. The state has become the invigilator of the family to a degree that would have scandalized the politicians and civil servants of one and certainly two centuries ago. (In those days society might as well have taken as its motto the words of a famous Irish actress who said that she did not care what people did "as long as they don't do it in the streets and frighten the horses.")

If there is any other thematic change that resonates throughout the history of family law, it is that the law has moved steadily, if very slowly, to bring justice to married women. Ontario went from being a province in which men had virtually every advantage and women had none to being one in which there have been gains, however mixed, for women. Overall, this has been the result of no grand design but of logic: there was almost nothing of substance left to confer on married men in eighteenth-century family law; change, any change, meant a diminution of their power and an increase in the power placed in the hands of women.

That unsentimental genius of American radicalism, Saul Alinsky, once said that power was having choices. And so it is. The law today offers choices – and power – of a kind unimaginable in Upper Canada. The result of that power and those choices has been far from what the reformers, past and present, might have imagined – or wished. There is only one certainty, human in its complexity and seeming paradox: in our search for intimacy, emotional safety, and nurture, for that "haven in a heartless world," we have never found a design more fraught with the potential for disappointment – and richer in possibilities – than the family.

Bibliographies

BOOKS

Abella, Irving and Troper, Harold. *None is Too Many: Canada and the Jews of Europe 1933-1948.* Toronto: Lester & Orpen Dennys, 1982.

Abrahamson, Una. *God Bless Our Home: Domestic Life in Nineteenth Century Canada.* Toronto: Burns and MacEachern Ltd., 1966.

Abrams, Alan. *Why Windsor?: An Anecdotal History of the Jews of Windsor and Essex County.* Windsor: Black Moss Press, 1981.

Acland, Alice. *Caroline Norton.* London: Constable and Co., Ltd., 1948.

Acton, Janice; Goldsmith, Penny; and Shepard, Bonnie, eds. *Women at Work 1850-1930.* Toronto: Women's Press, 1974.

Alinsky, Saul D. *Rules for Radicals.* New York: Random House, 1971.

Allen, Richard. *The Social Passion: Religion and Social Reform in Canada, 1914-1928.* Toronto: University of Toronto Press, 1973.

Allen, Robert Thomas. *When Toronto was for Kids.* Toronto: McClelland and Stewart Ltd., 1961.

Andersen, Margaret, ed. *Mother Was Not a Person.* Montreal: Black Rose Books, 1972.

Andrews, H.T.G. Judge, ed. *Family Law in the Family Courts.* Toronto: The Carswell Co., Ltd., 1973.

Armstrong, Christopher and Nelles, H.V. *The Revenge of the Methodist Bicycle Company.* Toronto: Peter Martin Associates Ltd., 1977.

Armstrong, Elizabeth H. *The Crisis of Quebec, 1914-1918.* Toronto: McClelland and Stewart Ltd., 1974.

Bailey, Thomas A. and Ryan, Paul B. *The Lusitania Disaster: An Episode in Modern Warfare and Diplomacy.* New York: Macmillan Publishing Co., 1975.

Bassett, Isabel. *The Parlour Rebellion: Profiles in the Struggle for Women's Rights.* Toronto: McClelland and Stewart Ltd., 1975.

Berger, Carl. *The Sense of Power, 1867-1914.* Toronto: University of Toronto Press, 1970.

Berton, Pierre. *The Invasion of Canada, 1812-1813.* Toronto: McClelland and Stewart Ltd., 1980.

Bible, The Revised Standard Version. London: Collins, 1952.

Blakeley, Phyllis R. and Grant, John N. *Eleven Exiles: Accounts of Loyalists of the American Revolution.* Toronto: Dundurn Press Ltd., 1982.

Bliss, Michael, ed., 2d ed. *The Woman Suffrage Movement in Canada.* Toronto: University of Toronto Press, 1974.

Blythe, Ronald, ed., rev. ed. *Writing in a War: Stories, Poems and Essays of 1939-1945.* Toronto: Penguin Books, 1982.

Bolger, Francis W.P. *The Years Before "Anne".* Charlottetown: The Prince Edward Island Heritage Foundation, 1974.

Bonis, Robert R. *A History of Scarborough.* Scarborough: Scarborough Public Library, 1965.

Bothwell, Robert; Drummond, Ian; and English, John. *Canada Since 1945: Power, Politics, and Provincialism.* Toronto: University of Toronto Press, 1981.

Bowerman, E.E. *The Law of Child Protection.* London: Sir Isaac Pitman and Sons, Ltd., 1933.

Bradley, A.G. *Sir Guy Carleton (Lord Dorchester).* Toronto: University of Toronto Press, 1966.

Braithwaite, Max. *The Hungry Thirties.* Toronto: Natural Science of Canada Ltd., 1977.

Brown, C.R.; Maxwell, P.A.; and Maxwell, L.F., compilers. *A Legal Biography of the British Commonwealth of Nations: Canadian and British-American Colonial Law.* London: Sweet and Maxwell, Ltd., 1957.

Brown, Robert Craig and Cook, Ramsay. *Canada 1896-1921: A Nation Transformed.* Toronto: McClelland and Stewart Ltd. 1974.

Campbell, P. *Travels in the Interior Inhabited Parts of North America in the Years 1791 and 1792.* Edited with an introduction by H.H. Langton and W.F. Ganong. Toronto: The Champlain Society, 1937.

Canadian Welfare Council. *The Juvenile Court in Law,* 4th ed. Ottawa, 1952.

Canniff, William. *History of the Province of Ontario (Upper Canada). Containing a Sketch of Franco-Canadian History – the Bloody Battles of the French and Indians, the American Revolution, Including Biographies of Prominent First Settlers. And the Census of 1871.* Toronto: A.H. Hovey, 1872.

Careless, J.M.S. *The Union of the Canadas: The Growth of Canadian Institutions 1841-1857.* McClelland and Stewart Ltd., 1967.

Carrigan, D. Owen, compiler. *Canadian Party Platforms 1867-1968.* Toronto: Copp Clark Publishing Co. Ltd., 1968.

Cartwright, The Hon. Richard. *Life and Letters of the Late Hon. Richard Cartwright.* Ed., Rev. Conway Edward Cartwright. Toronto: Belford Bros., 1876.

Cattermole, William. *Emigration: The Advantages of Emigration to Canada.* London: Simpkin and Marshall, 1831. Reprint, Coles Publishing, 1970.

Clark, C.S. *Of Toronto the Good.* Montreal: The Toronto Publishing Co., 1898. Reprint, Coles Publishing, 1970.

Cleverdon, Catherine L. *The Women's Suffrage Movement in Canada.* Toronto: University of Toronto Press, 1950.

Cook, Ramsay and Mitchison, Wendy, eds. *Their Proper Sphere: Women's Place in Canadian Society.* Toronto: Oxford University Press, 1976.

Cornell, Paul G.; Hamelin, Jean L.; Ouellet, Fernand; and Trudel, Marcel. *Canada: Unity in Diversity.* Toronto: Holt, Rinehart and Winston of Canada Ltd., 1967.

Craig, Gerald M. *Upper Canada: The Formative Years - 1784-1841.* Toronto: McClelland and Stewart Ltd., 1967.

________, ed. *Early Travellers in the Canadas, 1791-1867.* Toronto: Macmillan Co. of Canada Ltd., 1955.

Craig, John. *The Years of Agony: 1910-1920.* Toronto: Natural Science of Canada Ltd., 1977.

Creighton, Donald. *John A. Macdonald: Volume 2 – The Old Chieftain.* Toronto: Macmillan Co. of Canada Ltd., 1955.

Dafoe, John W. *Over the Canadian Battlefields: Notes on a Little Journey in France in March, 1919.* Toronto: Thomas Allen, 1919.

Dranoff, Linda Silver. *Women in Canadian Law.* Toronto: Fitzhenry and Whiteside, 1977.

Dymond, Allan M., K.C. *The Laws of Ontario Relating to Women and Children.* Toronto: Clarkson W. James, 1923.

Edgar, Mathilde (Rideout). *Ten Years of Upper Canada in Peace and War: 1805-1815, Being the Rideout Letters With Annotations, by Mathilde Edgar; Also an Appendix of the Narratives of the Captivity Among the Shawanese Indians, in 1788, of Thos. Rideout, Afterwards Surveyor-General of Canada and a Vocabulary, Compiled by Him of the Shawanese Language.* Toronto: W. Briggs, 1890.

Falconer, R.A. *The German Tragedy and its Meaning for Canada.* Toronto: University of Toronto Press, 1915.

Fitzgibbon, Mary Agnes. *A Veteran of 1812: The Life of James Fitzgibbon.* Toronto: William Briggs, 1894. Reprint, Coles Publishing, 1979.

Franklin, Stephen. *A Time of Heroes: 1940-1950.* Toronto: Natural Science of Canada Ltd., 1977.

Fryer, Mary Beacock. *Buckskin Pimpernel: The Exploits of Justus Sherwood, Loyalist Spy.* Toronto: Dundurn Press, 1981.

Garner, John. *The Franchise and Politics in British North America, 1755-1867.* Toronto: University of Toronto Press, 1969.

Garvin, John, ed. *Canadian Poems of the Great War.* Toronto: McClelland and Stewart Ltd., 1918.

Gay, Peter. *The Bourgeois Experience, Victoria to Freud Volume I: Education of the Senses.* New York: Oxford University Press, 1984.

Gemmill, John Alexander. *Bills of Divorce Including an Historical Sketch of Parliamentary Divorce.* Toronto: Carswell and Co., 1889.

Gillen, Molly. *Lucy Maude Montgomery.* Toronto: Fitzhenry and Whiteside, 1978.

Glazebrook, George Parker de T. *Life in Ontario.* Toronto: University of Toronto Press, 1968.

Government of Canada. *Report of the Royal Commission on the Status of Women.* Ottawa: 1970.

Granatstein, J.L. and Stevens, Paul, eds. *Canada Since 1867: A Bibliographic Guide.* Toronto: Samuel Stevens Hakkert and Co., 1977.

Graveson, R.H. and Crane, F.R., eds. *A Century of Family Law: 1857-1957.* London: Sweet and Maxwell Ltd., 1957.

Grayson, L.M. and Bliss, Michael, eds. *The Wretched of Canada: Letters to R.B. Bennett, 1930-1935.* Toronto: University of Toronto Press, 1971.

Guillet, Edwin. *Pioneer Settlements.* Ontario Publishing Co., 1938.

Hadfield, Joseph. *An Englishman in America, 1785, Being the Diary of Joseph Hadfield, Edited and Annotated by Douglas S. Robertson.* Toronto: Hunter-Rose Co., 1933.

Hale, Alice K. and Brooks, Sheila A., eds. *The Depression in Canadian Literature.* Toronto: Macmillan Co. of Canada Ltd., 1976.

Hardie, Frank. *The Political Influence of Queen Victoria.* London: Frank Cass and Co., Ltd., 1963.

Harkness, Ross. *J.E. Atkinson of The Star.* Toronto: The University of Toronto Press, 1963.

Hellerstein, Erna Olafson; Hume, Leslie Parker; and Offen, Karen, eds. *Victorian Women.* Stamford: Stamford University Press, 1981.

Hepworth, H. Philip. *Foster Care and Adoption in Canada.* Ottawa: Canadian Council on Social Development, 1980.

Hibbert, Christopher. *The French Revolution.* Toronto: Penguin Books, 1982.

________. *Edward VII, A Portrait.* Toronto: Penguin Books, 1982.

History of North America, Comprising a Geographical and Statistical View of the United States and of British Canadian Possessions. Leeds: Davies and Co., 1820.

Hoar, Victor. *The On to Ottawa Trek.* Toronto: Copp Clark Publishing Co., 1970.

Holcombe, Lee. *Wives and Property: Reform of the Married Women's Property Law in Nineteenth Century England.* Toronto: University of Toronto Press, 1983.

Holdsworth, Sir William. *A History of English Laws,* vol. 13 and 14. London: Methuen and Co., Ltd., 1964.

Holmested, G.S. *Matrimonial Jurisdiction in Ontario, and Quebec.* Toronto: Arthur Poole and Co., 1912.

Innis, Mary Quayle, ed. *The Clear Spirit: Twenty Canadian Women and Their Times.* Toronto: University of Toronto Press, for the Canadian Federation of University Women, 1966.

Ireland, G. and de Galindez, Jesus. *Divorce in the Americas.* Buffalo: Dennis and Co., Inc., 1947.

Irvine, William. *The Farmers in Politics.* Toronto: McClelland and Stewart Ltd., 1920.

Ishwaran, K., ed. *Marriage and Divorce in Canada.* Toronto: Methuen Publications, 1983.

________, ed., rev. ed. *The Canadian Family.* Toronto: Holt, Rinehart and Winston, 1976.

Johnston, William Victor, M.D. *Before the Age of Miracles: Memoirs of a Country Doctor.* Toronto: Fitzhenry and Whiteside Ltd., 1972.

Jones, Alfred. *The Loyalists of Massachusetts.* London: St. Catharines Press, 1923.

Jones, Mary Fallis. *The Confederation Generation.* Toronto: Royal Ontario Museum, 1978.

Kalbach, Warren E. and McVey, Wayne W. *The Demographic Bases of Canadian Society.* Toronto: McGraw-Hill, 1971.

Kerr, D.G.G. *Historical Atlas of Canada, 3rd Revised Edition.* Toronto: Thomas Nelson and Sons (Canada) Ltd., 1975.

Kingsford, R.E. *Commentaries on the Law of Ontario, Being Blackstone's Commentaries on the Laws of England Adapted to the Province of Ontario.* Toronto: The Carswell Co., Ltd., 1896.

Landon, Fred. *Western Ontario and the American Frontier.* Toronto: McClelland and Stewart Ltd., 1967.

Langton, H.H., ed. *A Gentlewoman in Upper Canada: The Journals of Anne Langton.* Toronto: Clarke, Irwin and Co. Ltd., 1950.

Lower, Arthur R.M. *Canadians in the Making.* Toronto: Longmans, Green and Co., 1958.

Lownsbrough, John. *The Privileged Few: The Grange and Its People in Nineteenth-Century Toronto.* Toronto: Art Gallery of Ontario, 1980.

MacDonald, Donald C., ed. *The Government and Politics of Ontario.* 2d ed. Toronto: Van Nostrand Reinhold Ltd., 1980.

Macdonald, Norman. *Canada Immigration and Colonization: 1841-1903.* Toronto: Macmillan Co. of Canada Ltd., 1966.

MacInnis, Grace. *J.S. Woodsworth, A Man to Remember.* Toronto: Macmillan Co. of Canada, 1953.

Mahood, Sally. *Women Unite.* Toronto: Canadian Women's Educational Press, 1972.

McCaughan, Margaret M. *The Legal Status of Married Women in Canada.* Toronto: Carswell and Co., Ltd., 1977.

McIlwraith, Jean N. *Sir Frederick Haldimand.* (*Makers of Canada* series). Morang and Co., Ltd., 1904.

McNaught, Kenneth. *A Prophet in Politics: A Biography of J.S. Woodsworth.* Toronto: University of Toronto Press, 1959.

Mendes da Costa, Derek, ed. *Studies in Canadian Family Law.* 2 vols. Toronto: Butterworth and Co. (Canada) Ltd., 1972.

Michelin Guide: Normandy. London: Michelin Tyre Co., Ltd., 1980.

Middlemas, Keith. *The Life and Times of Edward VII.* London: Weidenfeld and Nicolson, 1972.

Mika, Nick and Helen. *Places in Ontario.* Belleville: Mika Publishing Co., 1977.

Millgate, Linda. *Almanac of Dates.* New York: Harcourt, Brace and Jovanovitch, Inc., 1977.

Moir, John S. *Church and State in Canada, 1627-1867.* Toronto: McClelland and Stewart Ltd., 1967.

Moodie, Susanna. *Roughing it in the Bush.* Toronto: McClelland and Stewart Ltd., 1962.

Morton, W.L. *The Kingdom of Canada: A General History from Earliest Times.* 2d ed. Toronto: McClelland and Stewart Ltd., 1963.

Munro, Iain R. *Canada and the World Wars.* Toronto: Wiley Publishers of Canada Ltd., 1979.

Oliver, Peter. *Public and Private Persons: The Ontario Political Culture, 1914-1934.* Toronto: Clarke, Irwin and Co., 1975.

Pankhurst, E. Sylvia. *The Suffrage Movement: An Intimate Account of Persons and Ideals.* Toronto: Longmans, Green and Co., 1931.

Paterson, G.C. *Land Settlement in Upper Canada (1793-1840).* Toronto: Printed as the Sixteenth Report (1920) of the Bureau of Archives of Ontario, Alexander Fraser, Provincial Archivist. The King's Printer, 1921.

Penrose, Maryly. *Mohawk Valley in the Revolution.* Franklin Park, N.J.: Liberty Bell Associates, n.d.

Perkins, Jane Grey. *Life of Mrs. Norton.* London: J. Murray, 1909.

Porter, McKenzie. *Overture to Victoria.* Toronto: Longmans, Green and Co., 1961.

Power, W. Kent, K.C. *The Law and Practice Relating to Divorce and Other Matrimonial Causes in Canada.* Toronto: Carswell Co., Ltd., 1948.

Reaman, Elmore. *The Trail of the Black Walnut.* Toronto: McClelland and Stewart Ltd., 1957.

Richardson, Gus, et al, compilers; Read, Daphne, ed. *The Great War and Canadian Society: An Oral History.* Toronto: New Hogtown Press, 1978.

(Richardson, John). *Tecumseh or Warrior of the West, A Poem in 4 Cantos, with notes, by an English Officer.* London, 1818.

Riddell, William Renwick. *The Legal Profession in Upper Canada in The Early Periods.* Toronto: The Law Society of Upper Canada, 1916.

_________. *The Bar and the Courts of Upper Canada or Ontario.* Toronto: Macmillan Co. of Canada Ltd., 1920.

Robertson, Heather. *A Terrible Beauty: The Art of Canada at War.* Toronto: James Lorimer and Co., 1977.

Robertson, John Ross. *Landmarks of Toronto.* Belleville: Mika Publishing Co., 1977.

Robinson, Helen Caister. *Mistress Molly, The Brown Lady: Portrait of Molly Brant.* Toronto: Dundurn Press, 1980.

Rose, Phyllis. *Parallel Lives.* New York: Alfred A. Knopf, 1984.

Ross, Alexander. *The Booming Fifties: 1950-1960.* Toronto: Natural Science of Canada Ltd., 1977.

Royal Commission on the Liquor Trade, the Facts of the Case: For a Total Suppression of the Liquor Traffic. Compiled under the direction of the Dominion Alliance for the Total Suppression of the Liquor Traffic, F.S. Spence, Secretary. Toronto: Newton and Treloar, 1896.

Ryerson, Egerton. *The Loyalists of America and their Times: From 1620-1816.* Toronto: W. Briggs, 1880.

Scadding, Henry. *Toronto of Old.* Abridged and edited by F.H. Armstrong. Toronto: University of Toronto Press, 1966.

Schull, Joseph. *Ontario Since 1867.* Toronto: McClelland and Stewart Ltd., 1978.

Shorter, Edward. *The Making of the Modern Family.* New York: Basic Books Inc., 1975.

Shortt, Adam and Doughty, Arthur G. *Canada and its Provinces, A History of the Canadian People and Their Institutions, by One Hundred Associates.* Toronto: Brode and Co., 1913.

Simcoe, Elizabeth Gwillam. *The Diary of Mrs. John Graves Simcoe, Wife of the First Lieutenant-Governor of Upper Canada, 1792-6.* Edited by John Ross Robertson. Toronto: William Briggs, 1911. Reprint, Coles Publishing, 1973.

_________. *Mrs. Simcoe's Diary.* Edited by Mary Quayle Innis. Toronto: Macmillan Co. of Canada, 1965.

Splane, Richard B. *Social Welfare in Ontario, 1791-1893: A Study of Public Welfare Administration.* Toronto: University of Toronto Press, 1965.

Story, Norah. *The Oxford Companion to Canadian History and Literature.* Toronto: Oxford University Press, 1967.

Sutherland, Neil. *Children in English-Canadian Society: Framing the Twentieth-Century Consensus.* Toronto: University of Toronto Press, 1976.

Sweetenham, John. *Canada and the First World War.* Toronto: The Ryerson Press, 1969.

Taylor, Charles. *Six Journeys: A Canadian Pattern.* Toronto: Anansi Press, 1977.

Thomas, Clara. *Love and Work Enough: The Life of Anna Jameson.* Toronto: University of Toronto Press, 1967.

Toye, William, ed. *Supplement to The Oxford Companion to Canadian History and Literature.* Toronto: Oxford University Press, 1973.

Trevelyan, G.M. (George Macaulay). *British History in the Nineteenth Century and After: 1782-1919.* London: Longmans, Green and Co., Ltd., 1922.

Trofimenkoff, Susan M. and Prentice, Alison. *The Neglected Majority: Essays in Canadian Women's History.* Toronto: McClelland and Stewart, 1977.

Trotter, Bernard Freeman. *A Canadian Twilight and Other Poems of War and of Peace.* Toronto: McClelland, Goodchild and Stewart, 1917.

Waite, Peter. *Canada 1874-1896: Arduous Destiny.* Toronto: McClelland and Stewart Ltd., 1971.

Walker, David M. *The Oxford Companion to Law.* Oxford: Oxford University Press, 1980.

Webster, Donald Blake with Cross, Michael S. and Szylinger, Irene. *Georgian Canada: Conflict and Culture, 1746-1820.* Toronto: Royal Ontario Museum, 1984.

Weitzman, Lenore J. *The Divorce Revolution: The Unexpected Social and Economic Consequences for Women and Children in America.* New York: The Free Press, 1985.

"Wife of an Emigrant Officer." *The Backwoods of Canada.* London: Charles Knight, 1836. Reprint, Coles Publishing, 1980.

Williams, Neville. *Chronology of the Modern World.* London: Barrie and Rockliff, 1966.

Wilson, Barbara M. *Ontario and the First World War, 1914-1918.* Toronto: The University of Toronto Press, The Champlain Society for the Government of Ontario, 1977.

Wilson, Bruce. *As She Began.* Toronto: Dundurn Press, 1981.

Woodforde, James. *The Diary of a Country Parson, 1758-1802.* Passages selected and edited by John Bersesford. 5 vols. Toronto: Oxford University Press, 1924-1931.

Woodham-Smith, Cecil. *Lonely Crusader: The Life of Florence Nightingale.* New York: Bantam Books, 1963.

Ziegler, Olive. *Woodsworth, Social Pioneer (Authorized Sketch).* Toronto: The Ontario Publishing Co., Ltd., 1934.

SELECTED PAPERS, DOCUMENTS, AND OTHER MATERIALS

Note: Papers and records of the *Ontario Historical Society* are marked *OHS*.

Abella, Judge Rosalie. "New Developments in the Law of Remedies." In *Law Society of Upper Canada Special Lectures, 1981.* Don Mills: Richard De Boo, 1981.

Abrahamson, Una. "Social Life in the Community." In *Everyday Life in Nineteenth-Century Ontario, The Proceedings of a Seminar Sponsored by the Ontario Museum Association.* Ontario: 1978.

Allan, D. "Some of Guelph's Old Landmarks." In *OHS*, vol. 30, 1930.

An Historical Review of Ontario Legislation on Child Welfare. Toronto: 1958.

Allinson, C.L.C. "John Galt." In *OHS*, vol. 22, 1925.

Ardagh, W.D. and Harrison, Robert A. "The Married Women Question." In *Upper Canada Law Journal and Local Courts' Gazette,* vol. 3. Toronto: Maclear, Thomas and Co., 1857.

Backhouse, Constance. "Shifting Patterns in Nineteenth-Century Canadian Custody Law." In *Essays in the History of Canadian Law.* Flaherty, David, ed. Toronto: Osgoode Society, 1981.

Bastedo, Thomas. "Remedies in Family Law (Property)." In *Law Society of Upper Canada Special Lectures, 1981.* Don Mills: Richard De Boo, 1981.

Bliss, Michael. "Pure Books on Avoided Subjects: Pre-Freudian Sexual Ideas in Canada." In *Canadian Historical Association, Historical Papers,* 1970.

Bricker, I.C. "First Settlement in Central Western Ontario." In *OHS*, vol. 30, 1930.

Bryce, P.H. "Quinte Loyalists of 1784." In *OHS*, vol. 27, 1931.

"By a Well Known English Health and Beauty Specialist." *1000 Things Every Man and Woman Should Know.* Toronto: W.K. Buckley, Ltd., 1938.

Canada-Ontario Rideau-Trent-Severn Study Committee. *The Quinte-Kingston Area: Yesterday Today Tomorrow.* Toronto: 1973.

Canadian Advisory Committee on the Status of Women. "Outline of Matrimonial Property Laws in Canada." Ottawa: 1982.

Cartwright, Richard, Jr. "The Marriage Law in Upper Canada." In *Canadian Archives, Series Q.*279-1.

Census of Canada, Volume 4: 1665-1871. Ottawa: 1876.

Cox, Renée. *Juvenile Justice Process in Canada: History and Reform.* MA (criminology) thesis. University of Toronto: 1981.

Drew, Major George A. "The Truth About the War." In *Maclean's Magazine.* Toronto: July 1, 1928.

Early History of the Humane and Children's Aid Movement in Ontario, 1886-1893. Toronto: L.K. Cameron, 1911.

Elliot, John K. "Crime and Punishment in Early Upper Canada." In *OHS,* vol. 27, 1931.

First Annual Report of the Mothers' Allowance Commission, 1920-21.

Gaffield, Chad. "Schooling, the Economy, and Rural Society in Nineteenth-Century Ontario." In *Childhood and Family in Canadian History,* edited by Joy Parr. Toronto: McClelland and Stewart Ltd., 1982.

Government of Canada. *Divorce Law in Canada: Proposals for Change.* Ottawa: 1984.

Government of Canada. *Report of the Royal Commission on the Status of Women.* Ottawa: 1970.

Gregory, Frances. *Maintenance and Its Enforcement.* Course paper, photocopy, 1984.

———. *Issue 4: The purpose of maintenance is one of rehabilitation and not a guarantee of security for life – Con.* Course paper, photocopy, 1984.

Griffin, Justus A. "Richard Cartwright, UEL." In *Wentworth Historical Papers,* 1924.

Gundy, H.P. "Molly Brant – Loyalist." In *OHS,* vol. 45, 1950-1953.

Hallowell, Gerald A. "Prohibition in Ontario, 1919-1923." In *OHS Research Publication No. 2,* Toronto, 1972.

Health and Welfare Canada. *Current Status of Family Planning in Canada.* Ottawa: 1973.

Hepworth, H. Philip. *Foster Care and Adoption in Canada.* Ottawa: Canadian Council on Social Development, 1980.

Herrington, M. Eleanor. *Captain Jon Deserontyou and the Mohawk Settlement at Deseronto.* Presented to the Royal Society of Canada, 1921; Kingston.

Houston, Susan E. "The 'Waifs and Strays' of a Late Victorian City: Juvenile Delinquents in Toronto." In *Childhood and Family in Canadian History,* edited by Joy Parr. Toronto: McClelland and Stewart Ltd., 1982.

Innes, Mary Quayle. "Industrial Development of Ontario, 1783-1820." In *OHS*, vol. 32, 1937.

Johnston, Jean. "Molly Brant, Mohawk Matron." In *Ontario History,* 1964.

Journals of the Legislative Assembly, Province of Canada, 1856, 1857, 1858, 1859.

Kahn-Freund, O. "Inconsistencies and Injustices in the Law of Husband and Wife." (2 parts). In *Modern Law Review,* vol. 15, 1952; vol. 16, 1953.

Kelso, J.J. *Social Laws of Canada and Ontario.* Toronto: Government of Ontario, 1914.

Law Society of Upper Canada Bar Admission Course Materials. *Family Law, 1983-84.* Toronto: Carswell Legal Publications, 1984.

Leon, Jeffrey S. "The Development of Canadian Juvenile Justice, a Background for Reform." In *Osgoode Hall Law Journal,* 1977.

MacDonald, Donald C. "The Honourable Richard Cartwright." In *Three History Theses.* Toronto: Ontario Department of Public Records and Archives, 1961.

Macfarlane, Ronald O. "An Economic Interpretation of Loyalism." Mss. United Empire Loyalist Association.

Machar, Agnes M. "The Story of a Canadian Loyalist, Col. Joel Stone, founder of Gananoque." In *United Empire Loyalist Papers,* 1898-1902.

Mackinnon, V. Jennifer and Groves, J. Robert. *Child Custody: Within the Bounds of Reality.* Unpublished mss., 1983.

McKie, D.C.; Prentice, B.; and Reed, P. *Divorce: Law and the Family in Canada.* Ottawa: Ministry of Supply and Services, 1983.

Minister of Public Welfare. *Report of the Superintendent of Neglected and Dependent Children.* Toronto: 1918 and 1924.

Minister of Supply and Services. *Divorce: Law and the Family in Canada.* Ottawa: 1983.

Ministry of Community and Social Services. "Child Welfare in Ontario: Past, Present and Future." Toronto: 1979.

Mohr, J.W. "The Future of the Family, the Law and the State." Address to the People's Law Conference: The Family and the Law. Ottawa: 1984.

Morrison, Terrence R. "The Child and Urban Social Reform in Late Nineteenth-Century Ontario." Ph.D. thesis, University of Toronto. Photocopy, 1971.

National Council of Women of Canada (for distribution at the Paris International Exhibition, 1900). *Women of Canada: Their Life and Work.* Reprinted, 1975.

Ontario Law Reform Commission. *Report on Family Law.* Part 1: Torts; Part 2: Marriage; Part 3: Children; Part 4: Family Property Law; Part 5: Family Courts; Part 6: Support Obligations. Toronto: 1969-1975.

Ontario Status of Women Council. "Brief to the Government of Ontario Respecting Widow's Rights to Family Property." Toronto: 1980.

Parker, Graham. "The Century of the Child." In *Canadian Bar Review,* 1967.

________. "Some Historical Observations on the Juvenile Court." In *Criminal Law Quarterly,* 1967.

________. "The Juvenile Court Movement." In *University of Toronto Law Review,* 1976.

Parliamentary Papers (Great Britain) (1867-1868), 7. *Special Report from the Select Committee on Married Women's Property Bill,* testimony of the Hon. John Rose, July 3, 1868.

Public Services Bulletin. *Ontario Legislation, 1920.* Toronto: 1920.

Recherches Historiques. "Les femmes electeurs." Levis: Pierre Georges Roy, 1905.

Riddell, William Renwick. "The Duel in Early Upper Canada." No publication or date given.

________. "A Trial for High Treason in 1838." In *OHS,* vol. 18, 1920.

________. "Was Molly Brant Married?" In *OHS,* vol. 19, 1922.

________. "The Law Society of Upper Canada in 1822." In *OHS,* vol. 23, 1926.

________. "Quaker Marriages in Upper Canada." In *OHS,* vol. 24, 1927.

Roland, Charles G., M.D. "Health and Disease Among the Early Loyalists in Upper Canada." In the *Canadian Medical Association Journal,* vol. 128, 1983.

Roy, James. "The Honourable Richard Cartwright." In *The Canadian Historical Association Report 1946-1950.* Kingston: 1950.

Ruggle, Richard G. "We Protect the Little Ones: A History of Children's Aid in Halton." Burlington: The Children's Aid Society of the Regional Municipality of Halton, 1978.

Simcoe, John Graves. *The Correspondence of Lieutenant-Governor John Graves Simcoe (with Allied Documents),* vol. 1, 1789-1793. Edited (1924) by Brig. Gen. E.A. Cruikshank for the *OHS.*

Smith, Alison. "John Strachan and Early Upper Canada, 1799-1814." In *Ontario History,* 1960.

Smith, Michael. "A Geographical View of the Province of Upper Canada and Promiscuous Remarks Upon the Government." In *United Empire Loyalist Papers,* 1898-1902.

Spettigue, C. Owen. *An Historical Review of Ontario Legislation on Child Welfare.* Toronto: Ontario Department of Public Welfare, 1937.

Strachan, John. *A Sermon on the Death of the Honourable Richard Cartwright, September 3, 1815.* Montreal: 1816.

Tozer, Ron and Strickland, Dan. *A Pictorial History of Algonquin Provincial Park.* Toronto: Ministry of Natural Resources, 1980.

Waterbury, W.B. "Sketch of Peter Teeple, Loyalist and Pioneer, 1762-1847." In *OHS,* vol. 1, 1899.

Weisman, Norris, Judge. "The Second Family and the Law of Support." In 37 *Report on Family Law* (2d) 245.

West, Julia E.A. "The Married Woman and the Law." In *Women and the Law.* Written and compiled by de Sousa, Maria; Wernham, Richard S.; and West, Julia E.A. Ottawa: Carleton University for the Secretary of State, 1975.

Wilson, Lawrence Charles. "Juvenile Justice in Canada: The End of the Experiment." Master of Laws thesis. University of Manitoba, 1976.

ACTS

Adoption Act, 1921, S.O. 1921, c. 55

Adoption Act, 1926, S.O. 1926, c. 45

Adoption Act, 1927, S.O. 1927, c. 53

An Act for the Prevention of Cruelty to, and Better Protection of Children, S.O. 1893, c. 45

An Act for the Protection and Reformation of Neglected Children, S.O. 1888, c. 40

An Act for the Protection of Infant Children, S.O. 1887, c. 36

An Act for the Relief of John Stuart, S.U.C. 1841, c. 72

An Act Respecting Dower, R.S.O. 1887, c. 133

An Act Respecting Infants, R.S.O. 1897, c. 168

An Act Respecting Municipal Institutions, R.S.O. 1897, c. 223

An Act Respecting the Election of Members of the House of Commons and Electoral Franchise, S.C. 1920, c. 46

An Act Respecting the Guardianship of Minors, S.O. 1887, c. 21

An Act Respecting the Property of Married Women, R.S.O. 1887, c. 132

An Act Respecting the Support of Illegitimate Children, R.S.O. 1897, c. 169

An Act Respecting Truancy and Compulsory School Attendance, S.O. 1891, c. 56

An Act to Amend the Act to Provide for the Admission of Women to the Study and Practice of Law, S.O. 1895, c. 27

An Act to Amend the Deserted Wives' Maintenance Act, S.O. 1920, c. 44

An Act to Amend the Dominion Elections Act, S.C. 1919, c. 48

An Act to Amend the Factories Act, S.O. 1904, c. 26

An Act to Amend the Factories Act, S.O. 1908, c. 57

An Act to Amend the Factory, Shop and Office Building Act, S.O. 1914, c. 40

An Act to Amend the Law Enabling Married Women to Convey Their Real Estate Within Upper Canada, S.C. 1859, c. 35

An Act to Amend the Law Relating to the Custody of Infants, S.C. 1923, c. 126

An Act to Amend the Ontario Factories Act, 1884, R.S.O. 1887, c. 35

An Act to Amend the Shops Regulation Act, S.O. 1908, c. 58

An Act to Confer the Electoral Franchise Upon Women, S.C. 1918, c. 20

An Act to Extend the Rights of Property of Married Women, S.O. 1872, c. 16

An Act to Provide for Certain Amendments of the Law, R.S.O. 1877, c. 8

An Act to Provide for the Admission of Women to the Study and Practice of Law, S.O. 1892, c. 32

An Act to Regulate Maternity Boarding Houses and for the Protection of Infant Children, R.S.O. 1897, c. 258

An Act to Repeal Certain Parts of an Act Passed in the Fourteenth Year of His Majesty's Reign, Entitled "An Act Making More Effectual Provision for the Government of the Province of Quebec in North America and to Introduce the English Law as the Rule of Decision in All Matters of Controversy, Relative to Property and Civil Rights," S.U.C. 1792, c. 1

An Act to Secure to Married Women Certain Separate Rights of Property, S.C. 1859, c. 34

Canadian Charter of Rights and Freedoms

Children of Unmarried Parents Act, 1921, S.O. 1921, c. 54

Children of Unmarried Parents Act, 1927, R.S.O. 1927, c. 51

Children's Law Reform Act, R.S.O. 1980 (as amended by S.O. 1982, c. 20)

Children's Protection Act of Ontario, R.S.O. 1897, c. 259

Children's Protection Act, 1922, S.O. 1922, c. 92

Children's Protection Act, 1927, S.O. 1927, c. 78

Childrens Protection Act of Ontario, S.O. 1908, c. 59

Children's Protection Act of Ontario, S.O. 1913, c. 62

Constitution Act, 1867

Deserted Wives' and Children's Maintenance Act, 1922 S.O. 1922, c. 57

Deserted Wives' and Children's Maintenance Act, 1927, S.O. 1927, c. 48

Deserted Wives' Maintenance Act, S.O. 1911, c. 34

Deserted Wives' Maintenance Act, R.S.O. 1914, c. 152

Disqualification Act, 1919, S.O. 1919, c. 6

Divorce Act, S.C. 1925, c. 41

Divorce Act (Bill C-187), S.C. 1968, c. 24

Divorce Act, 1985, S.C. 1986, c. 4

Divorce Act (Ontario), 1930, S.C. 1930, c. 14

Divorce Amendment Act, 1984 (Bill C-10) (introduced but not passed)

Divorce Jurisdiction Act, 1930, S.C. 1930, c. 15

Election Law Amendment Act, 1917, S.O. 1917, c. 6

Factories Amendment Act, 1895, S.O. 1895, c. 50

Factory, Shop and Office Building Act, S.O. 1913, c. 60

Factory, Shop and Office Building Act, 1918, S.O. 1918, c. 44

Family Law Act, 1986, S.O. 1986, c. 4

Family Law Reform Act, 1978, S.O. 1978, c. 2

Family Law Reform Act, S.O. 1980, c. 152

Illegitimate Children's Act, S.O. 1914, c. 154

Infants Act, S.O. 1911, c. 35

Infants Act, R.S.O. 1914, c. 153

Infants Act, 1927, S.O. 1927, c. 50

Infants Amendment Act, 1923, S.O. 1923, c. 33

Legitimation Act, 1921, S.O. 1921, c. 53

Legitimation Act, 1927, S.O. 1927, c. 52

Manhood Suffrage Act, S.O. 1888, c. 4

Marriage Act, S.O. 1911, c. 32

Marriage Act, R.S.O. 1980, c. 256

Married Women (Maintenance in Case of Desertion) Act, 1888, S.O. 1888, c. 23

Married Women's Property Act, 1884, S.O. 1884, c. 19

Married Women's Property Act, R.S.O. 1897, c. 163

Married Women's Property Act, S.O. 1913, c. 29

Married Women's Property Act, R.S.O. 1914, c. 149

Married Women's Property Act, 1926, S.O. 1926, c. 44

Married Women's Real Estate Act, 1873, S.O. 1873, c. 18

Matrimonial Causes Act, 1931, S.O. 1931, c. 25

Military Voters Act, 1917, S.C. 1917, c. 34

Minimum Wage Act, S.O. 1920, c. 87

Minimum Wage Amendment Act, 1922, S.O. 1922, c. 91

Minors' Protection Act, 1927, S.O. 1927, c. 71

Mothers' Allowance Act, S.O. 1920, c. 89

Mothers' Allowance Act, 1921, S.O. 1921, c. 79

Municipal Institutions Act, R.S.O. 1914, c. 192

Ontario Election Act, R.S.O. 1897, c. 9

Ontario Election Act, 1918, S.O. 1918, c. 3

Ontario Election Act, 1919, S.O. 1919, c. 7

Ontario Factories Act, R.S.O. 1877, c. 256

Ontario Factories Act, 1884, S.O. 1884, c. 39

Ontario Franchise Act, 1917, S.O. 1917, c. 5

Ontario Law Reform Act, S.O. 1978, c. 2

Ontario Shops' Regulation Act, 1888, S.O. 1888, c. 33

Ontario Shops Regulation Act, R.S.O. 1897, c. 257

Parents Maintenance Act, 1921, S.O. 1921, c. 52

Parents Maintenance Act, S.O. 1927, c. 185

Parents Maintenance Act, 1927, S.O. 1927, c. 49

War-time Elections Act, S.C. 1917, c. 39

Women's Assembly Qualification Act, 1919, S.O. 1919, c. 8

Women's Municipal Franchise Act, R.S.O. 1917, c. 43

Women's Municipal Qualification Act, 1919, S.O. 1919, c. 47

Women's Rural School Board Qualification Act, 1919, S.O. 1919, c. 76

CASES

Bennett v. Edmonton (1922), 1 W.W.R. 861 (Alta. S.C.)

Blum v. Blum (1982), 132 D.L.R. (3d) 69 (Ont. Prov. Ct. Fam. Div.)

Bregman v. Bregman (1978), 7 R.F.L. (2d) 201 (Ont. S.C.)

Children's Aid Society of Metropolitan Toronto v. Mr. K. and Mrs. K. (unreported), (1985), Provincial Court, Family Division, before His Honour David R. Main

Edwards et al v. Attorney-General for Canada et al (1929), 3 W.W.R. (P.C.)

Farquar v. Farquar (1983), 35 R.F.L. (2d) 287 (Ont. C.A.)

Hanna v. Hanna, Lewis and Hanna (1983), 33 R.F.L. (2d) 335 (Ont. S.C., Master)

Hawn v. Hawn, [1944] 4 D.L.R. 173 (Ont. C.A.)

Joyce v. Joyce (1984), 41 R.F.L. (2d) 85 (Ont. C.A.)

Leatherdale v. Leatherdale (1982), 30 R.F.L. (2d) 225 (S.C.C.)

Manclark and Manclark (1925), 28 O.W.N. 78 (Div. Ct.)

Maroukis v. Maroukis (1981), 24 R.F.L. (2d) 113 (Ont. C.A.)

McKee v. McKee (1951), A.C. 352 (P.C.)

Messier v. Delage (1983), 2 S.C.R. 401

Murdoch v. Murdoch (1973), 41 D.L.R. (3d) 367 (S.C.C.)

R. v. Baxter, R. v. Snooks (1846), 2 U.C.Q.B. 370

R. v. Cyr (Alias Waters), (1917) 2 W.W.R. 1185 (Alta. C.A.)

R. v. Cyr (Alias Waters), (1917) 3 W.W.R. 849 (Alta. C.A.)

Schaffer v. Dumble (1884), 5 O.R. 716 (2.B.)

Shuttleworth v. McGillivary (1903), 5 O.L.R. 536 (C.A.)

Silverstein v. Silverstein (1978), R.F.L. (2d) 239 (Ont. S.C.)

Trusts Corporation of Ontario v. Clue (1896), 28 O.R. 116 (C.A.)

Webb v. Webb (1984), 39 R.F.L. (2d) 113 (Ont. C.A.)

Weir v. Weir (1978), 6 R.F.L. (2d) 189 (Ont. S.C.)

Index

Photo Credits

The author expresses her thanks to the sources listed below for the use of the photographs that appear in this book. The following abbreviations are used to indicate these sources:

Art Gallery of Ontario: AGO
Canapress: CP
Children's Aid Society of Toronto: CAS
City of Toronto Archives: CTA
Geological Survey of Canada, Ottawa: GSC
Glasgow Museums & Art Collection, Stirling Maxwell Collection: GMAC
Herb Nott & Co., Ltd., Toronto: Nott
Joan Magee, *Loyalist Mosaic*. Toronto: Dundurn Press, 1984: Magee
Mathieson Photo Services: MPS
Metropolitan Toronto Library: MTL
Miller Services: MS
National Portrait Gallery, St. Martin's Place, London: NPG
Notman Photographic Archives, McCord Museum of McGill University, Montreal: Notman
Ontario Archives: OA
Public Archives of Canada: PAC
R.M. Bruce, *The Loyalist Trail*. n.p., n.d.: Bruce
The Lord Chamberlain, St. James's Palace, London: TLC
The Picture Gallery of Canadian History, Vol. 2. Toronto: Ryerson Press, 1945: PGCH

The page number for each photo is followed by the credit; when two photos appear on the same page, the credits read from left to right or top to bottom.

xiv PAC C 6060
2 PAC C 111205
4 OA S2109
5 Magee
6 PGCH
7 Magee
8 MTL T 31584
10 PAC C 44633
14 OA S196
15 OA S1072
17 MTL: *The Diary of Mrs. Simcoe*
18 OA S2328
22 OA S4375; MTL: *The Diary of Mrs. Simcoe*
23 OA Simcoe Sketch 135
24 MTL T 10023
27 Bruce
29 OA S8506; OA S8507
31 Nott 84-522-2
33 PAC C 6487
35 OA S2901
36 PAC C 98755
37 OA S785; PAC C 13988
39 OA *Colonial Advocate Supplement*, 9/26/1833
39 TLC
40 GMAC PLi6
42 OA S2163
45 PAC C 123162
53 Notman 7952-I
54 Notman 66.178-I
55 OA S196
56 PAC C 20705
59 NPG X 26597
60 PAC C 3689
62 MTL: Broadside Collection, Jenny Lind, 10/22//851
64 PAC C56484
66 OA S4332
69 PAC PA 118217
71 CAS 199963; CAS 11 7143 49
72 AGO G.G.49; G.S. 111
73 AGO N-830
74 OA S13461
75 OA S8973
77 OA S15526
79 PAC C 2078
80 PAC PA 28924
82 Eaton's Archives
84 Popperfoto
86 CTA:James 279F
89 CTA:James 724
90 G.S.C. 17117
91 CTA:James 640
94 David Hall-Humpherson

95 OA 14364-12
96 PAC C 95738
97 CP
100 OA S15118
101 CTA:James 654
106 PAC C 18586
107 PAC C6908
108 OA S17387
109 PAC PA 136738
111 PAC C 54523
113 CTA:James 8054
117 OA S804
120 OA S17139
123 MS 398
125 PAC PA 119765; PA 51587
126 CP
127 The author
130 PAC PA 132394
133 PAC 13695
134 OA: 20th Legislature
135 PAC PA 128761; PA 128760
136 PAC PA 93538
137 PAC PA 93543; PA 93534
140 MPS 38123 #1
142 CP
143 *The Globe and Mail*, Toronto
149 CP
154 OA: R. McMurtry
156 Moira Armour
158 CP
159 Toronto Star Syndicate
162 AGO